School Discipline,
Classroom Management,
&Student Self-Management

To my wife, Julianna,
and (now adult) children—Jesse, David, Janna, and Justin:
For your love, support, caring, and presence. For keeping me grounded.
For supporting the important work that I do, even in the face of sacrifice and
absence. For allowing me to share your lives individually and our lives as a family.

To my colleagues in schools and communities across the country:
Thank you for sharing your professional and personal lives and experiences
with me. For challenging me, educating me, and including me. For helping
me to be practical, realistic, and real. For your persistence in the face
of unimaginable challenges and your insistence that we advocate
for every student, every school, and every family.

School Discipline, Classroom Management, & Student Self-Management

A **PBS** Implementation Guide

Howard M. Knoff

Foreword by Raymond J. McNulty

CORWIN
A SAGE Company

CORWIN
A SAGE Company

FOR INFORMATION:

Corwin
A SAGE Company
2455 Teller Road
Thousand Oaks, California 91320
(800) 233-9936
www.corwin.com

SAGE Publications Ltd.
1 Oliver's Yard
55 City Road
London EC1Y 1SP
United Kingdom

SAGE Publications India Pvt. Ltd.
B 1/I 1 Mohan Cooperative Industrial Area
Mathura Road, New Delhi 110 044
India

SAGE Publications Asia-Pacific Pte. Ltd.
3 Church Street
#10-04 Samsung Hub
Singapore 049483

Acquisitions Editor: Jessica Allan
Associate Editor: Allison Scott
Editorial Assistant: Lisa Whitney
Production Editor: Cassandra Margaret
   Seibel
Copy Editor: Michelle Ponce
Typesetter: C&M Digitals (P) Ltd.
Proofreader: Scott Oney
Indexer: Joan Shapiro
Cover Designer: Candice Harman
Permissions Editor: Karen Ehrmann

Copyright © 2012 by Corwin

Printed in the United States of America.

Library of Congress Cataloging-in-Publication Data

Knoff, Howard M.

School discipline, classroom management, and student self-management: a PBS implementation guide/ Howard M. Knoff; foreword by Raymond J. McNulty.

p. cm.

Includes bibliographical references and index.

ISBN 978-1-4129-9396-8 (pbk.)

1. School discipline—United States. 2. School discipline—United States—Case studies. 3. Classroom management—United States. 4. Community and school—United States—Case studies. I. Title.

LB3012.2.K63 2012

371.102′40973—dc23   2012008930

This book is printed on acid-free paper.

SUSTAINABLE   Certified Chain of Custody
FORESTRY   Promoting Sustainable Forestry
INITIATIVE   www.sfiprogram.org
   SFI-01268
SFI label applies to text stock

12 13 14 15 16 10 9 8 7 6 5 4 3 2 1

Contents

Foreword

With more than 39 years of experience in education serving as a teacher, principal, superintendent, commissioner of education, senior fellow at the Bill and Melinda Gates Foundation, and now president of the International Center for Leadership in Education, I have had the pleasure of meeting a number of great educators, but few rise to the level of Howie Knoff.

When a professional spends more than 20 years doing great work, we should admire him. But when someone spends more than 20 years doing great work, achieving great results, and *then* they take it to scale over and over again, I call it amazing! Those of us who know Howie Knoff don't expect any less of him. I first met Howie when I hired him as a waterfront instructor for a camp I directed for inner city children from Boston. Howie needed money for college and all I could offer him was a little bit—a very little bit. And yet, Howie took the job because he wanted to make a difference in the lives of the children, and he has been doing that ever since that summer long ago.

We live in an educational environment obsessed with test scores, control, and predictability, and because of that, we build most school improvement plans around quantitative (hard) data gleaned from test results in core curriculum areas. We design solutions to poor student performance around specific content weaknesses that we see in the data, and then we launch a solution and wait to see the performance rise and behaviors change. This is clearly not how it should happen.

In this book, Howie Knoff takes a systems perspective and approach to the challenges faced by educators around discipline, behavior management, and school safety. By that I mean that his is not an add-on to the system but a way to embed this important work into the culture of the system. Trying to bring solutions into a system by just adding them on ignores the importance of interacting with schools and building them into more effective systems.

This book also emphasizes the importance of teaching students social, emotional, and behavioral self-management skills as the most effective and preventative approach to school discipline and improved academic performance. This involves teaching all students—from preschool to high school—the interpersonal, social problem-solving, conflict prevention and resolution, and emotional coping skills that they need to be successful both inside and outside of school.

So after almost 20 years of implementation, field-testing, and validation, Dr. Knoff provides us with a step-by-step guide to implementing schoolwide positive behavioral support systems—at the student prevention, strategic intervention, and intensive wrap-around and crisis management levels. Guided by both research and established practice, this book provides the educational community with a pragmatic, easy-to-follow, three-year blueprint for Positive Behavior Support Systems (PBSS) implementation that will help systems, schools, and staff to integrate academics, instruction, and achievement with discipline, behavior management, and student self-management. It also integrates this work into an effective strategic planning and continuous school improvement approach that focuses on building organizational and staff capacity, guiding professional development with strong implementation, and strengthening parent and community outreach.

While zero tolerance has been emphasized as an administrative approach to discipline for many years, educators are now realizing that we need to develop relationships with students that connect them to their schools, establish positive school and classroom climates, teach students social skills, motivate them to make good choices, keep our common areas safe, and eliminate instances of teasing, taunting, bullying, harassment, hazing, and physical aggression. This is what our schools need, this is what our children need, and this is what this book delivers—in a step-by-step, user-friendly fashion.

Nice work, Howie; you always amaze me.

Raymond J. McNulty
President
International Center for Leadership in Education

Preface and Acknowledgments

The bell rings. It is 10:20 a.m. and a thousand middle school adolescents of all sizes and shapes pour into the hallway for the five minutes of chaos that goes with their transition from one classroom to the next. Ignoring the expressionless faces of the staff members supervising this school ritual, the students are in their own worlds and on their own terms—generating a cacophony of mindless chatter, good-natured ribbing, deliberate ridicule, and ego-shattering disdain.

During the five-minute frenzy, some students are celebrated and idolized; some are accepted and supported; some are ignored or rejected; and some are bullied, harassed, and intimidated. As in generations past, there are the emerging (when they get to high school) class superstars and supermodels, the cool kids, the preps, the brains, the jocks, the valley girls, the thespians, the geeks, the nerds, the losers, the Goths, the punks, the greasers, the burnouts, and, of course, just the average students fighting to fit in.

While some may say that the culture of a middle school (or elementary or high school) is a microcosm of a community and our society (and maybe it is), this should not make us passive and fatalistic. And it should not discourage us from taking the actions needed to improve the culture of our schools, communities, and society by helping everyone to learn and demonstrate the interpersonal, social problem-solving, conflict prevention and resolution, and emotional coping skills that they need to be successful—now and in the future.

At its core, this book is more about helping students to learn and use necessary social, emotional, and behavioral self-management skills than about minimizing student discipline problems. It is more about staff members enthusiastically infusing these skills into the fabric of their classrooms and instruction than about staff members trying to manage, coerce, or control student behavior. And it is more about a recognition that schools are successful when staff and students focus on communication, collaboration, caring, and celebration than when administrators focus on office discipline referrals and school suspensions or expulsions. When I began to write this book, I knew that I needed to be comprehensive, yet practical; visionary, yet realistic. I needed to present a blueprint that not only could be adapted to different schools and situations, but that also outlined the underlying science that makes it all work. Finally, I knew that I needed to reflect more on the practical insights of the 100,000-plus educators with whom I have worked across the country than on the theoretical discussions and debates that occurred when I was at the university.

Hopefully, as I complete the last sentences of this book, I have been successful. But if I have had any degree of success, I expect it is because I have tried to tell a story throughout this book. Briefly, the story is embedded in ten chapters:

• Chapter 1 (Integrating a Schoolwide Positive Behavioral Support System [PBSS] Blueprint Into an Effective Schools Process) provides an overview of an evidenced-based Positive Behavioral Support System (PBSS) and integrates it into an effective school and schooling model that has been implemented in hundreds of schools across the country. This schoolwide PBSS involves students, staff, administration, and parents who work together (a) to teach and reinforce students' interpersonal, social problem-solving, conflict prevention and resolution, and emotional coping skills; (b) to create and maintain positive, safe, supportive, and consistent school climates and settings; and (c) to strengthen and sustain school and district capacity such that the entire process becomes an inherent part of their school improvement planning and success.

• Chapter 2 (School Readiness and the Steps for PBSS Implementation) focuses on the organizational and motivational readiness and the strategic planning processes needed to begin a schoolwide PBSS initiative.

• Chapter 3 (The School Discipline/PBSS and Other Committees: Effective Team and Group Functioning) discusses the creation of a shared leadership approach and committee structure in a school that facilitates the buy-in, initial implementation, and long-term institutionalization of the PBSS. The mission, role, and function of the school discipline/PBSS committee is especially emphasized as are the other school-level committees that collectively support the multi-tiered system of services, supports, strategies, and programs needed to help all students to be successful.

• Chapter 4 (Behavioral Accountability, Student Motivation, and Staff Consistency) describes the importance of a schoolwide approach to identifying the behavioral expectations for students in their classrooms and across the common areas of the school (with positive responses or reinforcements) and the different intensities of inappropriate behavior (with corrective responses, consequences, administrative responses, and interventions). This approach is intended to motivate and hold students accountable for appropriate behavior while preventing, decreasing, and eliminating inappropriate behavior.

- Chapter 5 (Teaching Social, Emotional, and Behavioral Skills) describes the scientific principles underlying effective social, emotional, and behavioral skills instruction programs and emphasizes the importance of having general education teachers teach and reinforce these skills as part of classroom management and student self-management.

- Chapter 6 (School Safety and Crisis Prevention, Intervention, and Response) describes specific approaches that help staff and students to create positive and safe common school areas, respond to inappropriate behavior when it occurs, and analyze and address serious or significantly problematic situations when they occur in these settings. The functional components of a safety audit also are described, as are the ways to prepare for and address different crisis situations.

- Chapter 7 (Teasing, Taunting, Bullying, Harassment, Hazing, and Physical Aggression) discusses comprehensive, evidence-based, and ecologically sound approaches to address these problems at the whole-school, existing group, and individual student levels of prevention, strategic intervention, and crisis or intensive need. A functional assessment approach that helps explain why specific circumstances or events are occurring is described and then linked to the interventions needed to address these situations in the future.

- Chapter 8 (Functional Assessment and Why Students Become Behaviorally Challenging) describes the step-by-step data-based, functional assessment, problem-solving process that helps determine specifically why students are not demonstrating the social, emotional, or behavioral skills expected in different settings and situations. This is done in the context of looking at the classroom factors that might be contributing to a student's difficulties and the seven high-hit reasons why students present with specific challenges.

- Chapter 9 (Behavioral Interventions for Students With Strategic and Intensive Needs) links the results of the functional assessment approach from the previous chapter to specific instructional and intervention approaches that help to change student behavior. This is done in the context of a multi-tiered system that focuses on services, supports, strategies, and programs and not on the percentage of students served or where the services are delivered.

- Chapter 10 (Evaluating and Sustaining PBSS Outcomes) describes a range of approaches that are used to formatively and summatively evaluate PBSS outcomes at the student, staff, school, and system levels. In addition, a number of articulation strategies are discussed that facilitate the transfer of successes and lessons learned from one school year (and, sometimes, school building) to the next.

Relative to acknowledgments, many people have supported me and the development of this book from beginning to end. While there is always a risk of forgetting someone when you write your thank-you notes (please accept my apologies in advance), I do want to recognize the people who had a direct hand in guiding this book.

First, I greatly appreciate the collegiality, feedback, recommendations, and read-throughs of this book by Jennifer Gonzales, Positive Behavioral Support System (PBSS) coordinator with the State Personnel Development Grant (SPDG) at the Arkansas Department of Education; our colleague Lisa Johnson, a PBSS consultant with the SPDG; and my good friend Matt Kamins, former supervisor of psychological services and still a practicing school psychologist with the Montgomery Public School System. Thanks also to the Corwin-chosen practitioners who read both my original book proposal and the first manuscript for their insight, honesty, and dedication to the review process.

Next, Jessica G. Allan, the senior acquisitions editor at Corwin Press, has been a phenomenal colleague, sounding board, collaborator, and support system whose expertise is embedded in every page of this book. In addition, it has been a joy to work with the entire Corwin Press publications team throughout this journey: Lisa Whitney, editorial assistant; Cassandra Seibel, production manager; Candice Harman, cover designer; and Michelle Ponce, copy editor.

Finally, my heartfelt thanks to Ray McNulty for his gracious foreword and his support over the years. His dedication to students, staff, and schools everywhere is evident in every reflection, every story, and every presentation he makes.

Howie Knoff
Little Rock, AR

PUBLISHER'S ACKNOWLEDGMENTS

Corwin gratefully acknowledges the contributions of the following reviewers:

MaryAnn Baldwin
Counselor
Chamberlain High School
Tampa, FL

Sheila Fisher
Principal
Maria Weston Chapman Middle School
Weymouth, MA

Antanas "Tony" Levinskas
Core Faculty, School Psychology Specialization
Capella University, Harold Abel School of Psychology

Nancy Moga
Principal
Callaghan Elementary School
Covington, VA

Ronda Schelvan
Teacher (SPED)
Hathaway Elementary School
Washougal, WA

Sally Sentner
Assistant Professor (SPED)
Department of Special Education and Rehabilitative Sciences
Clarion University of PA
Clarion, PA

Angie Whalen
Instructor and Practicum Coordinator
COE-School Psychology Program
University of Oregon, SPED
Eugene, OR

About the Author

Howard M. Knoff, PhD, is the creator and director of Project ACHIEVE. After 22 years as a university professor, he is now a full-time national consultant, author, and lecturer, and he has been the director of the State Improvement/Personnel Development Grant for the Arkansas Department of Education—Special Education Unit since 2003. Formerly a professor of school psychology at the University of South Florida (USF) for 18 years and director of its school psychology program for 12 years, Dr. Knoff was also the creator and director of the Institute for School Reform, Integrated Services, and Child Mental Health and Educational Policy at USF.

As director of Project ACHIEVE, a nationally known school effectiveness and improvement program that was designated a National Model Prevention Program by the U.S. Department of Health & Human Service's Substance Abuse and Mental Health Services Administration (SAMHSA) in 2000, Dr. Knoff has trained over 1,500 schools or school districts in every state over a 25-year period.

As director of the Arkansas State Improvement/Personnel Development Grant (SIG/SPDG), a multimillion-dollar grant from the U.S. Department of Education, Office of Special Education Programs, he helps oversee the primary SPDG goals of the statewide implementation of Project ACHIEVE's Positive Behavioral Support System (PBSS) approach; literacy and mathematics interventions for at-risk students, underachieving students, and students with disabilities; Response-to-Instruction and Intervention and Closing the Achievement Gap technical assistance to schools and districts in school improvement status; and special education and related services recruitment, training, and retention.

Dr. Knoff received his PhD degree from Syracuse University in 1980 and has worked as a practitioner, consultant, licensed private psychologist, and university professor since 1978. Dr. Knoff is widely respected for his research and writing on school reform and organizational change, consultation and intervention processes, social skills and behavior management training, Response-to-Intervention, and professional issues. He has authored or coauthored 18 books, published over 75 articles and book chapters, and delivered over 500 papers and workshops nationally—including the *Stop & Think Social Skills Program* (preschool through middle school editions) and the *Stop & Think Parent Book: A Guide to Children's Good Behavior.* In addition, he was on the writing team that produced *Early Warning, Timely Response: A Guide to Safe Schools,* the document commissioned by President Clinton after the first wave of school shootings in the fall of 1998.

Dr. Knoff has a long history of working with schools, districts, and community and state agencies and organizations. For example, he has consulted with a number of state departments of education, the Department of Defense Dependents School District during Desert Storm, and the Southern Poverty Law Center. He has also served as an expert witness in federal court five times, in addition to working on many other state and local cases—largely for legal advocacy firms who represent special education and other students in need.

A recipient of the Lightner Witmer Award from the American Psychological Association's School Psychology Division for early career contributions in 1990 and over $18 million in external grants during his career, Dr. Knoff is a Fellow of the American Psychological Association (School Psychology Division), a nationally certified school psychologist, and a licensed psychologist in Arkansas, and he has been trained in both crisis intervention and mediation processes. Frequently interviewed in all areas of the media, Dr. Knoff has been on the NBC Nightly News as well as numerous television and radio talk shows, and he was highlighted on an ABC News *20/20* program titled "Being Teased, Taunted, and Bullied." Finally, Dr. Knoff was the 21st president of the National Association of School Psychologists, which now represents more than 25,000 school psychologists nationwide.

1

Integrating a Schoolwide Positive Behavioral Support System (PBSS) Blueprint Into an Effective Schools Process

> Almost all successful individuals and organizations have one thing in common—the power and depth of their vision of the future.
>
> Joel Barker

PBSS Implementation Case Study:
Hotchkiss Elementary School, Dallas, Texas

The counselor from Hotchkiss Elementary School in Dallas Independent School District, Texas, called on March 10, 1995, to inform me that I was going to work with their school. Hotchkiss was an inner city, predominantly Hispanic kindergarten through sixth grade school with 80% of its 900 students receiving federal free lunch support. Opening for the first time in August 1994 with a completely new staff, the school experienced over 4,500 office discipline referrals that year.

On April 1, 1995, we began a ten-year partnership to systematically implement the Project ACHIEVE Positive Behavioral Support System (PBSS) blueprint. Within less than a year, most of the PBSS was implemented or in progress. Over the next decade, the staff continued to adapt the PBSS to the needs of the students, school, and community—and they built their capacity to the degree that Project ACHIEVE activities were largely implemented independently and with the needed integrity and intensity.

The following outcomes were documented:

- Total discipline referrals to the principal's office dropped from 56.1 referrals per 100 students during the baseline year prior to project implementation to 13.0 referrals per 100 students during the first two years of the project (less than one referral per school day over an entire year). Total discipline referrals dropped to 3.0 referrals per 100 students during the last three years of implementation (less than one referral per week over the school year).
- The number of grade retentions was 2.0 retentions per 100 students during the baseline year, 2.5 students per 100 students for the first two years of project implementation, and 3.6 retentions per 100 students for the next three years.
- Special education placements were 1.9 placements per 100 students for the baseline year versus an average of 2.8 placements per 100 students for the first two years of the project versus an average of 3.0 placements per 100 students during the last three years of the project.
- On the Texas state proficiency test (Texas Assessment of Academic Skills; TAAS) reading section, taken by Hotchkiss's third through sixth graders, 68.7% of the students passed the test during the baseline year, 67.6% passed the test during the next two years, and 81.7% passed during the next three years through the 2000 school year.
- On the TAAS math section, again taken by the school's third through sixth graders, 55.1% of the students passed the test during the baseline year, 65.1% passed the test during the next two years, and 78.6% passed during the next three years.
- On the TAAS writing test, taken only by the school's fourth graders, 80.5% passed the test during the baseline year, 77.6% passed the test during the next two years, and 90.9% passed during the next three years.

INTRODUCTION

It is a simple fact that how students feel about themselves, behave, and get along with others strongly predicts their interactions and even their achievement in school. Indeed, if students feel pressured, bullied, or unsafe, they focus more on these emotional conditions than on academic instruction and learning. If they are unsure of themselves, lack self-confidence, or are self-conscious, they may not believe that they can succeed. If they do not have the behavioral skills to pay attention, work independently, or organize themselves, their academic work may suffer. If they cannot relate to others, work cooperatively in a group, and prevent or resolve conflicts, they will not survive socially.

We have known that students' social, emotional, and behavioral competency and self-management is essential to their academic and interpersonal success in school for decades (Cawalti, 1995; Wang, Haertel, & Walberg, 1993/1994; Ysseldyke & Christenson, 1993). While a strong academic program with effective instruction and a focus on real-world knowledge and skills is essential to student achievement and understanding, it is evident that a positive and supportive school and classroom climate with positive and productive student and teacher interactions and effective classroom management is necessary. Indeed, these components are among the top six predictors of students' academic achievement (Goodman & Schaughency, 2001; McNeely, Nonemaker, & Blum, 2002; Zins, Weissberg, Wang, & Walberg, 2004). More specifically, reviews of over 200 studies of school-based programs (Durlak, Weissberg, Dymnicki, Taylor, & Schellinger, 2011; Payton et al., 2008) revealed that classroom time spent on addressing the social, emotional, and behavioral skills and needs of students helped to significantly increase their academic performance and their social and emotional skills, and that the students involved were better behaved, more socially successful, less anxious, and more emotionally well-adjusted and earned higher grades and test scores.

This book discusses how schoolwide PBSSs are essential to helping students learn, master, and apply the skills needed for social, emotional, and behavioral competency and self-management and how PBSS activities facilitate the positive climates, prosocial interactions, and effective management approaches noted above across all classroom and school settings. Given this focus, this book is largely for district and school administrators, related service professionals (e.g., school psychologists, counselors, behavioral specialists), and general and special education teachers who, individually or as part of a team or committee, are responsible for developing, implementing, evaluating, and sustaining PBSSs. At the same time, a number of chapters (e.g., this chapter and Chapters 3, 4, 5, and 7) contain information that all classroom teachers should understand and be able to implement. Other chapters (e.g., this chapter and Chapters 6, 7, 8, and 9) are especially important for related service professionals.

This chapter introduces the six evidence-based components of an evidence-based PBSS along a three-tiered Response-to-Instruction and Intervention (RTI^2) continuum that is embedded in an effective school and schooling model. Initially, the competency and self-management goal of the PBSS is described along with the effective schools model that includes the PBSS as one of its primary components.

STUDENT COMPETENCY AND SELF-MANAGEMENT DEFINED

The ultimate goal of a PBSS is student social, emotional, and behavioral competency and self-management. While competency and self-management look different across the age span because of genetic, biological, and developmental factors, they are collectively defined as children's or adolescents' ability to

- be socially, emotionally, and behaviorally aware of themselves and others;
- demonstrate successful social, emotional, and behavioral interactions and skills; and
- effectively control their own emotions, so that appropriate proactive and prosocial behavior independently occurs.

Critically, competency and self-management exist along a continuum from social-emotional competency and self-management (i.e., how students feel) to cognitive-behavioral competency and self-management (i.e., what they think and then what they do). Using this cognitive-behavioral perspective, students' positive feelings, thoughts, beliefs, and attributions represent the cognitive goals and outcomes of a PBSS. Students' positive interpersonal, social problem-solving, conflict prevention and resolution, and social-emotional coping skills—both in their classrooms and in the common areas of a school—represent the behavioral goals and outcomes of a PBSS.

More specifically, on a social level, skills that are important to self-management include those that contribute to effective (a) listening, engagement, and responding; (b) communication and collaboration; (c) social problem-solving and group process; and (d) conflict prevention and resolution. On an emotional level, important self-management skills include (a) the awareness of one's own and others' feelings, (b) the ability to manage or control those feelings and other emotions as well as the ability to use coping skills to minimize the emotional effects of previous situations, and (c) the ability to demonstrate appropriate behavior even under conditions of emotionality. Finally, on a behavioral level, important self-management skills include those that help students to demonstrate appropriate behavior in the classroom and across the common areas of the school and to be actively engaged in their own learning—whether in the classroom or on a more independent level.

HOW A PBSS FITS INTO AN EFFECTIVE SCHOOL

If the ultimate PBSS goal is to help students learn, master, and apply social, emotional, and behavioral self-management skills, then this instructional goal needs to be integrated into a school's mission, role, and function. One way to begin this integration is to understand that a school's ultimate academic goal is to help students become independent learners, while its ultimate behavioral goal is to teach students to become self-managers. In order to accomplish these outcomes, schools need to dedicate themselves to effective school and schooling practices. To this end, the components of an effective school are described below.

The Components of an Effective School. During the past 30 years, a number of evidence-based effective school models have been developed by individuals such as Robert Marzano, Bill Daggett, Ted Sizer, Larry Lezotte, James Comer, and others. These models share a number of key constructs that create a foundation for any school's continuous improvement efforts and processes. These constructs involve a schoolwide commitment to

- a culture of high and realistic expectations for all students that is supported by a shared mission, vision, values, and goals;
- data-driven decision making that focuses on continuous improvement;
- validation, verification, evaluation, and accountability;
- articulated and differentiated academic and social, emotional, and behavioral (or health, mental health, and wellness) curricula;
- rigorous and relevant instruction delivered through a multi-tiered system of prevention, strategic intervention, and intensive services, supports, strategies, and programs;
- personalized learning, resulting in students who are college and career ready;
- professional learning communities where cross-disciplinary teaming focuses on effective instruction that results in student learning, mastery, proficiency, and the ability to solve real-world problems;
- partnerships that reach out to and actively engage families and community partners;
- positive and safe school climates that engage and connect students in sustained, meaningful relationships; and
- a formal and informal system of shared, multileveled leadership.

Beyond these key constructs, these models also have a common core of effective school components. While they may use different labels, these components have been integrated into an evidence-based school improvement model known as Project ACHIEVE (Knoff & Batsche, 1995; Knoff, Finch, & Carlyon, 2004). Project ACHIEVE is a comprehensive preschool through high school continuous improvement and school effectiveness program that has been implemented in hundreds of urban, suburban, and rural districts across the country since 1990. Project ACHIEVE was recognized by the U.S. Department of Health & Human Services' Substance Abuse and Mental Health Services Administration (SAMHSA) as an evidence-based model prevention program in 2000. Its effectiveness has also been recognized by the U.S. Department of Justice's Office of Juvenile Justice and Delinquency Prevention (OJJDP; in 2003); the Collaborative for

Academic, Social, Emotional Learning (CASEL; in 2002); and other regional and state groups. Project ACHIEVE is now listed on SAMHSA's National Registry of Evidence-Based Programs and Practices (U.S. Department of Health and Human Services, SAMHSA, 2010), and its implementation blueprints, procedures, and strategies are the foundation of most of the effective practices embedded throughout this book.

Working with some of the lowest to highest performing schools and in some of the poorest to most affluent communities nationwide, Project ACHIEVE's ultimate goal is to design and implement effective school and schooling processes that maximize the academic and social, emotional, and behavioral progress and achievement of all students. Project ACHIEVE also assists schools to implement effective and efficient problem solving and strategic intervention processes for students with academic and behavioral difficulties, while improving the staff's professional development and effective instructional interactions and increasing the quality and quantity of parent and community involvement and engagement. All of this is done through a strategic planning, capacity building, professional development, and technical assistance process that helps students, staff, schools, and systems to continuously improve and become independent over time. Adapting its evidence-based blueprints to diverse settings, Project ACHIEVE practices have been used in public schools, alternative schools, special education centers, psychiatric and juvenile justice facilities, Head Start and other preschool programs, and specialized charter schools.

Seven interdependent components form the foundation of Project ACHIEVE's effective school and school improvement process. These components are described below (see also Figure 1.1).

1. The *strategic planning and organizational analysis and development component* initially focuses on assessing the organizational climate, administrative style, staff decision making, and other interprofessional and interpersonal processes in a school. Activities then move into identifying and reinforcing or establishing and implementing the organizational policies, professional development and instructional practices, and year-round teaming and intervention approaches that support the academic and social, emotional, and behavioral success of all students. The ultimate products of this component are school improvement plans that help schools build capacity and autonomy; identify, develop, and deploy resources; facilitate communication, collaboration, commitment, and innovation; and sustain student, staff, and system success.

2. The *problem solving, teaming, and consultation processes component* focuses on the consistent implementation of data-based, functional assessment, problem-solving approaches that all staff learn and use (a) when implementing effective academic and behavioral instruction in the classroom, and (b) when addressing students who either are not responding to this instruction or are exhibiting serious academic or behavioral concerns.

For the latter students, a multi-tiered RTI^2 process is used (Knoff, 2009a; Knoff & Dyer, 2010) that integrates problem solving with consultation and intervention. Rejecting the more traditional RTI approach that advocates a universal intervention protocol, this RTI^2 process emphasizes the importance of linking the data-confirmed reasons why a student is not responding to effective instruction to strategic instructional or intervention approaches. These strategic approaches then are implemented by classroom teachers with consultative support (if needed) from other experts in the school. This RTI^2 process also recognizes that some students need adapted, differentiated, different, or more intensive instruction to address their needs, while other students need specific, focused, strategic or intensive interventions.

This component also extends problem solving and consultation beyond the classroom level, to grade-level RTI^2 teams (or instructional teams at the secondary level) and building-level RTI^2 teams, respectively. Project ACHIEVE utilizes grade-level RTI^2 team meetings to encourage collaborative data-based problem solving and collegial consultation among teachers at the same or adjacent grade levels. These meetings are especially effective when, for example, one teacher on a teaching team is not having success with a challenging student in a specific area, while

Figure 1.1   Organizational Model for Maximizing Student Achievement

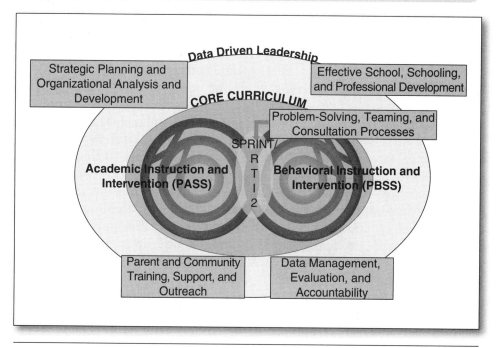

Source: Project ACHIEVE Press. Dr. Howie Knoff (author).

another teacher on the same team knows exactly what to do—based on previous training or experience—and can provide consultation and support.

The building-level RTI^2 team is staffed with the best academic and behavioral intervention specialists in or available to the school, resulting in more multidisciplinary problem solving and consultation. This team is important because some students are so complex or present such unique or intense challenges that multi- or cross-disciplinary assessment processes and instructional or intervention perspectives are needed to best understand and then address their needs.

Finally, this effective school and schooling component organizes instructional and intervention services, supports, strategies, and programs along a primary (whole school), secondary (strategic intervention), and tertiary (intensive need or crisis management) continuum to address the academic and behavioral needs of all students—including those who are at risk, underachieving, unresponsive, or unsuccessful. Critically, the foundation to the entire RTI^2 process is an effective classroom taught by a highly qualified teacher who uses effective instruction and classroom management techniques. Beyond that, the tiers of the multi-tiered model reflect the intensity of the services and supports needed by students—not where specific interventions are delivered (e.g., inside or outside a general education classroom) or how many students (e.g., all, some, or few) are receiving them (Knoff, Haley, & Gonzales, 2011).

3. The *effective school, schooling, and professional development component* focuses on the evidence-based professional development, clinical supervision, and evaluation practices—at the system, school, staff, classroom, and student levels—that ensure effective and differentiated instruction and effective and positive behavior management exists in every classroom for every student. This involves creating a culture and planning and implementing the processes whereby everyone recognizes that professional development occurs, formally and informally, every day for every staff person. With a goal of increasing staff knowledge, enhancing instructional and intervention skills, and reinforcing confidence and independence, the essential processes are research and self-study, professional development and in-service instruction, clinical supervision and collegial consultation, and case study practice and application using peer mentoring and professional learning communities. Functionally, instructional and intervention knowledge is systematically linked to individuals through whole-staff skill, confidence, proficiency, and independence through (a) "master classes" with experts who demonstrate specific, targeted skills; (b) guided staff practice that includes planned applications, supervision, and informed feedback; and (c) the transfer of this training into more challenging settings and situations with additional supervision and evaluation. As with the other effective school and schooling components, professional development activities extend beyond those establishing effective classroom practices to those addressing the coordination and implementation of the

tiered RTI² services, supports, strategies, and programs needed by students at more strategic or intensive levels.

4. The *academic instruction and intervention (or Positive Academic Supports and Services [PASS]) component* focuses on creating an effective Instructional Environment in every classroom within a school. The Instructional Environment consists of the interdependent interactions among teacher-instructional, student, and curricular processes in all classrooms. Expanding briefly, the Instructional Environment involves the integration of (a) the different academic curricula being taught in a classroom as well as their connection to state standards and benchmarks and district scope and sequence objectives (i.e., "What needs to be learned?"); (b) the teachers who are teaching these curricula and how they organize and execute their classroom instruction (i.e., "Are appropriate instructional and management strategies being used?"); and (c) the students who are engaged in learning, their ability and motivation to master the instructional material, and their responses to effective instruction and sound curricula (i.e., "Is each student capable, prepared, motivated, and able to learn, and are they learning?").

Critically, the data-based, functional assessment, problem-solving process and effective school and schooling practices, described earlier, work implicitly within this component. This occurs as the three facets of the Instructional Environment are analyzed proactively to determine how to design and implement the most effective instruction so that the highest number of students are academically successful. For those students who are unsuccessful, however, specific characteristics or processes within the three Instructional Environment components are analyzed to determine the reasons, individually or collectively, for their lack of success. Using the data-based, functional assessment, problem-solving process, for example, for a student with ongoing difficulties in third grade mathematics, a classroom teacher, independently or with the grade- or building-level RTI² team, might

- analyze the design and organization of the curriculum, its scope and sequence, its materials, and its contribution to the student's understanding, learning, and progress;
- evaluate his or her lesson plans, instructional delivery and pace, sensitivity and differentiation with the student, and accuracy in evaluating the student's understanding and mastery of material and skills over time; or
- assess the student's specific mastery of prerequisite skills, understanding of the instructional goals and directions, and progress when more concrete and sequential instruction, positive practice opportunities, or specific guidance and feedback are provided.

Once the reasons for a student's lack of success are validated, the results are linked to needed instructional or intervention services, supports, strategies, and programs. Here is where Project ACHIEVE's academic service-delivery blueprint, the PASS model, is used (see Figure 1.2).

Figure 1.2   The Positive Academic Supports and Services (PASS) Model:
A Service Delivery Continuum

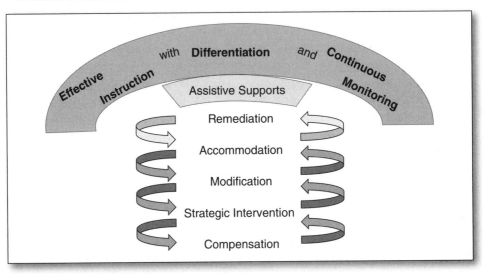

Source: Project ACHIEVE Press. Dr. Howie Knoff (author).

The PASS blueprint involves a continuum of academically focused instructional and intervention supports and services that are strategically implemented, across a multi-tiered system, at different levels of intensity. The foundation of the PASS blueprint is effective and differentiated classroom instruction where teachers use and continuously evaluate (or progress monitor) evidence-based curricular materials and approaches that are matched to students' learning styles and needs. As noted above, after a reasonable period of instruction, practice, and support, if students still have not mastered academic materials that are presented in effective ways, the data-based, functional assessment, problem-solving process is used. Results then are linked to different instructional or intervention approaches that are organized along the PASS continuum:

- *Assistive supports* involve specialized equipment, technologies, medical or physical devices, and other resources that help students, especially those with significant disabilities, to learn and function—physically, behaviorally, academically, and in all areas of communication. Assistive supports can be used anywhere along the PASS continuum.
- *Remediation* involves strategies that teach students specific, usually prerequisite, skills to help them master broader curricular, scope and sequence, or benchmark objectives.
- *Accommodations* change conditions that support student learning—such as the classroom setting or setup, how and where instruction is

presented, the length of instruction, the length or time frame for assignments, or how students are expected to respond to questions or complete assignments. Accommodations can range from the informal ones implemented by a classroom teacher to the formal accommodations required by and specified on a 504 Plan (named for the federal statute that covers these services).

- *Modifications* involve changes in curricular content—its scope, depth, breadth, or complexity.

Remediations, accommodations, and modifications typically are implemented in general education classrooms by general education teachers, although they may involve consultations with other colleagues or specialists to facilitate effective implementation. At times, these strategies may be implemented in "pull-out," "pull-in," or co-taught instructional skill groups so that larger groups of students with the same needs can be helped. If target students do not respond to the strategically chosen approaches within these three areas or if their needs are more significant or complex, approaches from the next three PASS areas may be needed:

- *Strategic interventions* focus on changing students' specific academic skills or strategies, their motivation, or their ability to comprehend, apply, analyze, synthesize, or evaluate academic content and material. Strategic interventions typically involve multidisciplinary assessments, as well as formal Academic Intervention or Individualized Education plans (AIPs or IEPs).
- *Compensatory approaches* help students to compensate for disabilities that cannot be changed or overcome (e.g., being deaf or blind, or having physical or central nervous system or neurological disabilities). Often combined with assistive supports, compensatory approaches help students to accomplish learning outcomes, even though they cannot learn or demonstrate specific skills within those outcomes. For example, for students who will never learn to decode sounds and words due to neurological dysfunctions, the compensatory use of audio or web-based instruction and (electronic) books can still help them to access information from text and become knowledgeable and literate. Both assistive supports and compensatory approaches are positive academic supports that typically are provided through IEPs.

While there is a sequential nature to the components within the PASS continuum, it is a strategic and fluid—not a lockstep—blueprint. That is, the supports and services are utilized based on students' needs and the intensity of these needs. For example, if reliable and valid assessments indicate that a student needs immediate accommodations to be successful in the classroom, then there is no need to implement remediations or modifications just to prove that they were not successful. In addition, there are times when students will receive different supports or services on the continuum simultaneously. For example, some students will need both modifications and assistive supports in order to be successful. Thus, the supports and services within the PASS are strategically applied to individual students. Moreover, while it is most advantageous to deliver needed supports and services within the general education classroom (i.e., the least restrictive environment), other instructional options could include co-teaching (e.g., by general and special education teachers in a general education classroom), pull-in services (e.g., by instructional support or special education teachers in a general education classroom), short-term pull-out services (e.g., by instructional support teachers focusing on specific academic skills and outcomes), or more intensive pull-out services (e.g., by instructional support or special education teachers). These staff and setting decisions are based on the intensity of students' skill-specific needs, their response to previous instructional or intervention supports and services, and the level of instructional or intervention expertise needed. Ultimately, the goal of this Project ACHIEVE component, and the PASS model, is to provide students with early, intensive, and successful supports and services that are identified through the problem-solving process, and implemented with integrity and needed intensity.

5.   The *behavioral instruction and intervention (PBSS) component* focuses on implementing a comprehensive positive behavioral support system within a school. Using Project ACHIEVE's evidence-based PBSS, this whole-school approach involves helping (a) students learn, master, and apply interpersonal, social problem-solving, conflict prevention and resolution, and emotional coping skills and interactions; (b) staff to create positive, safe, supportive, and consistent classroom climates and school settings that hold students accountable for their behavior; (c) schools to implement the strategic and intensive behavioral instruction or intervention needed to address students with nonresponsive, resistant, challenging, or extreme behavior; and (d) communities to reinforce these goals in home and other community settings. Like the academic instruction and intervention (PASS) component, this component and the PBSS are dependent on and implemented primarily in the Instructional Environment. Moreover, when students do not respond to effective social, emotional, and behavioral instruction, the data-based, functional assessment, problem-solving process is used at the student, classroom, grade, and building levels (the latter two through the early intervention School Prevention, Review, and Intervention Teams [SPRINT]; see Chapter 3) to determine why the situation is occurring and what instructional and/or intervention approaches are needed.

Ultimately, the primary goals of the PBSS are students who are socially competent and skilled in self-management; staff who can competently, confidently, and independently teach social skills and implement effective classroom-management strategies; and schools that can respond to students' strategic and intensive social, emotional, and behavioral needs. Thus, the self-management in Positive Behavioral *Self-Management* occurs at three levels: student, staff, and school. The evidence-based PBSS blueprint is described more extensively later in this chapter.

6. The *parent and community training, support, and outreach component* focuses on increasing the involvement of all parents but especially the involvement of parents of at-risk, underachieving, and chronically nonperforming students (Raffaele & Knoff, 1999). Unfortunately, parents in these latter three groups tend to be less involved in and supportive of the school and schooling process, and thus, parent involvement often discriminates achieving from underachieving students (Christenson, Rounds, & Franklin, 1992; Dunst, Trivette, & Johanson, 1994). Relative to the community, many schools do not use, and often are unaware of, the expertise and resources available to them. In addition, there are times when community agencies (e.g., afterschool programs) are providing services that schools could use to reinforce or extend their instructional, intervention, or other support activities. Finally, for students with significant, 24/7 academic or behavioral and mental health challenges, the need to coordinate and integrate school and community-based professionals and their services, supports, strategies, or programs is essential to the integrity of these approaches and the success of the students.

Among the parent and community activities that effective schools could demonstrate in this component are

- conducting needs assessments to look at the current and desired status of parent involvement and home-school-community collaboration and then designing and executing plans that meet identified needs;
- organizing building staff around collaboration and community outreach and establishing a school-level committee to specifically focus on more formal initiatives;
- creating parent drop-in centers to help parents see the school as a community resource for information and lifelong learning, increase their positive relationships and comfort levels with school staff, and encourage their participation in school activities;
- training parent mentors who can share information with other parents about the school's academic and social, emotional, and behavioral programs, and teach them how to support their children and adolescents at home relative to study skills, homework, academic proficiency, and social-behavioral success;
- completing community resource surveys resulting in resource directories that identify important organizations, agencies, and professional

programs, and important professionals with their specific skills and areas of educational, health and mental health, and related expertise; and

- reaching out to these community resources, formally and informally, to establish the communication, collaboration, and coordination that is especially needed relative to integrating services for at-risk, underachieving, and challenging students.

7.   The *data management, evaluation, and accountability component* focuses on actively evaluating, formatively and summatively, the status and progress of students' academic and behavioral mastery of information and skills as well as the processes and activities that support the other instructional, staff, and service components (see above) of an effective school. Part of this process involves collecting formative and summative data to validate the impact of a school's strategic planning and school improvement efforts; its professional development and capacity-building efforts; its selection, preparation, and implementation of academic and behavioral curricula and instruction; and its problem-solving, consultation, and multi-tiered RTI^2 services and supports for students not making appropriate academic or behavioral progress.

Another part of this process involves evaluating the interpersonal and interprofessional success of a school's shared leadership and committee and team processes as well as the contributions of administrative, related services, and instructional support personnel to system, staff, and student success. Relative to interpersonal and interprofessional relationships, evaluations should consider staff to staff, staff to parent and community, staff to student, and student to student interactions. All of these interactions collectively contribute to the climate and functioning of a school.

Summary. Beyond the research that correlates students' social, emotional, and behavioral status with their academic achievement, the interdependent relationship between classroom behavior and academic success is demonstrated through two essential questions. "Are there students in our classrooms who behaviorally act out or emotionally 'check out' because of academic frustration?" and "Are there students in our classrooms who do not academically succeed (or succeed as well as they might) because of social, emotional, or behavioral skill or motivational issues?" Knowing that the answers to these two questions are "Yes," this again reinforces the fact that curriculum, instruction, and academic achievement in any classroom is interdependent with discipline, behavior management, and student self-management. Moreover, the social, emotional, and behavioral factors are often prerequisite to the learning and achievement. Indeed, if students cannot sit in their seats, academic engagement decreases. If they cannot work independently, academic mastery may be reduced. If they cannot work, socially and behaviorally, in cooperative learning situations, their ability to apply and synthesize information may be hindered.

As an essential component of an effective school, a schoolwide PBSS is critical to students' academic and social, emotional, and behavioral learning, mastery, and proficiency. As the primary focus of this book, the six components of a scientifically based PBSS are described.

THE UNDERLYING SCIENCE AND SIX COMPONENTS OF THE EVIDENCE-BASED PBSS BLUEPRINT

Many states, districts, and schools have been implementing schoolwide PBSS using a number of available models for well over 15 years (e.g., Positive Behavioral Intervention Systems, Project ACHIEVE, Safe and Civil Schools, Fred Jones, William Glasser). In most cases, these models have adopted three-tiered RTI[2] approaches that focus on prevention, strategic intervention, and intensive need/crisis management services. Project ACHIEVE's PBSS (Knoff, 2009a) provides an evidence-based blueprint comprised of six functional components that organizes the behavioral side of the effective school and schooling process (see, again, Figure 1.1). Similar to the PASS, the PBSS is a continuum that begins with positive and effective classroom management and continues with social, emotional, and/or behavioral instructional or intervention services, supports, strategies, and programs that occur at different levels of intensity depending on student need. Before describing the six PBSS components, it is critical to emphasize that they exist within the context of ten scientific principles of behavior that directly relate to the ultimate goal of a PBSS—students' social, emotional, and behavioral competency and self-management. The ten scientific principles (Knoff, 2009b) are as follows:

1. We need to teach the social, emotional, and behavioral skills and the classroom and building routines that we expect students to demonstrate.

To accomplish this, students need to learn how to maintain physiological and cognitive self-control—that is, control over their physical/biochemical levels of emotionality and their thoughts, beliefs, attitudes, expectations, and attributions. Concurrently, students need to learn the steps or "scripts" required to demonstrate specific skills and the associated behaviors such that the skills are exhibited. This instruction is most successful when specific skills are explicitly taught and modeled by the teacher, behaviorally practiced (through role-play) by students along with explicit teacher feedback, and transferred (or applied) and infused into real-life situations.

2. When teaching social, emotional, and behavioral skills, we need to recognize that social and behavioral skills often occur under conditions of emotionality, and that students need to be taught emotional control skills.

Our definition of skill mastery is that "skills are mastered when a student can independently demonstrate these skills even under conditions of emotionality." Students learn how to respond successfully to emotional conditions when they are taught how to control their emotions—physiologically, cognitively, and affectively—and when the instruction includes simulations of these conditions, under supervision, so that students can successfully practice controlling their emotions and demonstrating appropriate behavior. Over time, this emotional control and coping instruction and the positive practice repetitions increase the probability that students will successfully use and demonstrate their skills when real emotional situations occur.

3. Many social, emotional, and behavioral skills are never fully mastered during childhood or adolescence, although the expectations for these skills increase over time. Thus, skill instruction must be ongoing and include instruction that teaches students to independently transfer the training across people, settings, situations, and conditions.

While students' potential for mastery and self-management increases developmentally and maturationally over time, skill instruction must be ongoing and continual. Relative to instruction, we need to continually give students guided learning opportunities to practice and apply their social, emotional, and behavioral skills with different people, in different settings and situations, and under varying conditions. These transfer of training opportunities, once again, increase the probability that students will more independently use and apply these skills successfully in actual situations.

4. For preschool through early elementary school students, mastered skills still need to be explicitly and externally prompted in order to be demonstrated. Middle elementary school students and beyond can self-prompt and independently demonstrate most mastered skills, but they still may need explicit and external prompts when under conditions of emotionality.

When preschool through early elementary school students have mastered specific social, emotional, and behavioral skills, adults still typically need to prompt or cue these skills before they will occur. That is, while the students have mastered these skills, they are not yet able to self-manage them. This is like having a software program already downloaded onto a computer but still needing to physically mouse-click it to activate it. Thus, after an adult prompt, these students demonstrate their skill mastery by responding to the social, emotional, or behavioral prompt within a reasonable amount of time and for longer and longer periods of time without the need for additional prompting.

When middle elementary school students (and beyond) have mastered specific social, emotional, and behavioral skills, they more independently recognize social, situational, or setting-specific cues; they self-prompt, guide, and demonstrate specific, needed skills; and they monitor, evaluate, and reinforce themselves for appropriate behavior or successful results. This is like having a virus protection program running continually on a computer so that when a virus tries to attack, the software automatically responds and disarms the threat.

Under conditions of emotionality, however, older elementary through middle school students (and beyond) still may need an adult to prompt a previously learned skill. This is because students at these age levels have not mastered emotional control skills at a level of automaticity and still need external support in these self-management areas.

5. Even when social, emotional, or behavioral skills have been mastered, students still need to be motivated to use these skills, and they need to be held accountable for their behavior. Ultimately, self-accountability is the highest level of social competency and self-management.

Students need to be motivated to learn new skills and, thereafter, to demonstrate these skills after mastering them. Some students need to be motivated to replace inappropriate with appropriate behavior. The foundations to motivation are incentives and consequences. Incentives are positive or reinforcing responses or experiences (e.g., positive statements or feedback, points or rewards, extra time or fun activities) that students value, want, or enjoy. Consequences are negative or aversive responses or experiences (e.g., negative feedback or calls home, the loss of points or opportunities to earn rewards, loss of free time or community service) that students do not want or enjoy and that they try to avoid. Incentives and consequences can be tangible, time or activity oriented, or provided (or lost) in a form (e.g., points or chips) that can be exchanged for something else. They can be (a) delivered verbally, nonverbally, or socially; (b) provided immediately or through different reinforcement schedules; or (c) given on an individual or group basis. They also can be extrinsic—coming from another person or from the environment—or intrinsic—coming from the student him- or herself.

When students have not learned and mastered specific skills, they are said to have a skill deficit in that area. The only intervention for skill deficit students is instruction. The question is, "Where, when, how, how often, at what level of intensity, and who will do the needed skill instruction with the student(s)?" Students who have mastered specific skills, but choose not to demonstrate them, are called performance deficit students. While the specific reasons for their refusal should be determined through a functional assessment process, any intervention for these students must include one or more motivational and/or accountability strategies.

Incentives best motivate performance deficit students to decrease and eliminate their inappropriate behavior and to establish or increase their appropriate behavior. At the same time, some performance deficit students are motivated to change their behavior only due to the consequences that may occur or that they have experienced in the past and want to avoid in the future. When used and effective, consequences do two things: they communicate that the student has behaved inappropriately, and they motivate the student to discontinue future inappropriate behavior and replace it with appropriate behavior. However, consequences do not change behavior by themselves; they create the conditions for change.

When the change process is working, performance deficit students recognize and acknowledge their inappropriate behavior and accept the resulting consequences. However, performance deficit students must also be held accountable for correcting their inappropriate behavior (e.g., by apologizing, cleaning or repairing an affected area, or completing community service activities), and they still must practice or demonstrate the expected, appropriate behavior—even if after the fact. Thus, performance deficit students are held accountable for both their inappropriate behavior and their choice to not behave appropriately.

6. Social, emotional, and behavioral skills need to be taught, learned, and mastered first in order for incentives and consequences to motivate future appropriate and independent behavior.

Clearly, if students have never learned and mastered a skill, no amount of motivation (i.e., incentives or consequences) is going to teach it to them. While motivation may enhance a student's desire to learn, effective instruction is the only thing that facilitates learning.

By way of analogy, if a student has not mastered the academic skills evaluated on a series of exams, the failing grades (the consequence for not learning) will not teach the student those skills. Similarly, if a student does not have the emotional skill of controlling his or her anger in class, disciplinary referrals to the office (again, the consequence) will not change this behavior. In fact, the only way to change this situation is to teach the student how to maintain emotional self-control or how to demonstrate specific conflict prevention or resolution skills when he or she is beginning to get angry.

When students are offered rewards for demonstrating skills or behaviors that they cannot do, an emotional and/or behavioral response typically results. Emotionally, the students may attempt to demonstrate the skill, fail, and become frustrated because they realize there is no hope for success. Behaviorally, the students may not attempt the skill for the same reason. Both scenarios may result in student distrust, anger, or withdrawal from with the person who offered a reward that was unattainable.

7. Incentives and consequences must be meaningful to the students, and they need to be strong enough to motivate students even when competing incentives and consequences are present. An effective accountability system in a school or classroom has both incentives and consequences available, as some students are motivated to receive incentives and others are motivated to avoid consequences.

When developing schoolwide student accountability systems, the expected behaviors should be clear and behaviorally described. In addition, the system should specify the incentives for appropriate behavior and progressive levels of consequences or responses to match different intensity levels of inappropriate behavior. While they may differ due to students' developmental and maturational differences, incentives and consequences must be meaningful to students and powerful enough to motivate appropriate behavior. If the incentives and consequences in a schoolwide accountability system are meaningful to the staff but not the students, the motivational system will fail.

In addition, we need to recognize that there are competing incentives and consequences in students' lives. For example, at times, there is a "triangulation" among an individual student, his or her teacher, and his or her peers. Thus, in the face of negative peer pressure, a student may not comply with a teacher, because compliance will result in later peer taunting, bullying, or rejection. When competing against each other, unless a teacher's motivational system is stronger than that of the peers, a student is likely to respond to the peers and not to the teacher.

Finally, we need to understand that incentives and consequences are contextual. Once again, effective incentives and consequences simply increase the probability that students will make good choices or demonstrate the appropriate social, emotional, or behavioral skills that they have learned. There are few 100% guarantees.

8. The intensity of a consequence should match the intensity of the offense. In addition, the most meaningful and powerful consequences are matched to each student and situation. The goal is to use the mildest consequence needed to motivate the quickest, largest, and most lasting change of student behavior.

When using consequences across different students, teachers need to know their students well enough so that they choose the consequence that has the most meaning and potential impact on each student. Relative to impact, the consequence that motivates the quickest, largest, and longest lasting change toward appropriate behavior should be chosen, recognizing that some students will receive different consequences even for the same inappropriate behavior.

In general, the mildest consequence needed to motivate a change of behavior should be used. If a major consequence is used to respond to a minor offense, then students may become angry at the inequity, refuse to accept responsibility and change their future behavior. They also may become accustomed to the more extreme consequence, requiring the same intensity in order to respond in the future. Thus, a school's accountability system should have a continuum of consequences and responses that are matched to different intensities of inappropriate behavior, from annoying to disruptive to antisocial to dangerous. As noted earlier, students will need to understand that while consequences are chosen to match the intensity of the offense, different students may receive different consequences at times.

9. If consequences are used, students must be held accountable for both their inappropriate and their (absent) appropriate behavior once they are finished. Thus, they need to correct or make amends for their inappropriate behavior and practice or demonstrate the absent or expected appropriate behavior. When consequences are needed, this combination of consequences, restitution, and positive practice is the formula that holds students accountable and responsible for appropriate behavior.

For performance deficit students especially, accountability must accompany motivation. That is, students who demonstrate inappropriate behavior still must demonstrate the appropriate behavior, even if after the fact. Our mantra here is, "If you consequate, you must educate." Thus, if students demonstrate an inappropriate behavior, there should be a consequence. As noted earlier, after the consequence is over, students should correct or remediate their inappropriate behavior (e.g., by apologizing, cleaning or repairing an affected area, or completing community service activities). They also need to return to the setting where the offense originally occurred and practice or demonstrate the appropriate behavior at least three times.

Naturally, the positive practice requirement should be done at times that are convenient for the teacher and others involved, but it should involve—as much as possible—the individuals (especially the adults) who were present for the original offense. Even if somewhat artificial, the goal here is to hold students accountable for appropriate behavior in specific settings with the people who typically are present in those settings. The positive practice also increases the probability that students will demonstrate appropriate behavior in the future because (a) they are motivated to avoid the positive practice requirement, and/or (b) the practice has taught or strengthened the appropriate behavior or choice.

10. Consistency, along with skill instruction, motivation, and accountability, are necessary, interdependent scientific components of student competency and self-management. While largely a process, consistency must be embedded within all of the other scientific principles and practices above.

Consistency, when setting social, emotional, and behavioral expectations, teaching competency and self-management skills, motivating and responding to students' use of these skills, and holding them accountable when inappropriate behavior occurs is essential to PBSS student, staff, and school outcomes (see Figure 1.3). Inconsistency weakens the instructional and motivational process, and it undermines adults' ability to hold students accountable. This often results in students who have not learned and mastered needed social, emotional, and behavioral skills and students who choose to demonstrate (continued) inappropriate behavior. Consistency is needed on an individual student level as well as across students, staff, settings, circumstances, and situations.

| Figure 1.3 | Consistency Across the Scientific Components of the Positive Behavioral Support System |

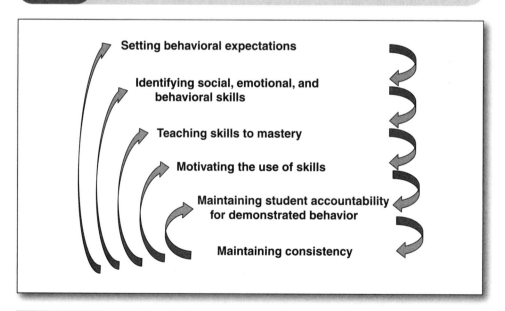

Source: Project ACHIEVE Press. Dr. Howie Knoff (author).

Relative to student competency and self-management, these scientific principles emphasize the importance of teaching, prompting, positively reinforcing, and helping students to internalize appropriate social, emotional, and behavioral skills. Relative to inappropriate behavior, these principles emphasize the importance of communicating and differentially responding to the intensity or severity of the behavior; holding students accountable for both inappropriate and expected, appropriate behavior; and taking actions that decrease or eliminate future inappropriate behavior and increase future appropriate behavior. Thus, when inappropriate behavior occurs, the goal is to positively change students' future behavior, not simply to punish or deliver consequences. As noted, these scientific principles are embedded in the seven goals and the six components of the PBSS process.

The Primary Goals of a Schoolwide PBSS Process. While the ultimate goal of a PBSS is student social, emotional, and behavioral competency and self-management, there are a number of complementary student, staff, and school goals.

Student Goals:
Student social, emotional, and behavioral competency and self-management as demonstrated by

- High levels of effective interpersonal, social problem-solving, conflict prevention and resolution, and emotional coping skills and behaviors by all students;
- High levels of critical thinking, reasoning, and social-emotional application skills and behaviors by all students; and
- High levels of academic engagement and academic achievement for all students.

Staff Goals:

- High levels of effective instruction and classroom management across all teachers and instructional support staff.
- High levels of teacher knowledge, skill, and confidence relative to analyzing why students are academically and behaviorally underachieving, unresponsive, or unsuccessful, and to implementing strategic or intensive academic or behavioral instruction or intervention to address their needs.

School Goals:

- High levels of the consultative resources and capacity needed to provide functional assessment leading to strategic and intensive instructional and intervention services, supports, strategies, and programs to academically and behaviorally underachieving, unresponsive, or unsuccessful students.

- High levels of parent and community outreach and involvement in areas and activities that support students' academic and social, emotional, and behavioral learning, mastery, and proficiency.
- High levels of positive school and classroom climate and low levels of school and classroom discipline problems that disrupt the classroom and/or require office discipline referrals, school suspensions or expulsions, or placements in alternative schools or settings.
- High levels of student success that result in high school graduation and postsecondary school success.

The Six PBSS Components. In order to accomplish these goals, Project ACHIEVE's evidence-based PBSS blueprint is described and used to organize the remainder of this book. The six components involve (a) *social skills instruction* for all students; (b) buildingwide *motivation and accountability* processes; (c) staff and administrative *consistency*; (d) *special situation* processes that focus on student behavior in the common areas of a school and teasing, taunting, bullying, harassment, hazing, and physical aggression; (e) school-based *crisis intervention and responses strategies*; and (f) *community and parent outreach* activities (see Figure 1.4).

Figure 1.4   The Positive Behavioral Self-Management (PBSS) Blueprint

Source: Project ACHIEVE Press. Dr. Howie Knoff (author).

Teaching Social Skills. The ultimate goal of a social skills program is to teach the interpersonal, social problem-solving, conflict prevention and resolution, and emotional coping skills that students need to become competent in these areas of their lives. In school and classroom settings, students with good social skills get along with teachers and peers, pay attention and cooperate with others, and demonstrate effective academic and social engagement and interactions. From a teaching perspective, social skills instruction involves the same steps as academic instruction. That is, students are taught the steps and behaviors that help them to prepare for and then behave in prosocial ways. Included in the teaching process are transfer of training activities and simulations to help students learn how to demonstrate their skills under conditions of emotionality.

For students who do not demonstrate appropriate social skill behavior after effective instruction, the data-based, functional assessment, problem-solving process is needed to determine why that is occurring. Some of these students, for example, might need more intensive or smaller group social skills instruction. Others might need more assistance in how to transfer their social skills training to actual situations. Still others might need more strategic or intensive emotional or self-control training to teach them how to demonstrate their social skills under these conditions. This information is discussed further in Chapter 5.

Accountability. Even when students have mastered their social skills, they still need to be motivated to use them. Indeed, when the peer group (that says, "be cool") competes against teachers and other educators (who say, "focus on school"), the importance of schoolwide accountability approaches is apparent. School accountability processes consist of meaningful incentives and consequences that motivate students to use their prosocial skills. These processes are important because (a) students with good social skills still need to be motivated to use their skills, (b) some (performance deficit) students lack this motivation, and (c) some students respond in situation-specific ways—making good choices when alone with adults but inappropriate choices when pressured by peers.

One way to establish a schoolwide behavioral accountability system is to develop a "Behavioral Matrix" (Knoff, 2007d). Created predominantly by staff and students, this matrix explicitly identifies, for all grade levels, behavioral expectations in the classroom and in other common areas of the school (connected with positive responses, incentives, and rewards) and different intensities or levels of inappropriate student behavior (connected with corrective responses, consequences, and interventions as needed). Relative to the latter, Intensity I behaviors involve annoying behaviors that teachers handle with corrective prompts; Intensity II behaviors involve more challenging, disruptive behaviors that teachers handle with prompts plus classroom-based consequences;

Intensity III behaviors are more serious persistent or antisocial behaviors that usually involve office discipline referrals followed by strategic intervention; and Intensity IV behaviors are the most serious code of conduct problems that generally involve office-based consequences, school suspensions, and then, intensive interventions.

Because the behaviors at each intensity level are agreed upon by staff and taught and communicated to students, their behavior is evaluated against a set of explicit behavioral standards. Moreover, when staff responses to both appropriate and inappropriate student behavior are consistent and predictable, students know how staff will respond in different situations and that they will be held accountable for their behavior. All of this facilitates a climate that reinforces student responsibility and self-management. This information is discussed further in Chapter 4.

When students do not respond to the skill instruction and behavioral accountability system over time or to a significant degree, or when they engage in persistent or significant Intensity III or IV behaviors, the need for functional assessment and strategic intervention becomes more apparent. This information is discussed further in Chapters 8 and 9.

Consistency. While social skills instruction and schoolwide accountability processes are necessary, a focus on consistency still is needed for student self-management and positive behavioral support success. Critically, consistency is more of a process than something that teachers explicitly teach (as in skills) or provide (as in incentives and consequences). Thus, the PBSS addresses skill consistency by evaluating the integrity of the social skills program's implementation in the classrooms and across the school; accountability consistency through the development and continuous monitoring of the Behavioral Matrix; and staff consistency by establishing staff processes that encourage positive staff communication, commitment, trust, collaboration, and celebration.

Consistency, however, also necessarily involves the students, who need to contribute to and sustain a prosocial atmosphere of prevention and communicate a no-tolerance attitude for inappropriate peer behavior. Thus, the PBSS helps schools create conscious and explicit values, expectations, norms, procedures, and interactions that prevent or respond to such behaviors as teasing, taunting, bullying, harassment, hazing, and aggression. This is best done by involving different student clubs and organizations, along with a school-level social marketing approach geared toward positive student and staff interactions.

Special Situations. Two types of special situations are incorporated into the PBSS to prevent or respond to situations and circumstances that most often occur at the peer group and school levels: setting-specific situations that occur in the common areas of the school (i.e., the hallways, bathrooms, buses, playground, cafeteria, or gathering areas) and student-specific situations that include teasing, taunting, bullying, harassment, hazing, and physical aggression incidents (often involving antagonists, victims, and active or passive peer bystanders). In order to develop strategic interventions for these situations, the school discipline committee (see Chapter 3) is taught to functionally analyze the ecology and dynamics of these special situations using the following domains: (a) student characteristics, issues, and factors; (b) teacher/staff characteristics, issues, and factors; (c) environmental characteristics, issues, and factors such as the physical plant and logistics within the specific setting; (d) incentives and consequences; and (e) resources and resource utilization (see Chapter 6). For student-specific special situations, analyses of peer group characteristics, issues, and factors are added. This is needed because many teasing through physical aggression incidents occur in the common areas of a school, and they are often influenced, explicitly or implicitly, by peer bystanders (Bosworth, Espelage, & Simon, 1999; Pellegrini, Bartini, & Brooks, 1999; Rigby, 2000; see Chapter 7). Once again, the results of these ecological, data-based assessments are linked to specific interventions to maximize problem solutions and resolutions.

Crisis Intervention and Response. This area involves an initial needs assessment of a school staff's ability to implement procedures to stop and stabilize situations during a crisis and then to address the security and social, emotional, and behavioral needs of students, staff, parents, and others after and in response to the crisis (Dwyer & Osher, 2000; Dwyer, Osher, & Warger, 1998). In the former area, schools and staff need to be prepared to address or de-escalate a wide variety of potential crisis situations as they are occurring (e.g., extreme weather conditions, racial harassment, gang fights, a faculty member's death, a hostage event). In the latter area, crisis response supports and strategies are needed to address procedural, wellness, and mental health needs in the aftermath of the crisis (i.e., one hour, six hours, 24 hours, three days, one week, and one month after the event). These supports and services include the interventions needed by those directly and indirectly affected by the crisis so that they can reconcile and resolve their involvement, experiences, and reactions on social, emotional, or behavioral levels. They also include the preventative and strategic interventions needed, for example, when crisis anniversary dates or other situations trigger emotional memories or reactions. This information is discussed further in Chapter 6.

Community and Parent Training and Outreach. Finally, this component focuses on increasing the involvement of community partners and the school's parents, as relevant, in all of the areas described above. Specific to community involvement, schools need to identify and use the expertise and resources available (e.g., from medical, social service, governmental, law enforcement, and other community agencies along with businesses, the faith community, and local or regional foundations) to reinforce and support their discipline, behavior management, and school safety programs. In a more direct way, parents especially need to be involved in the development and implementation of their school's social skills program, its schoolwide accountability system, and the special situation components within its PBSS initiative. In this way, parents and school staff can collectively give students explicit and consistent messages to reinforce their social and behavioral responsibilities and the fact that they will be held accountable for both appropriate and inappropriate behavior. Beyond this, school, community, and parent partnerships are critically important when behaviorally challenging students exist. Here, parent involvement is essential to the development and implementation of a coordinated treatment or intervention program, while community resources are often integral to the depth, breadth, and success of the identified program.

THE THREE TIERS WITHIN THE PBSS BLUEPRINT

When students do not respond to the preventative strategies within the six domains above, data-based functional assessments are conducted and linked to strategic social, emotional, or behavioral instruction or intervention approaches. These approaches are designed to address the underlying reasons for the problems and to prepare staff for effective and consistent implementation (Kerr & Nelson, 2010; Sprick & Garrison, 2008). These interventions may focus, for example, on the specific problems exhibited by a student (e.g., not completing homework, noncompliance, swearing, threatening others). Alternatively, they may focus on specific teacher behaviors, actions, or reactions that are triggering or inadvertently reinforcing inappropriate student behavior or are not prompting and reinforcing appropriate student behavior. More specifically, this may involve teachers who are not providing advanced organizers or appropriate behavioral feedback to one or more students, or teachers who are reinforcing inappropriate behavior through attention or inconsistent disciplinary practices.

To address the needs of non-responding, negatively responding, or inappropriately responding students, schools need staff members who have skills in behavioral observation, data collection and analysis, consultation, intervention, and evaluation. Relative to students with strategic and intensive needs, a multi-tiered instructional or intervention continuum that varies in intensity or needed specialization is outlined and described in Chapters 8 and 9 (see also Figures 1.5 through 1.7).

Figure 1.5 Prevention Services for All Students

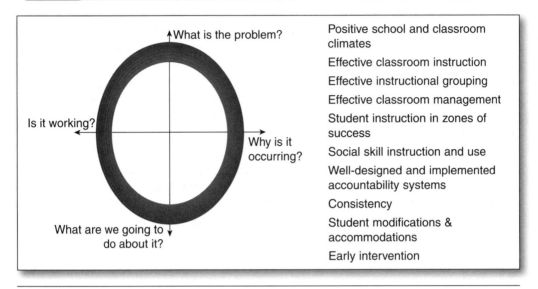

What is the problem?

Is it working?

Why is it occurring?

What are we going to do about it?

Positive school and classroom climates

Effective classroom instruction

Effective instructional grouping

Effective classroom management

Student instruction in zones of success

Social skill instruction and use

Well-designed and implemented accountability systems

Consistency

Student modifications & accommodations

Early intervention

Source: Project ACHIEVE Press. Dr. Howie Knoff (author).

Figure 1.6 Tier 2: Strategic Intervention Services for Some Students

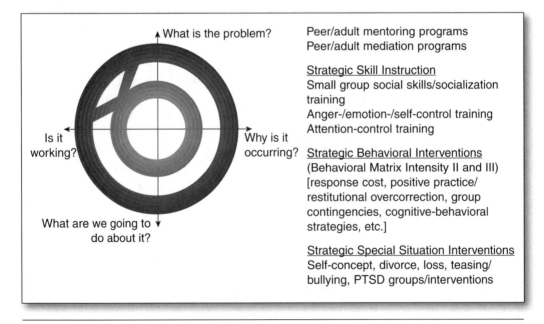

What is the problem?

Is it working?

Why is it occurring?

What are we going to do about it?

Peer/adult mentoring programs
Peer/adult mediation programs

Strategic Skill Instruction
Small group social skills/socialization training
Anger-/emotion-/self-control training
Attention-control training

Strategic Behavioral Interventions
(Behavioral Matrix Intensity II and III)
[response cost, positive practice/ restitutional overcorrection, group contingencies, cognitive-behavioral strategies, etc.]

Strategic Special Situation Interventions
Self-concept, divorce, loss, teasing/ bullying, PTSD groups/interventions

Source: Project ACHIEVE Press. Dr. Howie Knoff (author).

Figure 1.7 Tier 3: Crisis Management/Intensive Need Services

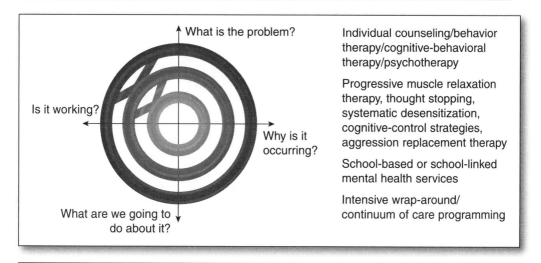

What is the problem?

Is it working?

Why is it occurring?

What are we going to do about it?

Individual counseling/behavior therapy/cognitive-behavioral therapy/psychotherapy

Progressive muscle relaxation therapy, thought stopping, systematic desensitization, cognitive-control strategies, aggression replacement therapy

School-based or school-linked mental health services

Intensive wrap-around/continuum of care programming

Source: Project ACHIEVE Press. Dr. Howie Knoff (author).

SUMMARY

This chapter provides a practical and research-based rationale for the schoolwide implementation of PBSS. It demonstrates the importance of embedding PBSS into the effective schools process and describes the scientific principles, the goals, and the six evidence-based components of the PBSS. The chapter concludes with a brief outline of the multi-tiered RTI^2 continuum to address the strategic and intensive needs of at-risk, underachieving, unresponsive, or unsuccessful students. Throughout this chapter, the ultimate goal of a PBSS is emphasized—for all students to consistently learn, master, and apply the skills needed for social, emotional, and behavioral competency and self-management in school (and other) settings. The remainder of this book addresses how to plan and implement the six PBSS components and what to do when students do not respond or respond in inappropriate or even extreme ways.

2

School Readiness and the Steps for PBSS Implementation

> In any endeavor, to be successful, you must begin with the end in mind.
>
> Stephen Covey

PBSS Implementation Case Study:
McDonald Elementary School, Seffner, Florida

McDonald Elementary School is in the Hillsborough County School District of Tampa, Florida, which is the tenth largest school district in the country. In 1998, we gave the School Leadership Team (SLT) and the entire school staff at McDonald an overview of the three-year Positive Behavioral Support System (PBSS) blueprint as part of our entry process. As we continued to work with the SLT and staff, we proceeded through a multifaceted organizational and motivational analysis of the readiness of the school for PBSS implementation. One aspect of the motivational analysis involved a formal vote by the staff to reflect their commitment to the three (or more) year process. A typical benchmark for readiness is a minimum 80% vote in favor.

Throughout the readiness process, a small, vocal number of staff members expressed concerns about (their resistance to) the initiative. When the vote was taken in late April, 83% of the staff voted in favor of the PBSS initiative, but the vocal negative staff members were among those who dissented—the only counselor in the building, the school's union representative, and one of the special education teachers.

In the follow-up SLT meeting in May, I expressed my concerns about the motivational readiness of the building given the dissenting staff and their formal and informal influence in the school. I recommended that we spend additional time to build the school's readiness and motivation, but the Team was not interested as the school year was ending and this would delay the first year of PBSS implementation in August. The principal replied, "I can handle the dissenters and bring them on board."

Against my better judgment, we began formal implementation in August. By the middle of the school year, it was apparent that the initiative was being undermined by the dissenters and that more dissenters had been brought on board. By the end of the year, the initiative was discontinued with no expectation that it could be resurrected by working again with the staff to rebuild the commitment needed.

INTRODUCTION

In order to effectively implement and scale up a PBSS in a school, across multiple schools in the same district, or across a state, it is important to have an evidence-based blueprint that can be adapted to meet the individual history, norms, needs, resources, and past and present outcomes at the school, district, or state level. As discussed in Chapter 1, this blueprint is implemented systematically and systemically across an entire school, and it is integrated into its effective school and schooling processes and its continuous improvement and strategic planning activities. At a district level, the same PBSS blueprint and process should be used across all schools, although some differentiation may occur at the elementary versus secondary levels.

Beyond the blueprint, the organizational and motivation readiness of a school and its staff is essential when planning, executing, maintaining, and sustaining a PBSS initiative. In addition, the importance of schoolwide planning and organization, capacity building and the use of resources, training and supervision, and implementation and evaluation is vital. Finally, the coordination and collaboration between school and district facilitates time-, cost-, and resource use efficiency, implementation integrity, and return-on-investment. Thus, while classroom teachers and support staff are the day-to-day PBSS implementers, the availability of resources and more intensive consultative support at the school and district levels facilitates implementation, maximizes momentum, and strengthens sustainability. This chapter focuses on the organizational variables and strategic planning processes needed when a school begins to consider a PBSS initiative. As such, we will begin with the end in mind by revisiting the most typical PBSS outcomes for a school and then describing a four-year implementation blueprint and how to prepare for its execution. Given the depth and breadth of this blueprint, this chapter is probably best read now and then reviewed after reading the remaining chapters in this book. In addition, it is essential to recognize how many individuals, groups, and committees will participate in the activities outlined here. Indeed, a schoolwide PBSS depends on schoolwide and district involvement. Thus, through this blueprint, important processes and activities are highlighted as well as how and where to link with district administrators and other resource professionals to maximize success.

While this PBSS blueprint is presented from a start-up perspective, schools that have successfully begun other more limited positive behavioral support programs can use this chapter to identify where and why they have been successful and what important value-added elements are needed to extend and strengthen their programs to a complete level of comprehensive implementation. This information also might help schools with unsuccessful programs or programs that have prematurely hit a plateau or an implementation wall to identify initial missteps, existing gaps, or activities that need to be revisited.

GOALS OF A SCHOOLWIDE
POSITIVE BEHAVIORAL SUPPORT SYSTEM

One of the first things that school staff members should do when beginning a new PBSS initiative is to think about (a) their desired or expected PBSS-related student, staff, and school goals and outcomes; (b) the current status of the school, staff, and students, and the school's outcomes over at least the last three years; (c) areas where they are not achieving desired PBSS-related outcomes (i.e., where there are negative, nonexistent, or slower-than-desired outcomes); and (d) the reasons for the school's existing accomplishments and non-accomplishments. By integrating all of this information with the primary PBSS goals and outcomes discussed in Chapter 1, the staff members should agree upon a core set of realistic and meaningful PBSS goals that need to be accomplished and that will guide their planning and initial implementation process.

Schools that are evaluating an existing positive behavioral support initiative need to consider and analyze the same four areas above. Sometimes, schools with existing positive behavioral support programs struggle because (a) they have not targeted students' social, emotional, and behavioral competency and self-management as their primary goal; (b) they have limited their focus to a single, deficit-related outcome (typically, decreasing office discipline referrals); and/or (c) they have not targeted important staff and school goals that contribute to student self-management outcomes. By considering the PBSS goals and objectives in Chapter 1 and the implementation elements and strategies throughout this book, schools using a different positive behavioral support model or approach may add essential components that result in deeper and more sustained outcomes and more comprehensive success.

Typically, the initial planning process that results in the identification of a school's core PBSS goals and outcomes is coordinated by the SLT (see Chapter 3), often in collaboration with the district administrators who oversee the following areas: health, mental health, and wellness; discipline, behavior management, and services for students with social, emotional, or behavioral challenges; and school safety and security. As the process proceeds, the PBSS goals and outcomes and the action steps needed to accomplish them are written into the school's annual school improvement plan, and the SLT actively facilitates their implementation. Eventually, most of these planning and execution processes are transferred to the school discipline/ PBSS committee that also becomes responsible for recommending the school's annual PBSS activities as the initiative progresses, expands, and succeeds.

A FOUR-YEAR PBSS IMPLEMENTATION BLUEPRINT

With the PBSS goals as a foundation, a four-year PBSS implementation blueprint is recommended for schools just beginning this process. Naturally, this blueprint may progress more quickly for schools (and districts) that have some elements already in place, and it might take longer for schools that need to secure resources, build capacity, or implement different elements more slowly. In the latter situation, school leaders need to recognize that a longer phase-in time might weaken momentum and motivation, especially if staff members do not see enough progress or positive outcomes over time. In the former situation, leaders should not move too quickly, putting implementation speed ahead of staff buy-in and consensus, the acquisition and deployment of resources, and the necessity for professional development and guidance.

The four-year PBSS blueprint devotes one year to planning and three years to phased-in implementation. During the planning year, activities within the blueprint involve the strategic planning and organizational analysis and development; behavioral instruction and intervention (PBSS); data management, evaluation, and accountability; and the parent and community training, support, and outreach components of the effective schools model discussed in Chapter 1. During actual implementation, all seven of the effective school and schooling components are involved. Below is an outline of the four-year PBSS planning and implementation process at the school level. Many of the actions and activities described can be adapted for use at the district level.

THE PLANNING YEAR: PRE-IMPLEMENTATION YEAR 1

Pre-implementation Year 1 activities involve three focus areas: (a) choosing a PBSS model and evaluating staff readiness; (b) organizational readiness and planning; and (c) preparation for implementation. These activities are organized below in a loose sequence, although many of them can be coordinated and completed at the same time. The pre-implementation year may extend across an entire school year or it may be concentrated from January through June. Regardless, in most cases, the first formal year of implementation starts just before the beginning of a new school year. Thus, those involved in PBSS planning and preparation need to complete the activities below so that the pre-implementation year moves seamlessly into the next year of formal implementation.

Focus Area 1. Choosing a PBSS Model or Approach and Evaluating the Motivational Readiness of the Staff and Others for the PBSS Initiative

Action 1.1: Initial PBSS Interest and Research Review and Study Team Selection. A school or district becomes interested in implementing a PBSS, and an initial research review and internet search of its generic goals, objectives, evidence-based components, activities, and outcomes is completed. The results of this review are reported to the entire faculty and, by virtue of a consensus of the faculty and the support of the administration, the SLT or a PBSS task force or study team with cross-staff representation is chosen to lead this part of the initiative.

Action 1.2: Initial Collection of Three Years of PBSS-Related School Data and Information. The study team collects at least three years of existing PBSS-related data, information, and outcomes from and about the school. This is collected from federal (Elementary and Secondary Education Act and Individuals with Disabilities Education Act), state, district, and school report cards and related databases and includes, for example, information about (a) student achievement and engagement; (b) students' social, emotional, behavioral health, mental health, and wellness status, programs, and needs; (c) perceptions and indicators of positive school climate and school safety; (d) office discipline referrals, student suspensions and expulsions, and special education or alternative school referrals and placements due to student behavior; (e) staff professional development and impact; and (f) parent and community involvement and outreach initiatives and outcomes.

Action 1.3: Completion of School Status and Longitudinal History Self-Study. Based on the self-study or self-evaluation in Action 1.2 above, the study team determines the current status of the school, staff, and students, and the school's PBSS-related outcomes over at least the last three years; problem areas and areas where the school is not achieving desired outcomes (i.e., where there are negative, nonexistent, or slower-than-desired outcomes); and reasons for the identified accomplishments and non-accomplishments. This begins the process of identifying what PBSS-related issues or outcomes the school needs to address through the chosen PBSS program or initiative and what existing activities or programs need to be maintained or discontinued, respectively.

Action 1.4: Completion of Staff, Stakeholder, and Consumer Motivational Analysis. As Actions 1.2 through 1.3 are proceeding, the study team or SLT completes a motivational analysis of the support, the potential support, and the opposition to the PBSS initiative across its staff and other stakeholder, constituency, and consumer groups, including community partners and parents. Through this analysis, the SLT also identifies those willing to publicize their commitment to the initiative and takes steps to gain the support of those who are on the fence or in opposition.

Action 1.5: Identification and Analysis of Effective PBSS Schools; PBSS Request for Proposals. If the study team wants to expand its Action 1.1 research review and internet search by identifying a number of already-existing effective PBSS programs, it locates these successful PBSS schools—nationally or within its state—matching them to the school's demographic and other student and staff characteristics. For schools willing to share their experiences and expertise, telephone or net-supported interviews, and/or virtual or actual school visitations then can occur.

Action 1.6: Choosing the Best PBSS Model and/or Project Director for the School. In order to choose the best PBSS model or approach, the study team matches the implementation and outcomes from the PBSS models or approaches researched in Action 1.1 to the problem areas and needs resulting from Action 1.3. At this point, especially if the school is going to independently implement the chosen PBSS model or approach, the team may have enough information to recommend a single model to its SLT and school staff.

If the school is planning to work with an outside (contracted) PBSS project director (or consultant) who will guide the implementation process, a formal Request for Proposals (RFP) asking for descriptions of applicants' background and expertise as well as the PBSS models that they use may be needed. Eventually, the team should interview the top two or three project director applicants responding to the RFP to determine who and whose model is best suited to their school. This process may include visits to one or more PBSS schools using each applicant, interviews, reviews of materials and products, and reference checks. As part of the interview process, each applicant might come on-site to the school, do a presentation for the PBSS study team or the entire staff, and meet with small groups of staff to allow for questions and discussion.

If the school is planning to use an internal (district- or school-employed) PBSS project director, the identification and selection process should be determined and implemented.

Action 1.7: Final PBSS Model and Project Director Recommendation. Here, the study team makes a final decision on its recommended PBSS model, approach, and PBSS project director and shares these results with the SLT and administration.

Action 1.8: Faculty Briefing, Discussion, Decision on PBSS Model and Project Director. With the endorsement of the SLT and administration, the study team shares their recommendation on the PBSS model, approach, and project director with the entire staff. Prior to this announcement, the administration and SLT need to decide how the staff will be involved in the final decision. That is, for example, are they advisory to an administrative decision, do they have a formal vote in the final decision, or is their consent desired but not necessary? Regardless of their formal or informal involvement, a staff consensus of at least 80% support typically is recommended to proceed.

Action 1.9: Administrative Agreement and Contracting. If needed, the school administrator discusses the formally recommended (and agreed upon) PBSS model, approach, and project director with the district administration and, if needed, the school board. If an external PBSS project director is used, he or she should agree to work with the school based on the match between his or her skills and expertise and the school's need for and commitment to the chosen PBSS model. If needed, contracts or memoranda of agreement with the PBSS project director are written and signed with the school or district.

Action 1.10: Initial Implementation Plan for Planning Meeting. An initial plan for planning meeting with the SLT, the PBSS study team, selected others, and the new PBSS project director (if relevant) is held. During this one (or multiple) meeting(s), a PBSS implementation readiness action plan is written that outlines the steps, activities, timelines, people, and resources needed for the next phase of PBSS implementation. Included in these next steps are a more formal needs assessment and resource analysis; the selection and formation of a building-level school discipline/PBSS committee (see Chapter 3); a review of the school's Response-to-Instruction and Intervention/School Prevention Review, and Intervention Team structure and process (see Chapter 3); the selection of a social skills program (see Chapter 5) and the development of a schoolwide behavioral accountability system through the Behavioral Matrix (see Chapter 4); and the execution of a number of critical end-of-year articulation or new-school-year preparation activities (see Chapter 10).

Action 1.11: Formal Public Announcement and Kickoff. The school administrator announces to the entire staff, as well as to the parents and community stakeholders and constituents, the final approval of the PBSS model and project director, and the tentative steps and timelines that will occur in the next phase of PBSS readiness.

Action 1.12: Disbanding of the Study Team. The study team is disbanded and thanked for its service to the school.

Focus Area 2. PBSS Organizational Readiness and Planning

Many of the next actions are guided by the new PBSS project director (if relevant), the SLT, any newly established committees (e.g., the school discipline/PBSS committee, the School Prevention, Review, and Intervention Team [SPRINT]), and the school's administration.

Action 2.1: Formation or Confirmation of the School Discipline/PBSS Committee and the Grade- and Building-Level SPRINT Teams and Structure. The SLT reviews the school's committee structure and establishes building-level school discipline/PBSS committee and grade- and building-level SPRINT teams if they do not yet exist (see Chapter 3). The discipline/PBSS committee will become responsible for guiding the implementation of the schoolwide PBSS process with the PBSS director. The SPRINT teams are the early intervention teams that implement the data-based functional assessment problem-solving process (see Chapter 8) when students do not academically or behaviorally respond to effective classroom instruction and classroom management.

Action 2.2: Selection of the School Discipline/PBSS Committee Chair, Recording Secretary, and Members' Terms of Office. Supported by the administration, a committee chair (or co-chairs) of the school discipline/ PBSS committee is (are) selected. If the PBSS project director is a member of the school's staff, he or she will typically be the committee chair. The committee also selects a recording secretary, a monthly meeting time (although the committee may need to meet more frequently during start-up), and the terms of office for different committee members (see Chapter 3).

Action 2.3: Completion of the Committee Mission, Role, and Function Document. During the next weeks or months, the school discipline/PBSS committee completes its committee mission, role, and function statement or document (see Chapter 3). In this document are the committee's mission, members, monthly meeting time and place, general and annual goals and objectives, fixed agenda items, and primary data and information sources.

Eventually, the school needs to integrate necessary school and district policies, practices, personnel, resources, waivers, and professional development into its three-year and next-year school improvement plan and have it approved at the district level.

Action 2.4: Completion of a Comprehensive Needs Assessment and Resource Analysis. With the PBSS director's involvement, the SLT completes a (or reviews its existing) needs assessment and resource analysis. The needs assessment expands on the data and information collected in Action 1.2 and analyzed during Action 1.3. The goal is to identify (a) what is working at high, moderate, low, and nonexistent levels relative to students' academic and social, emotional, and behavioral outcomes; (b) what is needed, at student, staff, school, district, and community levels to maintain high successes, strengthen moderate successes, and address low and nonexistent successes; and (c) how the needs should be prioritized.

Complementing the needs assessment is a Strengths, Weaknesses, Opportunities, Threats (SWOT) analysis completed, again, at student, staff, school, district, community, and regional or state levels. This analysis identifies existing resources (e.g., personnel, time, money, materials, products, buy-in, professional development, technology, innovation) and their return-on-investment (ROI) relative to time, cost, and effort. When crosswalked with the needs assessment, this analysis specifies the existing supports available to facilitate the PBSS initiative, organizational and resource gaps to close, existing barriers to overcome, and other factors that threaten to undermine the initiative.

Action 2.5: Completion of the Staff Resource Directory. As part of the resource analysis, the SLT develops a questionnaire and conducts a staff "skill and expertise" analysis to determine the expertise of everyone working full-time or part-time in the school (including, for example, all part-time or consulting related services professionals or community/agency professionals or volunteers). On the questionnaire, staff share their specific areas of expertise, for example, relative to (a) curriculum and academic instruction; (b) student behavior and classroom management; (c) technology or special instructional techniques; (d) student assessment and progress monitoring; (e) strategic or intensive academic and social, emotional, or behavioral instruction or intervention techniques; and (f) other areas of expertise, including out-of-school talents, hobbies, and interests. The goal of this activity is to identify the skills and resources that already exist in a school and to make everyone in the school aware of the different people who are available to consult with others in specific areas.

All of this information is published in a staff resource directory. This resource can be posted on the shared drive of the school's computer system, and it can be used informally by classroom teachers or more formally as part of the school's early intervening and multi-tiered SPRINT process.

Action 2.6: Completion of the Consultant Resource Directory. Beyond the school, districts should also prepare and publish a consultant resource directory, describing the specific skills of the instructional specialists or consultants, related services professionals, special educators, counselors or behavioral intervention specialists, and others with advanced areas of expertise who work in schools or other settings across the district. This directory helps schools find and obtain the expertise and consultative services from other parts of the district when they lack, for example, specific expertise for a student with unusual, complex, or intensive assessment, instructional, or intervention needs.

Action 2.7: Completion of the Behavioral Intervention Survey. As the staff and consultant resource directories are being created, participating staff also should complete an in-depth survey of their expertise across a number of specific Tier 1 through Tier 3 social, emotional, and behavioral interventions that might be needed by certain students or in certain situations (see Chapters 1, 9, and 10). The behavioral intervention survey, for example, describes a number of specific interventions and asks respondents to rate their expertise with each intervention along a five-point scale from 5—Expert in Both Consultation and Implementation to 1—No Knowledge of the intervention. The results of this survey are used to identify both the intervention expertise of specific professionals in the school and district and the intervention gaps that might require systematic professional development for selected professionals.

Action 2.8: Completion of the Community Resource Directory. Beyond school and district employees and consultants, the district also should prepare and publish a community resource directory—especially in the areas of social, emotional, and behavioral, or health, mental health, and wellness. The directory should specify the degrees and certifications or board licensure areas of expertise of anyone working in a specific agency or for any private practitioner or group practice. In addition, the types of student disorders addressed by agency personnel or private practitioners, the psychological orientations used (e.g., cognitive-behavioral, family systems, psychodynamic), and the specific clinical techniques available should be outlined. Finally, the scope of services, populations served, specific qualifying criteria (if any), and indicators of clinical success should be shared. With this directory, schools and districts can make strategic community-based referrals of students and parents when needed. The directory is particularly important when coordinating home-school-community, wrap-around, or continuum systems of care services for students with complex, significant, or multifaceted needs.

Action 2.9: Completion of the Scale of Staff Interactions and School Cohesion and Scale of Effective School Discipline and Safety. In order to evaluate the staff's perceptions of how well they interact with each other and the administration and of the existing discipline and behavior management attitudes and interactions across the school, the 25-item *Scale of Staff Interactions and School Cohesion* and the 58-item *Scale of Effective School Discipline and Safety* are completed (see Chapter 10). The results of these scales should be shared with the faculty at a meeting so they can be validated, clarified, and discussed. Activities to address the needs based on the results of the scales and follow-up discussions eventually are written into the PBSS section of the school improvement plan.

Action 2.10: Development of the Committee Implementation Plans. Based on the completed comprehensive needs assessment and resource analysis (Action 2.4), the school discipline/PBSS committee writes a three-year PBSS implementation plan and a one-year plan that is submitted to the SLT for integration into the next school improvement plan. An implementation preparation plan (if needed) also is written to cover the activities needed prior to Implementation Year 1 (see below).

Action 2.11: Review and Alignment of School and District Policies With PBSS Directions. If needed, the school makes sure that all of its internal policies are consistent with the existing PBSS initiative and its planned directions. The school discipline/PBSS committee, SLT, and administration discuss needed additions or changes to school or district policies and procedures—securing them either through the district's administration or school board or by receiving a waiver from those that cannot be changed.

Action 2.12: Review and Alignment of School Vision and Mission Statements With PBSS Directions. Based on all of the results and actions above, the SLT looks at its vision statement (if applicable) and mission statement to ensure that they are consistent with the PBSS initiative, making any changes desired or needed.

Focus Area 3. Preparation for PBSS Implementation

Action 3.1: Review and Redesign of Existing PBSS Multi-tiered System of Implementation. The discipline/PBSS committee reviews the programs, strategies, and approaches currently in place in the school that represent the current multi-tiered system of prevention, strategic instruction or intervention, and intensive needs and crisis management. This process identifies the strengths, weaknesses, barriers, gaps, and needs that should be addressed immediately, in the short term or in the long term. This process may result in a redesign of the multi-tiered system (see Chapter 1) to facilitate the accomplishment of specific PBSS goals and outcomes.

Action 3.2: Review of the PBSS Data Collection and Management System. The discipline/PBSS committee reviews the components of the existing PBSS data collection, tracking, analysis, and management resources and tools (e.g., software, databases, and other computer- or web-based programs), and their efficacy relative to helping the school to enter, organize, summarize, display, track, and evaluate PBSS data and information (see Chapter 10). Based on the results, the committee works with the administration, the school district's technology personnel, committee members, and others to design and set up the needed databases and other software or data management systems to close any apparent gaps.

Action 3.3: Review of the Social, Emotional, Behavioral Instruction System/Process. As part of Action 3.1 above, the discipline/PBSS committee reviews the programs, strategies, and approaches currently in place in the school that focus on teaching students social, emotional, and behavioral skills and their outcomes (see Chapter 5). These are cross-referenced to any state or district requirements in the areas of health, behavioral or mental health, and wellness. For example, at the secondary level, such requirements often involve topics related to drugs and alcohol, social skills and character education, cultural sensitivity and competence, bullying and sexual harassment, and sexual health and relationships.

As one result of this review, the committee validates or creates a scaffolded health, mental health, and wellness scope and sequence or curriculum map that includes the specific social, emotional, and behavioral topics and skills that will be taught across the grade levels in its school. A second result is that the committee validates the current social, emotional, and behavioral curriculum currently being used in the school, or it decides to research and choose a new approach.

Action 3.4: Validation or Selection of a Social, Emotional, and Behavioral Curriculum or Instruction Process. If the discipline/PBSS committee decides to pursue a new social, emotional, and behavioral skill instruction curriculum, it completes a systematic review and analysis of the evidence-based curricula available, and it chooses the curriculum that best meets its student-focused goals, outcomes, and needs. It then secures the permission and funding so that all of the necessary implementation materials are purchased and available prior to implementation year one.

Action 3.5: Development of the Behavioral Accountability Matrix. Guided by the grade-level representatives on the school discipline/PBSS committee, the Behavioral Matrix—a document that codifies the behavioral expectations at each grade level in the school—is completed (see Chapter 4). The Behavioral Matrix is the anchor to the PBSS's accountability process. It identifies expected behaviors in the classrooms and common areas of the school connected with positive responses, incentives, and rewards and four intensity levels of inappropriate behavior (from annoying behavior through code of conduct offenses) connected with research-based responses that hold students accountable for their inappropriate behavior while reinforcing and motivating future appropriate behavior.

Once the behavioral matrices are completed, the school discipline/PBSS committee prepares the staff for the implementation rollout of the process across the school and ensures that support materials and other necessities (e.g., Behavioral Matrix posters for all classrooms) are ready for the rollout.

Action 3.6: Social Skills Preparation by the Staff. Once the social, emotional, and behavioral curriculum chosen by the school or district is received (see Action 3.4), the school discipline/PBSS committee coordinates a book study whereby the materials are progressively read by everyone in the school and each reading assignment is discussed in small groups. This is an important step that precedes, if it is to occur, the formal in-service training where all staff are trained in how to implement the curriculum or program.

Action 3.7: Drafting of the Social Skills Calendar With Classroom and Building Routines. Given the results of Actions 3.4, 3.5, and 3.6, the school discipline/PBSS committee drafts a beginning-of-the-year social skills and student accountability implementation calendar in April or May. This calendar includes the rollout of the Behavioral Matrix accountability system on the first day of the new school year, teaching and reinforcing expectations and routines in the common areas of the school and in the classrooms, and teaching the social, emotional, and behavioral skills curriculum across the school year.

Action 3.8: Completion of the Get-Go and Student Briefing Reports Process. If ready, the school should complete the Get-Go process (see Chapter 10) in April. This end-of-year process involves a review of the academic and behavioral progress of all students and identification of students who need immediate interventions at the beginning of the new school year ("Get-Go" students) and those whose next-year's teachers need to be briefed as to the instructional and intervention approaches that helped them be successful this year ("At-Risk" students). Related to this activity is the completion of Student Briefing Reports for the students by their current teachers. These reports are given to the new teachers receiving these students prior to the beginning of the new school year.

Action 3.9: Special Situations Analysis. If possible, the school discipline/PBSS committee should complete a special situation analysis (see Chapters 6, 7, and 10) in April of student behavior in the common areas of the school, and relative to teasing, taunting, bullying, harassment, hazing, and physical aggression. Based on the results of this analysis, the committee could complete a focused special situation analysis on one of the areas identified to develop an intervention plan to address the selected area at the beginning of the next school year.

Implementation Year 1

As noted above, Implementation Year 1 typically starts at the beginning of a new school year during the staff preparation days just prior to the students returning to school. The activities below are largely coordinated by the school discipline/PBSS committee, but, given the interdependence between students' academic and social, emotional, and behavioral success, virtually all of the other school-level committees are involved at some point. This is especially true of the SPRINT teams who use the data-based functional assessment problem-solving process (see Chapter 8) when individual students are exhibiting progressive, resistant, or significantly challenging behavior. The activities below are organized in a preferred, but not absolute, sequence. Individual schools, guided by their SLT and school discipline/PBSS committees, need to make strategic decisions, based on staff, resources, and other aspects of their school improvement plan, as to the best timing and approaches for implementation.

Implementation Year 1, Semester 1

Action 1.1: Initial School Discipline/PBSS Committee Meeting. During the staff preparation days prior to the new school year, the school discipline/PBSS committee should have its first meeting of the year. During this meeting, it should review its annual goals, objectives, outcomes, and activities as well as the upcoming training and other events that will begin the schoolwide PBSS process for the new school year. If needed, group and other processes to help the committee function effectively will be reviewed along with any important information based on events during the summer.

Action 1.2: Social Skills Training for the Entire Staff. During the staff preparation days prior to the new school year, the entire staff participates in a full-day in-service training to learn the buildingwide implementation of the chosen social, emotional, and behavioral skills program.

This in-service should be followed up during the first weeks of school with (a) grade- or instructional-team meetings to allow teachers to develop and practice selected social skill lessons, (b) observations of social skill demonstrations in the classrooms by the primary in-service trainers (with opportunities to debrief these experiences), and (c) the implementation of real social skill lessons by all classroom teachers with appropriate supervision and feedback.

Action 1.3: First Day and Week of School PBSS Activities. Guided by the grade-level representatives on the school discipline/PBSS committee, the PBSS Behavioral Matrix and accountability system is rolled out on the first day of the new school year emphasizing and teaching the classroom and common school area expectations and behaviors as well as the system of incentives and consequences. In addition, classroom teachers begin to introduce the social skills curriculum and to teach the initial processes and skills.

Action 1.4: Extended Social Skills and Time-Out Training. Within the first six weeks of the school year, all staff members participate in additional in-service training to debrief and extend the buildingwide implementation of the social, emotional, and behavioral skills program to new and more complex skills and situations. In addition, the staff members have an opportunity to discuss the initial implementation of the Behavioral Matrix system and unexpected or unintended behavioral situations or outcomes. Finally, especially at the elementary and middle school levels, staff members are trained in a buildingwide application of an educative time-out process (see Chapter 9) which is integrated into the Behavioral Matrix and office discipline referral processes.

Action 1.5: School Discipline/PBSS Committee Follow-Up and Support. Immediately following Action 1.4 above, the PBSS director and other PBSS consultants should be available to grade-level teams and individual staff members with on-site technical assistance across a range of possible areas: demonstrating and videotaping sample social skill lessons in selected classrooms or using specific skills; demonstrating and videotaping sample time-out lessons or procedures in selected classrooms or with specific challenging students; observing and providing feedback to teachers conducting social skill lessons in their classroom; observing and providing feedback to teachers demonstrating the time-out process in their classrooms; meeting with grade-level teams to discuss the social skills or time-out process or to address specific students' more challenging behavior; meeting with the building-level school discipline team to discuss implementation issues; meeting with the administration to discuss implementation issues; and meeting with parent and community representatives to discuss building and extended community implementation and wrap-around.

Action 1.6: Initial SPRINT Team Training. Concurrent with the PBSS activities above, the building-level SPRINT team participates in an in-service on the data-based problem-solving process and begins to practice these skills using a guided case study approach.

Action 1.7: End-of-Semester Formative Evaluations. At the end of the semester, the school discipline/PBSS committee, in collaboration with the administration and SLT, conducts formative evaluations on the different facets of the PBSS so that strategic plans and implementation activities and processes can be adapted as needed. This review should especially focus on the social skills training and the Behavioral Matrix process. If needed, modifications to the social skills calendar and to specific behaviors on the Behavioral Matrices can be made at this time.

Implementation Year 1, Semester 2

From January through the remainder of the first year, the school discipline/ PBSS committee continues to meet at least monthly to plan, implement, and evaluate PBSS activities and data. Within the grade-level teams, teachers continue to implement, evaluate, and monitor the social skills, accountability, and consistency processes in their classrooms. The school discipline/PBSS committee, meanwhile, continues to support and periodically review the classroom, grade-level, and buildingwide accountability system; collect formative evaluation data; determine the need for additional social skills, time-out, or behavioral intervention training for the staff; track the use of the social skill process by secretaries, paraprofessionals, cafeteria workers, and custodians; develop drafts of the building's crisis response plans and processes (see Chapter 6); and extend the initiative's training and implementation into home and community settings.

Action 2.1: Schoolwide SPRINT Training. In January, a third schoolwide in-service is provided on the data-based functional assessment problem-solving process that teaches staff members how to functionally and behaviorally analyze students who are not responding to the preventive aspects of the PBSS system and who are presenting with more resistant or challenging behavior.

Action 2.2: Grade-Level SPRINT Practice. Once the Action 2.1 training has been completed, grade-level teams meet at least monthly to use and practice the data-based functional assessment problem-solving process, applying it to cases involving individual or groups of students presenting with challenging behaviors. These meetings are facilitated by a representative of the building-level SPRINT team (e.g., the school psychologist, social worker, school counselor, or special education teacher) so that the problem-solving process is practiced and used with integrity. This helps to establish the grade-level SPRINT process (see Chapter 3) that becomes a routine part of the monthly grade-level meetings in the school.

Action 2.3: Formal Special Situations Analysis Training for the School Discipline/PBSS Committee. If it has not yet taken place, the school discipline/PBSS committee is formally trained in how to conduct special situation analyses and develop special situation intervention plans based on their results.

Action 2.4: Extended Social, Emotional, and Behavioral Intervention Training for Selected Staff Members. During the course of this semester (or school year), and based on the results of the behavioral intervention survey (and other tools), selected staff members participate in strategic and intensive training in specific social, emotional, and behavioral intervention areas. For example, selected members of the school discipline/PBSS committee may receive more specialized training in Tier 1 and 2 (see Chapter 1 and 9) interventions, while members of the building-level SPRINT team may receive more specialized training in Tier 2 and 3 interventions.

Action 2.5: End-of-Year Articulation Activities. At the end of the school year, the school discipline/PBSS committee, along with all other staff, committees, and administrators, complete the PBSS-relevant articulation activities (see Chapter 10). At a minimum, this involves the strategic planning, committee, social skills, Behavioral Matrix, Get-Go and Student Briefing Report, and professional development planning articulation activities.

Action 2.6: End-of-Year Formative Evaluations. At the end of the school year, the school discipline/PBSS committee, in collaboration with the administration and SLT, conducts formative and summative (as relevant) evaluations on the different facets of the PBSS so that new strategic plans and implementation activities and processes can be identified and written into the new school improvement plan.

Action 2.7: Summer Facilitators' Institute. During June at the end of Year 1, the PBSS director (and others) may lead a summer institute for staff members who wish to become PBSS facilitators. During this institute, prospective facilitators learn how to (a) provide the in-service and professional development training needed in different areas of PBSS implementation, including the SPRINT data-based functional assessment problem-solving process; (b) implement the corresponding building- and classroom-based technical support and consultation follow-up such that the content of the professional development is implemented with integrity; and (c) coordinate the data collection and analysis process such that formative and summative evaluations are completed to validate the impact and success of the activities implemented.

Implementation Year 2

During Implementation Year 2, schools focus on institutionalizing as many Year 1 activities as possible, for example, the (a) consistent, schoolwide implementation of the social, emotional, and behavioral skills program; (b) grade-level and schoolwide use of the Behavioral Matrix; (c) effective internal functioning of the school discipline/PBSS committee; and (d) continued, effective facilitation and support of the entire PBSS initiative by the school discipline/PBSS committee with the entire school staff and community. This institutionalization includes the SPRINT's data-based functional assessment problem-solving process as the Committee works to extend the capacity of staff to implement more intensive social, emotional, and behavioral interventions, to the greatest extent possible, in all general education classrooms.

In addition, by the beginning of Implementation Year 2, school discipline/PBSS committee meetings should be occurring monthly, complemented by at least one grade-level meeting per month (at each grade level) focusing on PBSS goals and activities. At this point (if not before), grade-level teams should be receiving monthly reports that give them differentiated data relative to their social skill and other outcomes, including the number of office discipline referrals that occurred the previous month compared with data from the same month during previous years. Using these data, teams can compare and contrast each year's students and track their ongoing progress. Grade-level teams also can use their meeting times to problem solve more complex or resistant individual student or group discipline or behavior management problems using the data-based functional assessment process.

Concurrent with these and other relevant activities described in the first two PBSS years above, the school discipline/PBSS committee continues to implement, evaluate, and extend their PBSS activities in the following areas: (a) helping to develop, implement, and periodically review the classroom-, grade-level, and buildingwide accountability process; (b) fine-tuning the data management system and determining the need for additional social skills, time-out, or behavioral intervention training for the staff; (c) tracking the use of the social skills process by secretaries, aides, cafeteria workers, and custodians; (d) upgrading (as needed) the building's prevention, intervention, and crisis management and response plans and processes; and (e) extending PBSS training and implementation into home and community settings.

Implementation Year 2 Activities

Action 1.1: Boosters Sessions for Previously Trained Staff on PBSS Components. During the staff preparation days prior to the new school year and during the first month of school (as needed), booster in-service, consultation, and technical assistance sessions for all continuing staff occurs in the PBSS's social skills, time-out, data-based problem solving, and other classroom implementation components, skills, and activities.

Action 1.2: Fast-Track Training for All New Staff on PBSS Components. During the staff preparation days prior to the new school year and during the first month of school, fast-track training in the year one PBSS components for all new staff occurs. If available, this training is coordinated with the training provided to another PBSS school in the district that is beginning its Implementation Year 1 start-up. Regardless, this training includes concurrent mentoring by the PBSS director, selected facilitators, the school discipline/PBSS committee representative at the new teacher's grade level, and the new teacher's first-year coach or mentor (if relevant).

Action 1.3: Staff Training on Strategic Behavioral Interventions. During the staff preparation days prior to the new school year and during the first month of school, the entire staff participates in a full-day in-service workshop on the more strategic, classroom-based behavioral interventions that can be applied and used with more challenging students who are only partially responding to the building-based social skills and accountability system (see Chapter 9).

Action 1.4: Strategic Intervention Consultation Follow-Up. During the two to three months following the strategic intervention in-service in Action 1.3, on-site technical assistance is provided using actual student cases to facilitate the implementation of these interventions for existing challenging students.

Action 1.5: Staff Training on Crisis Prevention, Management, and Response. During the winter or spring, staff members receive training, support, and practice in how to prevent and, as needed, respond to different crisis situations (see Chapters 6 and 7). Such situations might include weather-related disasters, student or staff accidents or deaths, student fights, shootings or other acts of violence on campus, and so on. This training also involves briefings on how to handle situations involving home-based physical or sexual abuse, student harassment, student suicide threats, and other life crises. Concurrent with this training is the identification of those contacts or resources within the school, district, and community for each of the situations discussed.

Action 1.6: Parent and Community Outreach Program. During the winter or spring, the school discipline/PBSS committee should implement (if this has not yet occurred) a PBSS outreach program to parents, community agencies, and other community leaders and constituencies. This outreach could involve training that extends the school's PBSS, for example, to families, community-based social service and support agencies, day care or afterschool care and weekend programs, the faith community, or the business community. Alternatively, this outreach might involve a communitywide collaborative effort to extend the PBSS to as many community-based and family settings and circumstances as possible.

Action 1.7: Continued or Extended Social, Emotional, and Behavioral Intervention Training for Selected Staff members. During the course of this year, and based on the intervention needs of the challenging students who exist or are emerging in the school, selected school discipline/PBSS committee and SPRINT team members continue to participate in strategic and intensive training in specific social, emotional, and behavioral intervention (Tier 2 and 3) areas.

Action 1.8: End-of-Year Articulation Activities. At the end of the school year, the school discipline/PBSS committee, along with all other staff members, committees, and administrators, again complete the PBSS-relevant articulation activities involving, at minimum, the strategic planning, committee, social skills, Behavioral Matrix, Get-Go and Student Briefing Report, and professional development planning articulation activities (see Chapter 10).

Action 1.9: End-of-Year Formative Evaluations. At the end of the school year, the school discipline/PBSS committee, in collaboration with the administration and SLT, conducts formative and summative evaluations on the different facets of the PBSS so that new strategic plans and implementation activities and processes can be identified and written into the new school improvement plan.

Action 1.10: Summer Facilitators' Institute. During June at the end of Year 2, a summer institute is held for staff members who spent Implementation Year 2 as PBSS facilitators (this could include a second cohort of new facilitators who are beginning this advanced training). During this institute, facilitators receive advanced training and responsibilities for the coming year in the wide range of PBSS components and activities.

Implementation Year 3

During Implementation Year 3, the consolidation and institutionalization of different PBSS activities continues through the school discipline/PBSS committee and across the school's staff. In addition, the PBSS facilitators continue to assume a more independent and leading role over the PBSS director (if one is present).

Implementation Year 3 Activities

Action 1.1: Training Selected Staff in Behavioral and Ecological Classroom Observation. During the staff preparation days prior to the new school year, a select number of staff members are trained in behavioral and ecological classroom observation and how to functionally evaluate Instructional Environments and effective classroom instruction. Practice opportunities then are provided to this group during the first three months of the school year so that these staff members are available to provide these services during the last half of the school year.

Action 1.2: Training Intervention and Other Support Staff in Consultation Processes. During the staff preparation days prior to the new school year, the intervention specialists and other consultants working in the school are trained in consultation processes at the individual colleague, small group, and organizational levels. Practice opportunities then are provided to this group during the first three months of the school year so that these staff can integrate these processes into their day-to-day consultation interactions.

Action 1.3: Continued Staff Training on Strategic Behavioral Interventions. During the school year, the entire staff continues to participate in professional development activities focusing on the strategic, classroom-based behavioral interventions that can be applied and used with more challenging students (see Chapter 9).

Action 1.4: Continued or Extended Social, Emotional, and Behavioral Intervention Training for Selected Staff. During the school year, selected school discipline/PBSS committee and SPRINT team members continue to participate in strategic and intensive training in specific social, emotional, and behavioral intervention (Tier 2 and 3) areas.

Action 1.5: Continued Community and Family Outreach and School-Based Mental Health. Analyses of the school's available intensive (Tier 3) social, emotional, and behavioral assessment and intervention resources at the family and community levels continues. This includes formalizing relations with health, mental, and wellness community practitioners, including those involved in school-based and school-linked community mental health services for crisis management and intensive need students and families.

Action 1.6: Summer Facilitators' Institute. During June at the end of Year 3, a facilitator's summit is held to debrief the past school year, provide any additional training or mentoring, and prepare the facilitators for their fully independent implementation of the PBSS.

SUMMARY

The chapter provides a blueprint describing specific activities that schools should complete at the very beginning of their PBSS initiative through the end of their third year of full implementation. Embedded in this four-year blueprint are the most effective and efficient ways to accomplish the primary goals of a PBSS initiative using the effective school and schooling and PBSS components discussed in Chapter 1. It is important to recognize that this is a blueprint only. That is, schools need to use their needs assessments, resource analyses, and strategic planning processes to determine which activities to target and how to sequence them over a specific period of time. As such, some schools may complete the implementation parts of the PBSS blueprint in two years while others may take four or five.

This blueprint has been used in hundreds of schools across the country with well-documented student, staff, and school success. The remaining chapters of this book provide the specific details as to how to make this blueprint a reality at the prevention, strategic intervention, and intensive need and crisis management levels. With communication, commitment, collaboration, and a shared leadership approach, schools can implement a successful PBSS initiative resulting in social, emotional, and behavioral self-management outcomes that students will use in school, at home, and out in the community for the rest of their lives.

3

The School Discipline/ PBSS and Other Committees

Effective Team and Group Functioning

> The best way to predict the future is to create it.
>
> John Scully

PBSS Implementation Case Study:
Shelby County Educational Service Center, Sidney, Ohio

Shelby County, Ohio, is located in a largely agricultural section of western Ohio with a population of approximately 48,000 individuals. Its Project ACHIEVE Positive Behavioral Support System (PBSS) activities began in October 2006 at a three-day PBSS retreat sponsored by the Shelby County Educational Service Center (SCESC). From that retreat, the Sidney City, Fairlawn, and Hardin-Houston school districts and the county's alternative school, the Cooperative Learning Center, made a multi-year PBSS commitment.

The beginning of this commitment involved establishing, in each participating school, a school leadership team and a school discipline/PBSS committee to go along with the state-required Student Assistance (early intervention and problem solving) Team. These teams stayed together for the first four years of the initiative, receiving intensive professional development and on-site consultation and technical assistance. Under the leadership of the SCESC, four annual retreats were held for these teams each January—giving them an opportunity to solidify their collaborative efforts (both within and across districts) and to strengthen their capacity for more independent PBSS implementation.

When compared with baseline data, the schools reported the following outcomes over the first three years of implementation: (a) a 57% decrease in office discipline referrals, (b) a 47% decrease in grade retentions, and (c) a 57% decrease in placements of at-risk students into special education classrooms. Other improvements included increases in different ratings of positive school climate, teacher effectiveness relative to classroom-based interventions, and student behavior at home.

On the strength of these results, the SCESC was awarded a three-year federal counseling grant from the U.S. Department of Education in 2009 to expand Project ACHIEVE to all eight districts within the county.

INTRODUCTION

Underlying the successful implementation of any schoolwide PBSS initiative are activities that directly relate to (a) strategic planning, organizational development, and resource and personnel management; (b) staff buy-in, professional development, and support; and (c) implementation integrity, evaluation, and continuous improvement. Beyond these elements, it is essential that the initiative include active staff involvement though shared leadership and other collaborative approaches. Ultimately, the success of any PBSS initiative is more dependent on the involvement and participation of the staff and students than on the expectations and oversight of district or school administrators.

In order to facilitate staff members' ongoing commitment to a comprehensive, schoolwide PBSS initiative and to organize and sustain a school's shared leadership activities, it is important to establish and maintain school-level committees that work seamlessly with grade-level (for elementary schools) or instructional-level (for secondary schools) teams. This chapter uses the effective schools blueprint from Chapter 1 to recommend and describe a school committee structure, focusing eventually on the two committees that most directly guide the PBSS: the school discipline/PBSS committee, and the building-level School Prevention, Review, and Intervention Team (SPRINT). Beyond this, PBSS and SPRINT-related activities at the grade or instructional team levels also are described.

USING THE EFFECTIVE SCHOOLS BLUEPRINT TO ORGANIZE A SCHOOL'S COMMITTEE STRUCTURE

From an organizational perspective, an effective business needs to strategically plan, on at least an annual basis, for all of the components that are essential to its operational and functional success. To accomplish this, many businesses design their organizational maps or management charts to structure their divisions or departments in ways that mirror these essential components and facilitate their implementation success. Applying this business principle, an effective school's committee structure should mirror the seven interdependent components of the effective school and schooling model described in Chapter 1: the strategic planning and organizational analysis and development; problem solving, teaming, and consultation processes; effective school, schooling, and professional development; academic instruction and intervention (PASS); behavioral instruction and intervention (PBSS); parent and community training, support, and outreach; and data management, evaluation, and accountability components (see also Chapter 1, Figure 1.1). Given this blueprint, six primary committees are suggested (see Figure 3.1). Significantly, data management, evaluation, and accountability activities are not centralized into a single committee. Instead, they are infused into the six recommended committees in ways that are relevant to each committee's respective goals, objectives, activities, and expected outcomes.

Figure 3.1   A Blueprint for an Effective School-Level Committee Structure

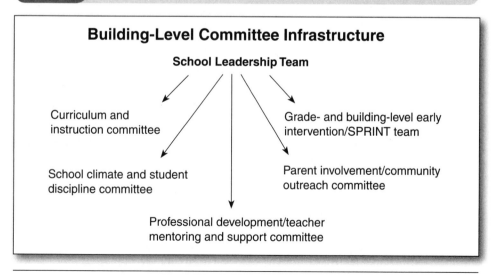

Source: Project ACHIEVE Press. Dr. Howie Knoff (author).

Briefly, the School Leadership Team (SLT) coordinates and guides all of the shared leadership planning and implementation processes in a school, overseeing the activities of the five other committees and the grade-level or instructional teams. This committee is made up of the school's administrators and the chairs or co-chairs of the other school-level committees and a representative sample of teachers, related services staff, support staff, and selected others. While district administrators, parents, community leaders, and students may be invited to attend some meetings, they are not permanent or standing members of the SLT.

The SLT is primarily responsible for overseeing activities related to the strategic planning and organizational analysis and development component within the effective school and schooling model. Thus, it makes many site-based management and related organizational and fiscal decisions, and it is ultimately responsible for planning (e.g., through the annual school improvement plan) and evaluating all school-level and student-specific outcomes. Like all of the other committees, the SLT meets on a monthly basis, usually just before or after these other school-level committee meetings. With the chairs or co-chairs present as members of the SLT, they can report on their respective committee meetings and activities each month so that all SLT members are duly briefed and can coordinate and collaborate, as appropriate, across school committees, teams, and staff. All of this facilitates a seamless bottom-up (i.e., from individual staff to grade levels to school-level committees to SLT and administration) communication process, as well as a top-down (i.e., from the administration on down) decision-making process.

While the SLT is the oversight committee to which all other committees report, there still is a clear delineation between the mandated and district-designated responsibilities of the school's administration and the shared leadership responsibilities of the SLT. In the former area, the SLT may be advisory to the school's administration, which still makes many final decisions. In the latter area, the SLT has many of its own decision-making responsibilities, as agreed upon by the administration.

The curriculum and instruction committee looks at the most effective ways to teach, infuse, progress monitor, and help all students to master and apply the information and skills in all of the academic areas within the school (and, if chosen, in other areas such as technology, music, art, physical education, health, etc.). Most critically, this committee especially guides the instruction and integration of the primary academic disciplines of literacy, mathematics, written and oral expression, and science throughout the school day and year. Meeting on at least a monthly basis with goals and outcomes connected to the school improvement plan (SIP), this committee also oversees the implementation and evaluation of new and existing district- and building-level curricula into the classroom such that they are taught in effective, differentiated ways to all students.

The membership of this committee includes representatives from every grade or instructional or teaching team or level, and it includes academic department chairs at the secondary level as well as instructional support, intervention, and special education representatives at both elementary and secondary levels. This committee is ideally chaired or co-chaired by a teacher or instructional support consultant, and school administrators are ex officio members (as they are for all school-level committees). At times, this committee may meet with other schools' curriculum and instruction committees or with district-level supervisors or administrators. At the school level, the committee has multiple layers—extending from the school level down to the grade (or instructional team) level and down to individual teachers' classrooms. Thus, this committee often is as differentiated as the curricula being taught across the school and, in large schools, it may have curriculum-specific subcommittees or use other organizational designs as needed, to facilitate the instruction and achievement of all students.

Relative to students' social, emotional, and behavioral status, this committee is important to the extent that students' academic success often affects how they feel and think about school, their teachers, and their classroom instruction; their social status within their peer group; their emotional and behavioral frustration; and their expectations for future short- and long-term success. Thus, this committee needs to collaborate closely with the school discipline/PBSS committee and the grade- and building-level SPRINT teams, and it often helps to coordinate the continuum of multi-tiered instructional and intervention services, supports, strategies, and programs represented in the PASS model presented in Chapter 1.

The school discipline/PBSS committee is the building-level committee that oversees the school's social climate and interactions, discipline and behavior management, safety and crisis intervention, and positive behavioral support and intervention activities and processes. Meeting on at least a monthly basis with goals and outcomes connected to the SIP, this committee looks at the most effective ways to teach, infuse, and facilitate the implementation of positive interpersonal, social problem-solving, conflict prevention and resolution, and social, emotional, and behavioral coping skills and interactions across students and staff such that students feel connected to the school, engaged in classroom instruction, and safe across the school's common areas.

The school discipline/PBSS committee also addresses large-scale issues of teasing, taunting, bullying, harassment, hazing, and physical aggression—working to prevent these situations across the school and student body and responding to them by completing special situation analyses (see Chapters 1, 6, and 7) linked to strategic or intensive interventions, as needed. In addition, this committee oversees the school's crisis prevention, intervention, and response processes, and selected members are prepared to intervene when crises occur. Finally, this committee works to involve the school's support staff (e.g., custodians, cafeteria workers, secretaries, bus drivers) in its efforts, and it reaches out to parents, community agencies, and other community leaders in collaborative efforts to extend PBSS activities and outcomes to home and community settings.

Clearly, the school discipline/PBSS committee is the anchor to the school's PBSS processes. As such, this committee is responsible for planning and implementing the different facets of the PBSS process described in Chapter 1. The role and responsibilities of this committee are discussed more specifically later in this chapter.

The professional development/teacher support and mentoring committee oversees, facilitates, and evaluates the school's professional development (PD) and formal and informal collegial supervision and support activities. These activities should help all staff feel professionally and personally connected to the school and its organizational, planning, instruction, and continuous improvement processes and motivate them to interact instructionally and personally with students and each other at the highest levels of effectiveness.

Meeting on at least a monthly basis with goals and outcomes connected to the SIP, this committee can help evaluate the short- and long-term implementation and outcomes of the school's PD program, making recommendations to ensure that all PD initiatives (a) are delivered using appropriate adult learning approaches; and (b) are implemented so that staff received the depth of training, job-embedded practice, supervision and feedback, and time needed to be successful. Ultimately, this committee facilitates a process such that the information and knowledge provided during any PD training transfers into instructional skill and confidence over time, and that the school's PD program and process collectively results in meaningful student outcomes.

The professional development/teacher support and mentoring committee also can help welcome and orient staff who are new to the building each year, coordinate the teacher mentoring program for teachers who are new to the profession, and guide others who have completed this induction process and are moving toward earning tenure. In addition, this committee might stay abreast of new pedagogical or technological advances in the field, periodically briefing the faculty on these new approaches and how they could improve the school and schooling process.

The SPRINT team is the school-level committee that facilitates the use of functional assessment and data-based problem-solving processes that identify the strategic or intensive instructional or intervention services, supports, strategies, or programs needed academically and behaviorally by students who are not responding to effective classroom instruction or behavior management. At the building level, the SPRINT team consists of the strongest academic and behavioral intervention specialists in or available to the school, along with the teacher (or teaching team) that is presenting a student of concern. The SPRINT team meets on a regularly scheduled basis (weekly is recommended) during the school day (or at least when every member of the team is present without other time constraints).

Grade- or instructional-level SPRINT teams also meet at least monthly to analyze and develop within-team approaches for student concerns that can be addressed at this level. These grade-level SPRINT teams consist of teachers who all teach at a specific grade or student group level and at least one representative from the building-level SPRINT team.

As noted in Chapter 2 (Implementation Year 1, Semester 2, Action 2.1), everyone in the school is trained on the same functional assessment and data-based problem-solving process so that these processes consistently occur at an individual teacher, grade, or building SPRINT level. This creates a Response-to-Instruction and Intervention (RTI^2) continuum where academic or behavioral information and data are collected, analyzed, and addressed similarly for all at-risk, underachieving, unresponsive, or unsuccessful students (see Knoff, 2009b, for a comprehensive discussion of SPRINT teams and RTI^2 processes).

As the building-level SPRINT team focuses predominantly on individual student concerns, it concurrently guides many of the school's goals and activities that relate to the problem-solving, teaming, and consultation process component of the effective school and schooling blueprint and that are written into the annual SIP. This SPRINT team also collaborates closely with the curriculum and instruction and school discipline/PBSS committees, as these latter committees oversee the respective academic and behavioral planning, instruction, intervention, and evaluation processes at the school, grade, and student-group levels, while the building-level SPRINT team oversees these same processes at an individual student level. Indeed, there are times when the curriculum and instruction or school discipline/PBSS committee identifies specific students at their meetings—often, when reviewing group academic achievement or student discipline data, respectively—and then recommends these students into the classroom teacher, grade-, or building-level SPRINT process.

Ultimately, when students (a) do not respond to progressive instructional or intervention services, supports, strategies, or programs; (b) demonstrate serious or intense academic or behavioral difficulties; or (c) exhibit signs that a possible disability is impacting their educational progress, the building-level SPRINT team typically initiates the process whereby a student's eligibility to receive special educational services is investigated. When this is needed, specific SPRINT team members, who are also on the school's special education eligibility team, should take the lead. When staff members serve on both the SPRINT and eligibility teams, a seamless transfer of information and experience occurs from the early intervening services provided through the SPRINT process to the assessment process that investigates a student's eligibility to receive special education services.

Finally, the parent involvement/community outreach committee is responsible for planning, implementing, and evaluating the activities described in the effective schools parent and community training, support, and outreach component in Chapter 1 that are written into the school's annual SIP. As such, based on ongoing needs assessments of the school's different parent and community groups and constituencies and asset analyses of their resources, interest, and capacity, this committee focuses on establishing and sustaining the collaborative approaches needed to address students' academic and social, emotional, or behavioral needs in home or community settings and on increasing the support, involvement, and leadership of parents, community agencies, and other organizations in accomplishing the school's mission and goals.

While many schools point to their parent-teacher associations (PTAs) as their parent and community involvement and outreach committees, these organizations—while important and needed—are outside-in groups. The parent involvement/community outreach committee is an inside-out group. Thus, this committee consists of a representative cross section of staff from within a school, it meets on a monthly basis, and it reaches out to and supports its PTA leaders and members. But this committee also collaborates with other community agencies and organizations, establishes partnerships with relevant businesses and foundations, and becomes, formally or informally, the public face and public relations unit for the school.

In the end, many schools need to establish this committee because they have never thought to organize an inside-out committee to spearhead the important activities described above. When established for the first time, this committee should devote considerable time and discussion to establishing its group norms and processes, completing its needs assessments and resource analyses, and determining its mission, goals, objectives, and initial action plan. This start-up process should be carefully planned and thoughtfully implemented, and it should emphasize the building of strong, positive, and sustainable relationships rather than quick, superficial, and one-sided gains. As the most public of a school's committees, this one has the greatest potential to enhance a school's positive reputation among its parents and community. Conversely, one significant misstep by this committee or one of its members could impair the school's standing in the community for many years to come.

Adapting the Committee Blueprint to Individual Schools. Reinforcing a school's commitment to shared leadership and representational governance, every staff member is expected to serve on at least one school-level committee. This increases staff members' feelings that they can positively participate in and influence important school decisions, and it decreases the resentment that sometimes occurs when a small number of staff are doing more than their share of the committee leadership and work. At the same time, some staff will still serve on more than one committee. This often involves those who have special SPRINT functional assessment or intervention expertise or those who are on the SLT because they chair or co-chair one of the five other committees.

Critically, the school committee blueprint (see Figure 3.1 again) is flexible and must be adapted to a school's strategic needs, organizational realities (e.g., state statutes, school size, local politics), and desired outcomes. For example, a school with a smaller staff may fuse two or more committees together, distributing the responsibilities of the committees it cannot formally establish to one or two others. Or the smaller school might pool specific grade-level teachers together (e.g., into Kindergarten/Grade 1, Grade 2/3, and Grade 4/5 teams) and have one teacher represent the interests of two grade levels. Other schools might assign more staff members to some committees and not others, reflecting the relative importance of some committees' annual goals and objectives over others. Or they might assign stronger, more experienced, and fewer staff to certain committees on a short-term basis. Finally, schools with strategic needs in one or more specialized areas may reach beyond their existing committee structure by assigning skilled staff members to a short-term task force or study group that intensively addresses these specialized needs, suggests approaches and directions, and then disbands.

The point here is that a school's organization and committee structure should be aligned to effectively and efficiently accomplish the student, staff, school, and parent and community outreach goals identified on its annual SIP. While a school's committee structure is generally reviewed every three to five years, it may need to be reconfigured if significant changes have occurred within the school that make the existing structure untenable or ineffective.

CHARACTERISTICS OF EFFECTIVE COMMITTEES

Beyond the existence of a logical and effective committee structure, committees still need to use sound leadership and collaborative practices that result in effective and efficient decisions and actions. And yet, few educators have ever been formally trained in these practices and processes. Below is a brief summary of some of the characteristics or processes that help committees to run smoothly and effectively.

Effective Committee Processes. All committees

- have representatives from every grade-level or instructional team (except for the SPRINT team) as well as from all relevant school-level and other support staff;
- are organized so that most staff members have staggered three-year terms of office;
- have a designated chair (or co-chairs) and a recorder who takes the minutes of all meetings;

- have a written mission, role, and function statement or document that is consistent with the school's mission statement;
- have annual written goals and objectives that have been included in the annual SIP;
- meet at a fixed (whenever possible), predesignated time each month;
- have a set agenda that is consistent from month to month and a fluid agenda that may change, according to the committee's goals or activities, from month to month;
- have meetings that are consistently attended by at least 80% of members;
- have agreed-upon meeting expectations and processes for making decisions; and
- publicly post minutes or summaries of all meetings that are available to all school staff within two to three days following each meeting.

Effective Meeting Processes (Branigan & Jones, 2006; Conzemius & O'Neill, 2002). All committees adhere to or demonstrate these effective practices:

- An agenda is prepared and distributed before each meeting.
- Members arrive on time for the meeting and stay until the meeting is over.
- The meeting starts and ends on time.
- The chair and others with assignments or reports are prepared.
- Team members adhere to the ground rules and norms agreed upon and needed for effective team meetings.
- Meeting agendas are clearly defined, are understood by all members, and relate in a meaningful way to the team's overall goals and objectives.
- The committee chair and others with relevant responsibilities (e.g., timekeepers, recorders, group process observers) effectively manage the meeting and other interactional processes.
- Committee discussions are on-task, relevant, focused, and concise and help to accomplish committee and meeting goals.
- Information is presented so that it is understood by everyone, and committee members are comfortable asking clarifying questions.
- Committee members know in advance how different decisions will be made (e.g., by simple majority vote or consensus, or by the chair with member input), and decisions are made in a collaborative fashion.
- Tasks are assigned to individuals who have the ability to complete them, with clear and realistic goals and timelines. For lengthy or complex tasks, specific action plans are developed.
- Committee members know what they are expected to do to continue the team's work between meetings and in preparation for the next meeting.

- The chair and others summarize the meeting's decisions, accomplishments, and assignments.
- The quality of interprofessional and interpersonal processes that occurred during the meeting are discussed, and relevant feedback is shared.

Committee Membership Within Grade Levels and Rotating Committee Members Across Grade Levels. In order to maintain a shared leadership approach across a school's committees, it is important that every instructional staff member be on at least one school-level committee. Beyond this, it is recommended that, to the greatest degree possible, different teachers on the same grade or instructional team also should be distributed across a school's different committees. For example, if a school's third grade team has four teachers, one teacher should be on the curriculum and instruction, school discipline/PBSS, professional development/teacher support and mentoring, and parent involvement/community outreach committees, respectively (remember that the SPRINT team is a more specialized committee). At the secondary level, where there are more teachers at different instructional levels, a logical and representative distribution of teachers into the respective committees is needed.

Once assigned to a committee, it is recommended that the teachers serve three-year terms (that may be renewed once) and that the committee terms be staggered so that only one-third of a committee's membership rotates off a committee in any one year. For example, within an elementary school's school discipline/PBSS committee, the kindergarten and third grade teachers, the first and fourth grade teachers, and the second and fifth grade teachers, respectively, would serve the committee in the same cohort. Thus, at the end of any year, only one of the three cohorts would be scheduled to rotate off the committee and be replaced by teachers at the same grade levels. This rotational approach maintains the history, continuity, integrity, and momentum of the committees and ensures that they have appropriate teacher representation, energy, and new perspectives over time. Parenthetically, if a brand-new committee were being formed at any point in time, the easiest way to set up this staggered rotational system would be, for example, to give the kindergarten and third grade representatives an initial two-year term, the first and fourth grade representatives a three-year term, and the second and fifth grade representatives a four-year term.

THE COMMITTEE MISSION, ROLE, AND FUNCTION DOCUMENT

As recommended in the effective committee process section above, when a committee is newly established or at the end of every school year, its mission, role, and function document should be written or reviewed. This document summarizes each committee's mission, goals, outcomes, and evaluation processes to ensure that the committee is working in ways that are consistent with both the school's mission and its annual SIP. In addition, this document provides a month-to-month overview of the most important activities that occur at each committee meeting and the fixed and fluid agenda items at those meetings. The fixed agenda items are those items that are discussed or reported on at virtually every monthly meeting. The fluid agenda items are those that occur less frequently, perhaps only one to four times per year.

A sample mission, role, and function document for the school discipline/PBSS and building-level SPRINT committees is available in Appendices 1 and 2, respectively, at the end of this chapter. Both of these committees are emphasized because of their direct importance to the PBSS process (see the committee descriptions earlier in this chapter). Once written, the SLT ensures that the committee mission, role, and function documents from every school committee are compiled into a single document that is available to the entire staff. This helps everyone to understand the individual responsibilities of each committee as well as how specific committees need to interface and collaborate.

THE MOST TYPICAL SCHOOL DISCIPLINE/ PBSS COMMITTEE ACTIVITIES AND THEIR INFUSION INTO GRADE-LEVEL OR INSTRUCTIONAL TEAM ACTIVITIES

As outlined in Chapter 2 and described in greater detail in this chapter's Appendix 1, there are a number of critical schoolwide activities that the school discipline/PBSS committee oversees on an ongoing basis. These include (a) the school's social climate and staff-student connectedness, interactions, and engagement; (b) the implementation of the social, emotional, and behavioral skills program (which may include the health, mental health, and wellness program at the secondary level); (c) the implementation of the Behavioral Matrix and the student accountability system; (d) attention to incidents of teasing, taunting, bullying, harassment, hazing, and fighting, and staff-student interactions in the common areas of the school; (e) attention to school safety and crisis prevention and readiness; (f) the involvement of the school's support staff (e.g., custodians, cafeteria workers, secretaries, bus drivers); (g) collaboration with other school-level committees, and grade-level or instructional teams; (h) collaboration with parents, community agencies, and other community leaders in a collaborative effort to extend its activities and outcomes to home and community; and (i) the evaluation of all of these activities.

In a parallel fashion, grade-level teams (at the elementary level) and instructional teams (at the secondary level) should meet (once per month is strongly recommended) to discuss the implementation of the PBSS at their levels. Guided by their representative(s) to the school discipline/ PBSS committee, these teams should discuss the implementation of the activities above that are relevant to their classrooms and students. Once again, the shared leadership and representational governance processes inherent in the effective school and schooling and committee blueprint allows for seamless planning, implementation, discussion, and decision-making. This collaboration occurs from the school discipline/PBSS committee down to the grade or instructional teams and from these teams up to the committee level.

SUMMARY

This chapter uses the effective schools blueprint from Chapter 1 to recommend and describe a school committee structure, focusing eventually on the two committees that most directly guide the PBSS: the school discipline/PBSS committee and the building-level SPRINT team. After the committees are described briefly, the characteristics of effective committees are outlined, and the importance of developing a mission, role, and function document for each committee is emphasized. The chapter concludes with a brief description of the most typical school discipline/PBSS committee activities as well as those recommended at the grade or instructional team levels.

Appendix 3.1

Prototype School Discipline/PBSS Committee
Mission, Role, and Function Overview

Name of School: Date:

Chair of Committee:

Committee Secretary:

Other Committee Members (with Terms of Office):

Monthly Meeting Day/Time:

Charge/Mission of the Committee:

The school discipline/PBSS committee oversees the school's social climate and interactions, discipline and behavior management, safety and crisis intervention, and positive behavioral support and intervention activities and processes. This committee also looks at the most effective ways to teach, infuse, and facilitate the implementation of positive interpersonal, social problem-solving, conflict prevention and resolution, and social, emotional, and behavioral coping skills and interactions across students and staff such that students feel connected to the school, engaged in classroom instruction, and safe across the school's common areas.

The school discipline/PBSS committee addresses large-scale issues of teasing, taunting, bullying, harassment, hazing, and physical aggression—working to prevent these situations across the school and student body and responding to them by completing special situation analyses linked to strategic or intensive interventions, as needed. In addition, this committee oversees the school's crisis prevention, intervention, and response processes, and selected members are prepared to intervene when crises occur. Finally, this committee works to involve the school's support staff (e.g., custodians, cafeteria workers, secretaries, bus drivers) in its efforts, and it reaches out to parents, community agencies, and other community leaders in a collaborative effort to extend its activities and outcomes to home and community.

Primary Committee Goals, Objectives, and Outcomes:

1.   Facilitates and tracks the implementation of the grade- and teacher-level social skills calendar and instruction at the teach, apply, and infuse level. Looks at the implementation of the social skills language and process across the school—with all instructional, administrative, and support staff—and including the appropriate and effective use by students.

2.   Facilitates the development and tracks the implementation of the Behavioral Matrix and its ability to motivate and hold students accountable for appropriate and inappropriate behavior. This includes ensuring that sound behavioral response decisions are made when students exhibit Intensity 1, 2, 3, or 4 offenses; that students are appropriately referred to the SPRINT team when teachers' use of the matrix is not changing student behavior; that the matrix is publicly available and used (e.g., through posters, in the parent handbook, through classroom management systems); that the time-out and office discipline referral process is effectively integrated into matrix activities and responses; and that positive responses, incentives, and rewards are used appropriately leading to positive classroom and school settings and environments.

3.   Identifies the need for and conducts (often through a task force or subcommittee) special situation analyses to address behavioral problems in common areas of the school or as related to teasing, taunting, bullying, harassment, hazing, and fighting.

4.   Ensures that support staff (e.g., secretaries, custodians, bus drivers, cafeteria workers, paraprofessionals, cafeteria and playground supervisors) receive training in the social skills language and implementation, the Behavioral Matrix, and other setting- or situation-specific strategies and approaches that will help them facilitate and reinforce appropriate student behavior.

5.   Monitors the data management system (e.g., the Automated Discipline Data, Review, and Evaluation Software System—ADDRESS) used to track the outcomes and success of the program at student, teacher, grade, and building levels and analyzes and reports (e.g., to the staff and administration) the ADDRESS and other relevant data on at least a monthly basis.

6.   Involves students, parents, community agencies and programs, and other community leaders in a collaborative effort that supports all of the goals above and that extends the committee's goals, objectives, strategies, and processes to home and community.

7.   Develops and helps to implement building-level prevention, intervention, and crisis response plans and processes.

8.   Writes the first draft of each year's school discipline/PBSS committee entry into the SIP, identifying needed resources, including professional development, training, and practice.

Year-at-a-Glance Agenda:

April: Choose new committee members and new committee chair/secretary

April–June: Hold at least three meetings with the outgoing and incoming committee membership to plan new school year transition; one meeting focused on summative evaluation of goals and outcomes

August preplanning: First committee meeting of new year

September–October: Monthly meetings

November: Goal-focused formative evaluation and planning meeting for next four months' activities

December–January: Monthly meetings

February: Committee drafts committee goals, objectives, needed resources, and needed funding for next year's SIP for submission to SLT

March: Goal-focused formative evaluation and planning meeting for next three months

Monthly Agenda:

Committee meets monthly and completes specific tasks:

- Collects the lists of social skills that are being taught at each grade level each month, compiling them on a monthly master calendar that is sent to all of the elective teachers, non-instructional staff, and relevant others across the school for their information and use.
- Discusses how the social skills are working at the grade levels and across the building.
- Discusses ways to continue using the social skills language continuously across the building by all staff and with all students.
- Identifies the existence of any building-level special situations (e.g., in the cafeteria, the hallways, at recess, on the playground, or on the bus) and completes any needed special situations analyses and subsequent interventions.

Over time, the Committee also undertakes additional activities:

- Helps to develop, implement, and periodically review the classroom, grade-level, and buildingwide accountability system that identifies expected student behavior (with corresponding incentives) and different levels of inappropriate student behavior (with corresponding consequences or administrative responses).

- Creates a climate that helps staff feel comfortable and competent with the social skills and (later) the time-out process, and that encourages and reinforces the consistent use of the social skills and accountability systems developed.
- Monitors the data management system that is tracking the outcomes and success of the program at student, teacher, grade, and building levels. Included here can be buildingwide celebrations for staff and students who have made continuous good choices.
- Determines the need for additional social skills, time-out, or behavioral intervention training for the school staff.
- Tracks the use of the social skills process by secretaries, aides, cafeteria workers, custodians, and so on; the need for booster training with these groups; and the ways to continue encouraging their appropriate use of the social skills language and process.
- Develops, implements, and evaluates building-level prevention, intervention, and crisis response plans and processes.
- Involves students, parents, community agencies and programs, and other community leaders in a collaborative effort that supports all of the goals above and that extends the PBSS training and implementation to home and community.

Data Sources to Evaluate Committee Outcomes:

- ADDRESS (Automated Discipline Data, Review, and Evaluation Software System)
- Student academic and behavioral intervention plans
- Referrals to the SPRINT team
- Special education referrals or placements for students with behavioral issues
- Formative evaluations of the social skills program implementation
- Tracking of progress on the social skills implementation calendar
- Periodic assessments with the Scale of Effective School Discipline and Safety
- Behavioral walk-through data and other observations of the classrooms and common areas of the school

Source: Project ACHIEVE Press. Dr. Howie Knoff (author).

Appendix 3.2

Prototype SPRINT Team Mission, Role, and Function Overview

Name of School: **Date:**

Chair of Committee:

Committee Secretary:

Other Committee Members (with Terms of Office):

Monthly Meeting Day/Time:

Charge/Mission of the Committee:

When students demonstrate ongoing or persistent academic or behavioral difficulties that do not respond successfully to classroom-based problem solving, functional assessment, and interventions, the SPRINT process is used to address these circumstances through more intensive, multidisciplinary action. The building-level SPRINT team's primary responsibility is to supervise this more intensive problem-solving, consultation, and intervention process—whether at a grade level or at the building level, such that all students in need receive early intervention services, as much as possible, in the general education classroom through working with the regular classroom teacher(s). The building-level SPRINT team also evaluates referrals for problem solving over time to identify referral trends, preventative strategies, and professional development needs so that teachers are prepared to provide strategic intervention or to support intensive intervention services to students in need. Finally, the building-level SPRINT team is responsible for tracking the number and type of students receiving 504 accommodations and special education/ IEP services, for coordinating manifestation and other discipline-related assessments for individual students, and for evaluating the school's success relative to the state-monitored special education triggers (e.g., least restrictive environment, disproportionality, adequate yearly progress, graduation and drop-out rates).

Primary Building-Level SPRINT
Team Goals, Objectives, and Outcomes

1. To oversee the implementation of the SPRINT process in the school, including the school's adherence to federal, state, and district policies and procedures; the identification (and, at times, provision) of professional development and practice opportunities; the creation or review of needed forms, databases, data collection or evaluation instruments, or other progress monitoring vehicles; and the completion of ongoing and needed community and family outreach activities.

2. To provide timely problem-solving and functional assessment, consultation, and early intervention services at the grade level and building level for students whose teachers are concerned with their academic or behavioral responses to teacher generated and delivered classroom interventions.

3. To track the progress of existing student interventions individually and collectively and to identify trends and professional development opportunities such that the individual students make successful progress in their targeted areas and the school's staff members are able to prevent or respond earlier and more independently to similar problems for other students.

4. To facilitate the communication and consistency, across staff, in the implementation and use of strategic interventions for students receiving them and to ensure that interventions and lessons learned about students are transferred systematically and in a timely way across relevant staff members from one school year to the next.

5. To collect and report individual and group student data such that the SPRINT process is formatively and summatively evaluated, it maximizes all students' academic and behavioral progress and skill mastery, the school meets and adheres to all Elementary and Secondary Education Act (ESEA) and Individuals with Disabilities Education Act (IDEA) requirements and mandates, and the strengths of the process are maintained and the weaknesses of the process are addressed.

Year-at-a-Glance Agenda for the Monthly
SPRINT Team Meetings

Even though the building-level SPRINT team meets on a weekly basis to address new student cases and to review current student cases, the team also should devote part of one or more weekly meetings each month to the activities below. These activities help to maintain effective underlying

SPRINT team processes, and they assist the team in making sure that annual goals, objectives, and outcomes are being evaluated on an ongoing and conscious basis.

During April: As needed, assign new SPRINT team members to the team for the next school year and choose a new team chair and secretary or recorder

During April–June: Hold at least six SPRINT team meetings with both outgoing team members and any incoming team members in attendance

During April–June: Conduct the various end-of-the-year articulation activities that help the team to plan for the transition to the new school year; one of the activities needs to focus on completing a summative evaluation of SPRINT goals, objectives, and outcomes written into the SPRINT section of the SIP Articulation activities needed:

o Complete and analyze the consultation referral audit
o Conduct a SPRINT forms analysis and update or prepare any needed forms
o Facilitate the Get-Go review process of the year's early intervention referral, IEP, 504, and other students
o Participate in the academic achievement audit
o Facilitate the writing of the Student Briefing Reports

August staff preplanning time (the staff preparation days prior to the new school year): The SPRINT team should have its first team meeting of the new school year during this time and should make a presentation for the entire faculty to review or update the SPRINT process along with any new forms

September–October: Hold weekly SPRINT meetings

November: Conduct a formative evaluation of the team's progress relative to the SPRINT goals, objectives, and outcomes in the current SIP and conduct a planning meeting to identify and coordinate all SPRINT activities for the next four months

December–January: Hold weekly SPRINT meetings

February: The team should draft the SPRINT team's section (including early intervening, and strategic/intensive academic and social, emotional, and behavioral instruction and intervention needs) for the next SIP, which should include team goals, objectives, resources, funding, activities, timelines, outcomes, and evaluation procedures; should be submitted to the SLT for review

March: Conduct a formative evaluation of the team's progress relative to the SPRINT goals, objectives, and outcomes in the current SIP and conduct a planning meeting to identify and coordinate all SPRINT team activities for the next four months

Typical SPRINT Team Meeting Agenda:

- The SPRINT team meets once per week for two hours per meeting.
- The first 90 minutes involves three 30-minute Initial Case Reviews.

General Initial Case Review Process:

1. Classroom teacher presents the case using the Records Review Form (10 minutes). (A SPRINT team member also completes the Records Review Form to ensure no loss of critical information.)

2. Round robin: Anyone on the SPRINT team with direct contact or additional information shares that information (5 minutes).

3. Initial summary: Chair or the SPRINT member on the classroom teacher's grade-level SPRINT team summarizes the major concerns (2 minutes).

4. Q&A: Additional clarifying questions, identification of relevant unknown information or hypotheses to explain the concerns from the SPRINT team (10 minutes).

5a. Too many relevant unknowns: Assign individuals to collect the information and determine when to reconvene at a future SPRINT meeting (3 minutes).

5b. Sufficient information to proceed: Assignment of a master consultant to work with the teacher in the classroom on functional assessment to interventions.

6. Determination of when the first Consultation Case Review will occur (3 minutes).

- The last 30 minutes involves Consultation Case Reviews of previously considered cases to update their progress.

Data Sources to Evaluate Committee Outcomes:

- ADDRESS (Automated Discipline Data, Review, and Evaluation Software System)
- Student academic and/or behavioral intervention plans
- Referrals to the SPRINT team for early intervention services

- Number of referrals successfully addressed or resolved by the grade-level SPRINT team
- Special education referrals or placements for students
- Number of students moving to less restrictive settings or programs, or who no longer need services through an academic or behavioral intervention plan
- The Consultation Referral Audit
- The Get-Go process and its outcomes
- The Academic Achievement Audit

Source: Project ACHIEVE Press. Dr. Howie Knoff (author).

4

Behavioral Accountability, Student Motivation, and Staff Consistency[1]

> Character is doing the right thing . . . when no one is watching.
>
> J. C. Watts

PBSS Implementation Case Study:
Turtle Mountain Community Schools, Belcourt, North Dakota

In 2003, a multi-year consultation with the Turtle Mountain Community Schools in Belcourt, North Dakota, began with a focus on helping the district to implement a schoolwide Positive Behavioral Support System (PBSS) across its elementary, middle, and high schools, along with an early intervention/response-to-intervention system. During the initial walk-through of the high school, a number of ninth-grade faculty cornered me in the hallway and shared that the ninth graders were "disorganized, unruly, out of control, and unable to manage their own behavior" during the first month or more of each new school year.

A walk-through of the middle school revealed a well-organized school that had virtually no office discipline referrals. Upon further observation and review, it became apparent that all of the students were escorted or supervised in all areas of the school, during every class bell and transition. Thus, for 180 school days times three years, the students' behavior was managed and the faculty (rather than the students) was held accountable for student behavior. Moreover, the students were not taught self-management skills, nor were they given opportunities to positively practice and be reinforced for these skills.

Clearly, the low number of office discipline referrals at this middle school was more reflective of the faculty's behavior than the students' behavior. More important, the failure to teach and hold the students accountable for their self-management skills in middle school negatively impacted their ability to transition effectively to the high school, and it resulted in a loss of academic time and instruction during the first months of their freshman years.

INTRODUCTION

Accountability is defined as "being willing to accept responsibility for one's actions." While it is important for students (and others) to accept responsibility for their social, emotional, and behavioral actions and interactions after they have done something, from a self-management perspective it is more important that they think and prepare to act responsibly before a specific interaction. To facilitate this, students need to have a framework, blueprint, or roadmap that identifies expected positive prosocial behaviors in different school settings and different levels of inappropriate behavior so that they understand that some inappropriate behaviors are more serious than others. While these frameworks are more external and adult-guided with younger students, an important self-management goal is to help students internalize different behavioral accountability frameworks over time so that they can respond to the increasing levels of social complexity that extend from preschool through high school and beyond. Indeed, when students internalize a sound social, emotional, and behavioral accountability framework, they learn to stop and think before certain interactions, to consider the advantages (or incentives) versus disadvantages (or consequences) of appropriate or inappropriate behavior, respectively, and to select the appropriate choices.

Given this, schools need to develop, teach, and consistently implement schoolwide behavioral accountability systems at the grade or instructional classroom level and across the different common areas of the school, respectively. As introduced in Chapter 1, the classroom accountability system is anchored by the Behavioral Matrix (Knoff, 2007c), a framework that specifies the behavioral expectations, connected with positive responses, motivating incentives, and periodic rewards at each grade level for students in their classrooms. The Behavioral Matrix also identifies four progressive intensity levels of inappropriate behavior connected with corrective responses, conse-quences, and administrative actions, so that students (a) are aware of how inappropriate behavior will be responded to, and (b) are motivated to avoid these responses by demonstrating appropriate behavior.

Critically, the Behavioral Matrix is developed and implemented with administrator, student, and parent input by each grade-level team in a school so that the social, emotional, and behavioral development and maturation across different age-groups of students is accounted for over time. Significantly, when developed collaboratively by a grade-level team, teachers need to come to a consensus as to (a) what behavioral expecta-tions to teach and emphasize to their students, (b) how to organize differ-ent inappropriate behaviors across the four intensity levels, (c) how to most effectively respond to different intensity levels of behaviors, and (d) how to address specific or unique behavioral situations in strategic ways. When implemented collectively by grade-level teams with elective teachers (e.g., music, art, technology/media, health, physical education), related services staff (e.g., counselors, psychologists, behavioral special-ists), support staff (e.g., paraprofessionals, secretaries, custodians, cafeteria servers, bus drivers), administrators, and extracurricular staff (e.g., after-school club advisers and athletic coaches), students realize that they will be held accountable for their appropriate and inappropriate behavior, and that their appropriate behavior is far more rewarding.

Relative to the common areas of a school (e.g., hallways, bathrooms, buses, playground, cafeteria, auditorium, sports fields and venues, and other common gathering areas), the Behavioral Matrix has setting-specific behavioral expectations that are common across all of the grade-level matrices. While these expectations are taught in developmentally appro-priate ways for students at different age levels, they also include incentives and consequences, relevant to each setting, to motivate students to con-form to and perform these expectations.

The Behavioral Matrix is essentially a behavioral standards document with explicit expectations that students are taught and held accountable to. The explicit goal of the Behavioral Matrix is to create a positive, respon-sive, schoolwide accountability system that results in high levels of posi-tive and prosocial classroom engagement and school safety, progressively higher levels of self-managed student behavior, and low levels of negative student interactions and office discipline referrals. The implicit goal of the Behavioral Matrix is to maximize the consistency needed to accomplish the outcomes above across students, staff, and administration.

These goals are accomplished by applying the science underlying the PBSS process (see Chapter 1). Indeed, the Behavioral Matrix (a) identifies many of the social, emotional, and behavioral skills and classroom or building expectations that students must be taught to move them to social competency and self-management (Principle 1); (b) recognizes, from preschool through high school, that these skills and expectations evolve developmentally and maturationally over time (Principle 3); (c) encourages the use of explicit, meaningful, student-centered incentives and consequences to motivate and hold them accountable for appropriate behavior (Principles 5, 7, and 8); and (d) facilitates a consistent focus on the essential behaviors and interactions expected of all students, and the ways to respond to students demonstrating different levels of inappropriate behavior (Principle 10). Critically, when the matrix's different elements are agreed upon by the staff across the school, taught and communicated consistently to students, and implemented with integrity and intensity, high and appropriate levels of responsibility, account-ability, and self-management result for most students.

This chapter describes the step-by-step development of the Behavioral Matrices within a school. At the preschool level, only one Behavioral Matrix (for ages three to five) typically is needed. For elementary schools, a separate Behavioral Matrix is developed at every grade level when there are three or more teachers at each grade level. For elementary schools with only one or two teachers per grade level, separate merged Kindergarten/ Grade 1, Grade 2/3, and Grade 4/5 matrices are recommended. For mid-dle schools, the size of the faculty, the number of faculty members that teach at multiple grade levels, and the maturational differences across the students need to be considered. When there are five or more teachers per grade level and they teach predominantly at one grade level, the middle school may develop separate sixth, seventh, and eighth grade matrices. If the sixth grade students are at a different functional level of social, emo-tional, and behavioral development than the seventh and eighth grade students, if the school physically separates the sixth graders from the other students, or if a sixth grade academy approach is being used, the middle school may have a sixth grade matrix that is separate from a merged Grade 7/8 matrix. Finally, for most high schools, a separate Grade 9 and a merged Grades 10–12 Behavioral Matrix is most typical.

As emphasized below, there is a high degree of overlap in where indi-vidual items are placed on different matrices as they progress from grade level to grade level. At the same time, grade-level teachers need to consis-tently use their own matrix so that they are responsive to the developmen-tal and maturational differences across students.

THE COMPONENTS WITHIN THE BEHAVIORAL MATRIX

Because it specifies the social, emotional, and behavioral expectations and interactions that contribute to student self-management and positive, safe, prosocial, and productive classroom and school settings, the Behavioral Matrix is the "heart" of the PBSS. This is one reason why the Behavioral Matrix is developed during Pre-implementation Year 1 (see Chapter 2) as one of the first functional, visible elements of the PBSS. Structurally, the

Behavioral Matrix has four related quadrants (see Figures 4.1 and 4.2): (a) the specific behavioral expectations in the classroom for the specific grade level covered by a particular matrix and the universal schoolwide behavioral expectations in the different common areas of the school (Quadrant I) that are connected with (b) setting-specific positive responses, incentives, and rewards (Quadrant II); and (c) the four different intensity levels of inappropriate student behavior (Quadrant III) connected with (d) the research-based corrective responses, consequences, or administrative responses focused on changing students' behavior in the future (Quadrant IV). Briefly, the four Quadrant III levels are Intensity I: annoying behaviors; Intensity II: disruptive or interfering behaviors; Intensity III: persistent or antisocial behaviors; and Intensity IV: severe or dangerous behaviors.

Functionally, the Behavioral Matrix facilitates the primary PBSS goal of teaching and motivating students' social competency and self-management by targeting and increasing appropriate student behavior while decreasing or eliminating inappropriate student behavior both preventatively and after it occurs. More specifically, Quadrant I helps identify the specific social competency and self-management behaviors that students need to

Figure 4.1 The Organization of the Behavioral Matrix

Grade _____

Expected, Prosocial Behaviors (I)   **Response (II)**

Classroom   ⟶   Positive responses,
Common areas of the school   incentives, rewards

- -

Inappropriate, Challenging Behaviors (III)   **Response (IV)**

Intensity I: annoying behavior   ⟶   Corrective responses

Intensity II: disruptive/interfering behavior ⟶   Corrective responses
                                                          plus consequences

Intensity III: persistent/antisocial behavior* ⟶   Consequences plus
                                                          interventions

Intensity IV: severe/dangerous behavior*   ⟶   Administrative
                                                          response plus wrap-
                                                          around intervention

*Functional assessment with strategic or intensive intervention

Source: Project ACHIEVE Press. Dr. Howie Knoff (author).

Figure 4.2 An Example of a Fourth Grade Behavioral Matrix

4th Grade

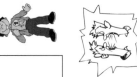

Expected Classroom Behavior:

Listening, following directions, focusing on completing work, raising hand to get teacher, waiting for your turn, positive words and voice, respect for others, treating property with respect, apologizing when needed

Incentives and Rewards:

Praise, smile, positive reinforcement, special privileges, happy notes home, extra free time at computer or games, class cheer, terrific student time

Intensity 1 (Annoying) Offenses:

Passive off-task behavior, not listening or following directions, uncooperative, leaving seat or area, noises that disrupt, tilting or falling out of seat, talking out, distracting others

Teacher/Corrective Responses:

Stop and Think Social Skills prompt, model/role-play, the "look," nonverbal redirect or prompt, proximity or touch prompt, verbal redirect or warning, change color card or mark, move student to another seat, loss of free time

Intensity 2 (Disruptive) Offenses:
Continuing Intensi1 behaviors

Arguing, passive or active defiance, teasing, bullying or threatening, name-calling, pushing or poking, inappropriate physical contact (no injury), horseplay, minor swearing, insubordination, rude or unacceptable language or tone

Classroom-Based Consequences:

Stop and think prompt, loss of points on reinforcement system, ending the activity, Level 1 or 2 time-out, loss of privileges, classroom service, notification of parents

Intensity 3 (Antisocial) Offenses:
Continuing Intensity 2 behaviors

Significant defiance, major swearing, safety issues, throwing rocks, fighting to hurt someone, stealing, cheating

Out-of-Class Consequences:

Classroom or community service, Level 3 or 4 time-out, parent notification or conference, responsible thinking classroom

Intensity 4 (Code of Conduct) Offenses:

Repeated violations of Intensity 2 or Intensity 3 behaviors, code of conduct violations

Administrative Response:

Follow district rights and code of conduct handbook, procedures, and guidelines

Source: Project ACHIEVE Press. Dr. Howie Knoff (author).

learn and demonstrate. Quadrant II describes ways to motivate and reinforce the use of these behaviors. Quadrant III identifies progressive levels of inappropriate behaviors for students to avoid. Finally, Quadrant IV describes the differential responses to the Quadrant III behaviors designed to motivate students to avoid these inappropriate behaviors or to eliminate them (if they occur) and replace them with appropriate behavior. Critically, Quadrant IV is not about stopping inappropriate behavior through punishment. It is about motivating students to decrease or eliminate their inappropriate behavior and replace it with appropriate behavior.

The expected classroom behaviors in Quadrant I generally come from three sources: (a) the specific interpersonal, social problem-solving, conflict prevention and resolution, and emotional coping skills and behaviors that students need, at specific grade levels, to be socially, emotionally, and behaviorally competent or successful; (b) the appropriate behaviors that are the opposite of the inappropriate behaviors found at the Intensity I and II levels of Quadrant III; and (c) research-based and other more common-sense behaviors that are needed for classroom success. The expected behaviors in the different common areas of the school are based on functional analyses of the logistical routines and interpersonal interactions needed for success. For example, expectations should be developed for the three logistical phases that contribute to effective hallway behavior (a) exiting the classroom and entering the hallway, (b) passing down the hallways and navigating any staircases, and (c) walking directly to the next scheduled class or setting (unless a locker stop is needed) and entering that room. In the cafeteria, behavioral expectations should be developed for each of the five logistical phases in that setting: (a) entering the cafeteria and lining up in the food line, (b) entering the serving area and receiving your food, (c) exiting the serving area and sitting at a table to eat your food, (d) finishing your food and cleaning up, and (e) exiting the cafeteria.

The positive responses, incentives, and rewards specified in Quadrant II are best generated by observing and interviewing the students at the respective grade levels of the different behavioral matrices. Clearly, this will increase the probability that the incentives will be meaningful and powerful to the targeted students, and that they will be valued by the peer group as a whole. Beyond this, there are many lists of developmentally arranged incentives and rewards available online by searching the appropriate terms on the internet.

Relative to Quadrant III, the four intensities define different levels of inappropriate student behavior:

- Intensity I (Annoying) Behavior: Behaviors in the classroom that are annoying or that mildly interrupt classroom instruction or student attention and engagement. Teachers can handle these behaviors with a minimum of interaction by using a corrective response (e.g., a nonverbal prompt or cue, physical proximity, a social skills prompt, reinforcing nearby students' appropriate behavior).

- Intensity II (Disruptive or Interfering) Behavior: Behavior problems in the classroom that occur more frequently, for longer periods of time, or to the degree that they disrupt classroom instruction or interfere with student attention and engagement. Teachers handle these behaviors with a corrective response and, usually, a classroom-based consequence (e.g., loss of student points or privileges, a classroom time-out, a note or call home, completion by the student of a behavior change plan).
- Intensity III (Persistent or Antisocial) Behavior: Behavior problems in the classroom that significantly (as a single incident) or persistently (increasing in severity over time) disrupt classroom instruction or engagement or that involve antisocial interactions toward adults or peers. These inappropriate behaviors require some type of out-of-classroom response (e.g., time-out in another teacher's classroom, removal to an in-school suspension or student accountability room, an office discipline referral), followed up by a payback response (e.g., an apology, cleaning up or repairing damaged property or a messed-up classroom, community service), a consequence, and, if needed, an intervention to eliminate a reoccurrence of the problem behavior.
- Intensity IV (Severe or Dangerous) Behavior: Extremely antisocial, damaging, or dangerous behaviors, on a physical, social, or emotional level that typically are cited and addressed in a district's student code of conduct handbook. These inappropriate behaviors require an immediate administrative referral and response (e.g., a parent conference, suspension, or expulsion), followed by a payback response and an intervention to eliminate a reoccurrence of the problem behavior.

Specific lists of possible inappropriate behaviors at each of these intensity levels have been collected over the years and are presented later in this chapter. Right now, however, we want to establish the relationship between the four intensity levels of inappropriate behavior and the research-based responses that address the inappropriate behavior, while motivating more appropriate behavior in the future (see the boxes and explanations below).

INTENSITY I (ANNOYING) BEHAVIOR IS RESPONDED TO WITH A CORRECTIVE ACTION

The corrective responses in the Behavioral Matrix are organized along a continuum of effective teaching responses ranging from least intrusive to more directive. While teachers should use the least intrusive corrective action possible, these are matched to the specific student involved. That is, for a specific student, the teacher should choose the corrective action that communicates most effectively that he or she is being annoying and that most quickly stops the annoying behavior, replacing it with appropriate behavior.

When developing a Behavioral Matrix, different grade-level teams rarely change the sequence of the effective teaching and corrective responses for Intensity I behaviors. This sequence includes corrective actions:

- Teacher visual, nonverbal, or physical prompt or cue
- Teacher proximity
- Teacher verbal or nonverbal redirect to the appropriate behavior needed
- Teacher warning
- Student is moved to another seat in the classroom
- Teacher ends the activity for the student; student waits until the next activity is introduced
- Teacher calls home with student from the classroom*
- Teacher sends a note home (written by the student) with parent signature required*

INTENSITY II (DISRUPTIVE OR INTERFERING) BEHAVIOR IS RESPONDED TO WITH A CORRECTIVE ACTION OR A CONSEQUENCE

The goal of a classroom-based consequence is to communicate to students that their behavior is inappropriate and motivate them to decrease or eliminate their inappropriate behavior while increasing their appropriate, prosocial behavior. That is, consequences do not change behavior; they create the conditions that facilitate behavioral change. Critically, if a student has not learned and mastered a desired appropriate behavior, no amount of incentives or consequences will produce that behavior (because it does not exist). What may occur, instead, is that the skill deficit student becomes frustrated. This occurs because the student eventually realizes that there is no hope of earning the incentive and no hope of escaping the consequence. Over time, the frustration is displayed along a spectrum from anger, aggression, and acting out, to anxiety, low self-concept, and checking out.

Typically, there are a number of consequences at every grade level to best respond to Intensity II behaviors. As with identifying incentives (see above), the best consequences are generated by observing and interviewing students. Significantly, though, some of the best consequences involve taking away a student's opportunity to earn an incentive or to participate in a preferred extracurricular activity. In this way, there is no physical or tangible loss of already-earned activities, points, or rewards, and students

---

*Done as a communication strategy for self-correction; not as a consequence.

typically are more motivated to demonstrate the appropriate behavior so that they can regain the right to earn these incentives.

When delivering consequences, especially at the Intensity II level, teachers should be mindful of additional behavioral principles:

1. Students need to learn and understand all of the components, behavioral interactions, and contingencies that make up the Behavioral Matrix. For example, through instruction and role-play, they should be taught what proximity control looks like and what behavioral responses are expected when it is used. Similarly, they should be taught how to accept a consequence when it is delivered and what will occur if they accept or resist a consequence.

2. When needed, teachers should individually select the mildest consequence needed to motivate specific students toward future (hopefully, immediate) appropriate behavior. While Intensity II consequences are less intrusive or intensive (i.e., milder) than Intensity III consequences, different students may respond more quickly to different Intensity II consequences. Thus, when teachers know their students on an individual and personal level, they can strategically select, for each student, the consequences that motivate him or her toward the quickest change of behavior with the least amount of effort.

3. In general, most Intensity II consequences are effective with most Intensity II inappropriate behaviors. However, based on research or experience, some Intensity II behaviors (e.g., lying, taking materials or personal items without permission) have one or two consequences that have the highest probability of resulting success. These specific behaviors and consequences somehow need to be connected on the matrix.

4. The behavioral principle of "If you consequate, you must educate" (see Chapter 1) needs to be followed after a consequence is delivered and completed. That is, after a consequence is over, students need to make amends for their inappropriate behavior and return to the setting where the offense originally occurred to practice the appropriate behavior they should have demonstrated at least three times.

5. The consistent use of the Behavioral Matrix helps students understand that it truly is a foundation to the classroom's discipline and behavior management system and their personal self-management system. While teachers need to decide whether to deliver an Intensity II consequence publicly or privately with specific students, a periodic public delivery communicates and demonstrates that students will continuously be held accountable for both appropriate and inappropriate behavior.

INTENSITY III (PERSISTENT OR ANTISOCIAL) BEHAVIOR IS RESPONDED TO WITH AN OUT-OF-CLASSROOM CONSEQUENCE, FOLLOWED BY AN INTERVENTION

An out-of-classroom consequence communicates to individual and groups of students that their behavior is very inappropriate. Critically, the consequence is not the removal of the student from the classroom setting; it is what occurs in the out-of-class setting (and, later, when they re-enter the original classroom setting). Thus, Intensity III consequences involve specific teacher, administrator, or parent actions and interactions with a student focused on responding to his or her inappropriate behavior while motivating a behavioral change resulting in future appropriate behavior. Often, Intensity III consequences are an extension of Intensity II consequences, with administrative or parental involvement, or they involve the precursors of Intensity IV (code of conduct) administrative responses. With appropriate adaptation, the behavioral principles discussed for Intensity II consequences above should be followed here with Intensity III consequences.

Beyond the points immediately above, when a student exhibits an Intensity III infraction, the student's social, emotional, or behavioral status and history and the severity or intensity of the offense should be considered to determine if a data-based functional assessment using the SPRINT (School Prevention, Review, and Intervention Team) process (see Chapters 1 and 8) is needed. Represented in the first asterisk on Figure 4.1, this assessment helps determine if an Intensity III consequence will resolve the behavioral situation for the future or if a more targeted, strategic intervention is needed. A functional assessment is definitely indicated when a student exhibits ongoing Intensity III offenses. This suggests that the student is not positively responding to the Intensity III responses, consequences, and positive practice re-entry and accountability procedures.

INTENSITY IV (SEVERE OR DANGEROUS) BEHAVIOR IS RESPONDED TO WITH AN ADMINISTRATIVE RESPONSE, FOLLOWED BY AN (INTENSIVE) INTERVENTION

An administrative response is generally neither a consequence nor an intervention in a technical sense. Initially, it involves an action or response that helps to stabilize a student, group of students, classroom, or common school area when a significant or dangerous disciplinary situation occurs. Eventually, the administrative response includes an action, typically included in the school or district's code of conduct, involving a high impact consequence meant to both communicate the serious nature of the infraction and motivate an immediate change of behavior.

Critically, as administrators implement consequences with students (typically involving their parents), the following question is essential: "Will this (for example) three-day suspension, while an appropriate consequence, also act as an intervention such that it immediately decreases or eliminates future inappropriate behavior while increasing immediate and future appropriate behavior?" If the answer is "Yes," then the consequence is also an intervention. If the answer is "No," then the administrator should immediately convene the building-level SPRINT team to begin the data-based functional assessment, problem-solving process.

In the case of a suspension, there are a number of advantages of starting the SPRINT process at the beginning of the suspension and before the student returns to school. The most notable advantages include the following: (a) the behavioral situation can be effectively debriefed prior to re-entry; (b) a diagnostic process can begin to identify the underlying reasons for the inappropriate behavior; (c) a re-entry plan can be developed; and (d) an intervention plan, based on the results of the diagnostic process, to change the student's future behavior may be ready. More specifically, the following actions should be completed during the time of the suspension:

1. Debriefing interviews can be completed to describe and analyze the dynamics of the critical incident—thus beginning the functional assessment process. These interviews can be conducted jointly by administrators and mental health or related services staff. They can be conducted in a neutral setting (e.g., a district office or community setting) and at a time when the emotionality that often exists immediately after the event and in the principal's office is removed—in both time and place. Finally, these interviews can involve, as needed, parents, staff, and other students (e.g., in the case of a fight) so that the critical incident can be completely debriefed, re-entry steps can be outlined, and everyone involved can receive a clear message that all of the students involved will be held accountable for their inappropriate behavior.

2. Diagnostic or psychological interviews and other assessments, as needed, can be completed with the student(s) involved. These assessments help identify underlying social, emotional, or behavioral factors contributing to the inappropriate behavior, linking them to strategic or intensive interventions that will change the precipitating triggers or conditions. If these assessments are completed and the resulting intervention plans are developed prior to a student's return to school following the suspension, a higher level of comfort and confidence may exist that the past behavior has been resolved, and the potential for future appropriate behavior has been established.

3. Some interventions may actually occur. For example, in the case of a student fight, the involved students may be required to re-enact and debrief the original situation, and then role-play (a) social, emotional, or behavioral ways to prevent similar situations from reoccurring and (b) related ways to de-escalate or resolve these situations, without physical aggression, if the issues or a confrontation begin again. These interventions hold the students accountable for their inappropriate behavior, increase the probability that the situation has been resolved prior to the end of the suspension, and increase the probability that future appropriate behavior will prevail.

In the end, while the code of conduct may limit their responses to some Intensity IV offenses, administrators still can accomplish the PBSS goals of holding students accountable for their behavior and facilitating their self-management. This begins when they recognize that most suspensions will not change a student's future behavior, and they initiate the SPRINT process as an inherent part of the suspension decision.

DEVELOPING THE BEHAVIORAL MATRIX

Across a school, the development of each respective grade-level Behavioral Matrix is guided by the grade-level representative(s) who is a member of the school discipline/PBSS committee (see Chapter 3). Because this committee has at least one representative from each grade level, there is a seamless communication and collaboration link between the committee trained to oversee the entire schoolwide accountability system and the school's grade-level teams responsible for establishing and implementing student-specific accountability processes. Indeed, after training, the grade-level representatives are expected to guide the activities within the different stages of matrix development at both the committee (school) and grade levels. In all, the development and implementation of the behavioral matrices typically occur in six phases (Knoff, 2007c):

Phase 1: At the grade-level teams

- Completion of the first draft of the Behavioral Matrix by each grade-level team

Phase 2: At the school discipline/PBSS committee

- Analysis and comparisons of each grade-level matrix by the school discipline/PBSS committee
- Completion of first draft of the behavioral expectations and incentives or consequences for the common areas of the school

Phase 3: At the grade-level teams

- Grade-level review of the feedback from the school discipline/PBSS committee and review of matrices from adjacent grade levels (if relevant)
- Student and parent input and suggestions for the matrix
- Finalization of the grade-level matrix
- Analysis and final approval of the behavioral expectations and incentives or consequences for the common areas of the school

Phase 4: At the school discipline/PBSS committee

- Final review and committee and administrative approval of the grade-level matrices
- Review of the feedback and finalization of the behavioral expectations and incentives or consequences for the common areas of the school
- Preparation for a faculty meeting for final matrix adoption

Phase 5: With the entire school faculty

- Faculty adoption of the matrices, and preparation for rollout and implementation

Phase 6: With all faculty and students

- Schoolwide Behavioral Matrix rollout and implementation

These phases and their typical activities are described below, with specific suggestions for the best results.

PREPLANNING: AT THE SCHOOL DISCIPLINE/PBSS COMMITTEE

Initially, the school discipline/PBSS committee is trained in the matrix development process, the use of the forms needed to develop a grade-level matrix, and the information relevant to developing expectations for the common areas of the school (Knoff, 2007c). Knowing that the matrix development process takes from six to twelve weeks (in order to be realistic given other meetings and activities planned and needed across the school), the committee and the school's administration agree on a schedule to complete the six phases outlined above. The above time frame is suggested because the development of the matrix requires a series of group meetings, in-depth discussions, and consensus-building processes that are better accomplished through a series of shorter meetings than through a single daylong professional development session. (When the latter is used, the process of facilitating staff consensus and consistency often is sacrificed for the completion of the forms and the matrix itself.) This results in a lack of commitment and consistency when implementing the final product. Typically, behavioral matrices can be developed and implemented at any time of the year as long as there are realistic goals and expectations when they are implemented at Phase 6.

Below is a chart with two sample matrix development schedules, one starting at the beginning of the school year and another starting in the middle. Typically, the rationale for the development of the matrix and the schedule with the goals and objectives for each phase is presented at a faculty meeting or a series of grade-level team meetings. At times, one or more samples of a Behavioral Matrix are provided so that staff members have a clear picture of the final result.

Phase of Development	Completion Time	Sample Deadlines for Completion: Start of the Year	Midyear
Phase 1	2 weeks	September 15th	February 1st
Phase 2	3 weeks	October 7th	February 20th
Phase 3	2 weeks	October 31st	March 7th
Phase 4	3 weeks	November 20th	April 1st
Phase 5	2 weeks	December 7th	April 15th
Phase 6	**Rollout Date:**	**First Day Back From Winter Break**	**First Day of School**

Phase 1: At the Grade-Level Teams

This phase begins when all staff members receive the Behavioral Matrix forms and are asked to complete them independently and return them to their grade-level school discipline/PBSS committee representative by a specific date. These include separate forms for classroom expectations, incentives, Intensity I, II, and III inappropriate behaviors, and Intensity II and III consequences (see Figure 4.3 for some examples). Elective teachers (e.g., music, art, physical education, etc.) separate themselves across the different grade levels in the school, completing the matrix process as part of that team. Special education teachers and others are distributed more strategically across the grade levels.

| Figure 4.3 | Developing a Schoolwide Behavior Management and Incentive Matrix: Sample Worksheets for Individual Teacher Completion |

Sample Worksheet 2A: Expected Behavior—Classroom

Grade Level _____

> **Directions:** Teachers should check off and then add (as needed) any additional relevant behaviors expected for students while in their classrooms.
>
> **NOTE:** Behavioral expectations come from desired social skills, the replacement (or opposite and desired) behaviors for the Intensity I and II behaviors listed on Worksheets #1A and B, and commonsense expectations for the classroom.

Expectations	Check Here If Considered an Appropriate Classroom Behavioral Expectation
Demonstrating good listening	
Following directions quickly and the first time	
Beginning work promptly	
Working quietly and completing work without disturbing others	
Focusing on and completing work in a timely way	
Keeping arms, feet, and body to one's self—in own space	
Making requests politely or asking for help in a nice way	
Waiting to be called on to speak	
Ignoring distractions successfully and consistently	
Bringing all needed materials to school each day	
Walking safely	
Staying appropriately in own space	
Using an appropriate tone, volume, and pitch of voice	
Talking with others positively and supportively	

Expectations	Check Here If Considered an Appropriate Classroom Behavioral Expectation
Ignoring distractions	
Accepting consequences quickly and appropriately	
Apologizing appropriately	
Treating classroom furniture, books, and other materials with respect	
Treating others' personal property with respect	
Asking adults for help to solve serious problems or to stay safe	
Being kind to others	
Cooperating with others	
Sharing with others	
Joining others appropriately	
Being aware of one's own feelings and the feelings of others	
Treating others with dignity and respect	
Discussing disagreements in a calm manner	
Taking responsibility for one's own actions and statements	
Telling the truth	
Responding appropriately to teasing, rejection, or being excluded	
Responding appropriately to losing	
Responding appropriately to answering a question incorrectly or getting a bad grade	
Dealing appropriately with peer pressure	
Starting and finishing a conversation appropriately	
Giving and accepting a compliment appropriately	
Being able to self-evaluate correctly	
Being a good leader and a good follower	
Other:	

Sample Worksheet 2B: Positive Responses, Incentives, Reinforcers

Grade Level _____

> **Directions:** Teachers should check off and then add to the relevant research- or experience-based positive responses, incentives, or rewards that are known to work with these behaviors.

Incentives or Rewards	Check Here If Considered an Appropriate Classroom Incentive or Reward
Praise or compliments	
Positive phone calls or notes home	
Positive notes to students in their mailboxes or in their classroom planners	
Lottery	
Treasure box—daily, weekly	
Bumper stickers	
Award certificates or badges	
T-shirts	
Rotating trophy	
Stickers to save for center time or privileges	
Stamps to save for center time or privileges	
"No homework" pass	
Tickets for drawings or buying rewards	
Centers or playtime	
Giving the student an additional responsibility or having him or her run an errand	
Letting the class have five minutes at the end of the class period as free time	
Letting the student visit the principal for a special treat or reward	
Recognizing the student as "student of the day or month" over the PA	

Incentives or Rewards	Check Here If Considered an Appropriate Classroom Incentive or Reward
Treats	
Magical money	
Coupons for class store	
"Love notes" in student folders	
Recognition in front of the class (the principal, a school assembly)	
Whole-class cheer or applause	
Good behavior stamp daily for weekly rewards	
Teams that keep stars daily get rewarded	
Fish coupons—catch 'em being good	
Gold tickets for lottery	
Gumball picture for team or whole class	
Marbles or beans in bowl	
Extra recess, free time, free reading time, free computer time, free game time	
Rewards or written feedback (stickers, happy note, certificates)	
Rewards or tangible feedback (pencils, grab bag, tokens, points, special bookmarks)	
Rewards or acknowledgments (student of the week, class cheer, special job or designation)	
Positive calls or notes home	
Class parties, snacks in the lunchroom, or field trips	
More gym/PE, free time in the gym or on the playground	
Extra art time or periods	
Certificates, good behavior grades on report card	
Opportunities to do desired job in classroom or school (take care of class pet, sort papers, help the custodian, run an errand to the office)	

(Continued)

(Continued)

Incentives or Rewards	Check Here If Considered an Appropriate Classroom Incentive or Reward
Opportunities to help a lower grade classroom (e.g., read to them, supervise them)	
Extra fun papers or worksheets	
Extra time in the library or media room	
Hugs, high fives, applause, pats on the back	
Free time to visit with friends, free choice of a partner for a project or assignment	
Opportunity to work with an upper grade student	
Special lunch with teacher (from classroom or another teacher in the school)	
Special lunch with principal	
Special banquet with parents and staff	
Executive dining room privileges	
Special lunch with teachers or staff as waiters	
Special activity with teacher—reading a special story to selected students or class	
Taking an internet field trip	
Spelling, math, or science bees	
Opportunity to listen to music in the class	
A special science experiment	
Opportunities to use arts and crafts materials or time in the classroom or on the computer	
Earn a special class position (e.g., line leader, be excused to go home first)	
Help design and teach a special class lesson	
Help design and put up a special class or building bulletin board	
Help design and put on a special class play or social skills lesson	
Other:	

Sample Worksheet 1B: Intensity II Behaviors and Consequences

Grade Level _____

Directions: Teachers should check off the behaviors below that they feel represent Intensity II behaviors for students at their age or grade level (feel free to add to this list as needed). They then should check off the relevant research- or evidence-based consequences that are known to work with these behaviors and add their own teacher-tested responses or consequences as appropriate. In general, teachers will strategically choose those consequences that have the higher probability of decreasing or eliminating the Intensity II behavior.

Intensity II (Disruptive or Interfering) Behavior: Behavior problems in the classroom that teachers handle with a more directed intervention (loss of student points or privileges, a classroom time-out, a note or call home, completion by the student of a behavior action plan).

INTENSITY II—Disruptive or Interfering Behaviors	Check Here If Considered an Intensity II Infraction
Continued or more intense Intensity I behaviors	XXX
Not following directions or passive or active defiance	
Arguing with the teacher or talking back	
Poor attitude or rudeness	
Talking to neighbors or others without permission	
Chronic socializing with peers	
Inappropriate language (e.g., racial, sexual)	
Inappropriate hand gestures	
Staring or attempting to nonverbally intimidate another student	
Leaving seat without permission	
Not being in a designated or specified area	

(Continued)

(Continued)

INTENSITY II—Disruptive or Interfering Behaviors	Check Here If Considered an Intensity II Infraction
Running in class	
Talking out of turn	
Inappropriate tone or volume of voice	
Non-speech noises that disrupt the class	
Rocking, tilting, falling out of seat	
Calling, shouting, blurting out answers	
Teasing	
Tattling	
Name-calling	
Distracting others	
Pushing or poking inappropriately another student	
Inappropriate physical contact—no injuries	
Horseplay or play fighting	
Bullying or verbally threatening behavior	
Physically threatening behavior	
Swearing	
Lying	
Stealing	
Sexual harassment	
Throwing furniture or dangerous materials	
Spitting (on floor or others)	
Vandalism	
Cheating	
Other:	

INTENSITY II—Responses/Consequences	Check Here If Considered an Appropriate Intensity II Consequence
Move the student to another seat in the classroom	
Loss of the opportunity to earn reinforcement tickets	
Loss of extra privileges	
Loss of reinforcement tickets	
Loss of free time (on a graduated scale)	
Write in discipline logbook	
Loss of recess time	
Student writes an action and remediation plan	
Student models the appropriate behavior	
Student repairs or replaces damaged items	
Teacher ends activity for the student; makes him or her watch the other students until they have completed their activity	
Letter to parent written by the student	
Notes home written by the teacher	
Time-out in class	
Detention	
Phone contact with parent	
Parent-teacher conference	
Other:	

Source: Project ACHIEVE Press. Dr. Howie Knoff (author).

Once grade-level representatives receive all of their respective colleagues' forms, they pool all of the data onto worksheets for each completed form. At this point, the representatives look for items that have been endorsed (or not) by a majority of their grade-level peers. For example, if there are five teachers on a fourth grade team (e.g., four classroom teachers and the art teacher representing her elective area colleagues), any item that is endorsed by four or five teachers should be included at a specific classroom expectation or intensity level. Any item endorsed by none or only one of the teachers should not be included at the level. Finally, any item endorsed by two or three teachers should be placed on a list to be discussed by the entire team during a grade-level meeting.

With a good orientation to the Behavioral Matrix process and attention to the definitions on the forms, most grade-level colleagues agree on 85% to 95% of the items. This allows the school discipline/PBSS committee representative, who usually chairs the grade-level meeting, to emphasize the high degree of consensus at the beginning of the team meeting, increasing the potential that the items on the discussion list can be constructively discussed. If there is less than 85% agreement on the items, the representative must decide how to strategically approach the meeting, consulting with other colleagues or administrators to get their advice. Indeed, when there is a high percentage of items on the discussion list or when it is common knowledge that there are group process issues within a team, an administrator may assign an outside individual or two to lead the Phase 1 meeting, thus taking the grade-level representative out of the middle of a potentially difficult situation.

During the actual grade-level meeting, it is important that all teams follow the effective meeting processes discussed in Chapter 3. While the goal of the meeting is to synthesize and finalize all of the Behavioral Matrix forms, this can be accomplished in different ways. What is essential, however, is that everyone should have access to all of the data, and everyone should feel comfortable discussing any individual item. Ultimately, participants will need to resolve all of the items on the discussion list (e.g., by consensus, a voice vote, a secret ballot) and any others of concern. If, however, there still are items that are so controversial that agreements are impossible, these can be placed on a list that will be reviewed and discussed later by the school discipline/PBSS committee and administration during Phase 2.

At times, administrators will make executive decisions and place disputed items somewhere on the matrix. At other times, especially when a matrix is first being developed by a grade-level team, these items are simply tabled until the team has used the matrix for three months or more. At that point, given the experience of actually using the matrix, some disputed items are no longer controversial. In the final analysis, if three or four items on any matrix level need to be tabled, there typically is little or no functional impact on staff or student implementation.

Phase 2: At the School Discipline/PBSS Committee

In Phase 2, the school discipline/PBSS committee reviews each of the completed grade-level matrices, especially analyzing which items are on the Intensity I, II, and III forms from grade level to grade level (e.g., comparing the Intensity II items identified by a middle school's sixth, seventh, and eighth grade team, respectively). This is done to make sure that there is a logical, developmental progression of items at the same intensity level across adjacent grades. Indeed, at times, a school may have one grade level that is behaviorally more lenient or punitive than its adjacent grade-level teams.

By looking across the completed forms, this phenomenon can be caught, and corrective feedback can be given to a specific grade level during Phase 3.

During this part of the meeting, the school's administrators also analyze the different behavioral matrices to ensure that each item is assigned to the most appropriate intensity level. While the building principal is ultimately responsible for certifying all of the behavioral matrices, he or she especially needs to attend to items that are sensitive from a legal, regulatory, district policy, and community or public relations perspective. Typically, administrators make changes at either the Intensity II or III level where they move (a) an Intensity II behavior to Intensity III status (e.g., to ensure that periodic teasing does not progress to persistent teasing); or (b) an Intensity III behavior to Intensity II status (usually because they believe that the behavior should be or is better handled, for example, in the classroom than in the principal's office). When administrative changes are made to items on a matrix, staff should receive an explanation so that they are sensitized to the issues at hand. Moreover, when an Intensity III behavior is moved to an Intensity II level, staff should discuss how they are going to handle the behavior in the classroom and identify what resources they may need to be successful.

The Phase 2 meeting is also when the school discipline/PBSS committee completes the first draft of the behavioral expectations and incentives or consequences for the different common areas of the school. When discussing this, the committee needs to task analyze the primary goal(s) in each area and specify the desired behaviors (see Chapter 6). For example, when walking down the hall, the goal is to safely walk from point A to point B in a calm and quiet (or silent, if desired) manner. Thus, the almost universal hallway expectations are (a) eyes forward, (b) hands by your sides, (c) mouth/voice quiet or silent, (d) walk to the right, and (e) watch the space in front of you and to your right and left (Knoff, 2007e). What else is needed? Clearly, there is no advantage in stating these expectations more globally by asking students to "be safe, be responsible, and be respectful." Indeed, these more global expectations (i.e., safety, responsibility, respect) are higher-ordered constructs that are not cognitively understood by preschool and elementary students and that are not interpreted similarly by secondary students (or even adults). Students need expectations that are behaviorally specific. Global constructs create interpretation issues and detract from the target behaviors that need to be performed.

During these discussions, the committee also decides whether certain common areas need to be subdivided into smaller phases or areas with more phase- or area-specific expectations. For example, while behavioral expectations in the hallway and bathroom, respectively, can be communicated using one set of expectations, those in the cafeteria and on the playground vary by where students are within those settings. Indeed, in the cafeteria, there are different expectations when students are (a) in line,

(b) getting their food and exiting the serving area, (c) eating at their tables, (d) cleaning up their tables, and (e) exiting from the room. On the playground, there are different expectations when students are (a) going out, (b) playing, and (c) coming in. Moreover, there are different expectations for different playground equipment, when playing certain games, or when moving from one area to another. Figure 4.4 provides some examples of behavioral expectations in four different common areas. Because of the importance of the common school areas as special situations (see Chapter 1), they are discussed further in Chapter 6.

At the end of the Phase 2 meeting, the grade-level representatives prepare to discuss the questions, recommendations, and decisions that have

Figure 4.4   Sample Expectations for the Common Areas of a School: Hallway, Bathroom, Bus, and Cafeteria

Sample Expectations for the Common Areas of a School

Hallway	Bathroom
Eyes forward	Enter/walk on the left
Hands by your side	One at a time at a stall or urinal/flush once when done
Mouth quiet	Mouth quiet
Walking to the right	Keep your space/respect others' privacy
Watching your space	Wash your hands/one towel . . . in the trash

Sample Expectations for the Common Areas of a School

Bus	Cafeteria
Walk on the bus and to the first open seat . . . starting in the back	Enter/walk on the right
Always sitting, eyes forward, hands in your space	Eyes forward, hands by your side, mouth quiet, space
Inside voice, one-seat talking, positive talk	Always walking, positive talking, six-inch voice, Always Good Choices
Exit only when bus in stopped	Food on your tray or in your mouth
	Raise hand for help
	Table clean, throw away your own trash

Source: Project ACHIEVE Press. Dr. Howie Knoff (author).

been made with their grade-level colleagues at the Phase 3 grade-level meetings. An additional outcome from all of the Phase 2 discussions might be the identification of universal classroom expectations across the entire building and a schoolwide positive incentive, reward, and celebration program. If this occurs, this also will need to be discussed during Phase 3, and a commitment from all or most of the grade levels will be needed. All of this, again, reinforces the benefits of having grade-level representation on the school discipline/PBSS committee as information is seamlessly shared from Phase 1 to Phase 2 and from Phase 2 to Phase 3, and as the communication and collaboration needed to develop effective Behavioral Matrices is maximized.

Phase 3: At the Grade-Level Teams

In Phase 3, each grade-level team revisits their Behavioral Matrix, considering the school discipline/PBSS committee's feedback, decisions, and questions. As part of this process, the team also may look at the matrices from the grade levels adjacent to them to see if, for example, they have novel incentive or consequence ideas that they also can use. In addition, the team reviews the draft expectations for the different common areas of the school and any other proposals or feedback requested by the committee. Finally, the team decides how to involve students and parents in the matrix-building process so that they can provide both input and ideas to the matrix before it is finalized.

To involve the students, some grade levels separate the matrix, asking different classes to provide feedback on one or two specific sections. Other grade levels choose a representative focus group of students and let them read and provide feedback on the entire matrix. To involve the parents, some grade levels present their matrix at a regularly (or specially) scheduled parent-teacher meeting. Other grade levels collectively use the leadership from their parent-teacher association (PTA) or parent-teacher organization (PTO) to decide how to best get feedback on different matrices. Clearly, involving students and parents in the matrix process is very important. The student feedback, for example, often helps to validate and expand the lists of incentives and consequences, increasing the potential that they are both meaningful and powerful. The parent involvement often helps to strengthen communication, collaboration, and consistency from school to home and reinforce a message to the students that they are behaviorally accountable in all settings.

Eventually, each grade-level team finalizes its matrix and responds to all other school discipline/PBSS committee requests. At this point, the grade-level representatives bring everything to the Phase 4 committee meeting. While Phase 3 may involve more than one meeting in each grade level, these meetings are instrumental in resolving any final disagreements relative to the matrix's contents or use and in solidifying the staff's collective commitment to the grade and school accountability process.

Phase 4: At the School Discipline/PBSS Committee

In Phase 4, the school discipline/PBSS committee completes a final review of all of the matrices, integrating and collating them into a final document, and prepares to lead a faculty meeting where the results are presented and formally approved. The committee also (a) discusses ways to roll out the matrix to the entire school (and community) once faculty approval has been secured, (b) begins to identify the resources and materials that will facilitate the rollout process, and (c) outlines the steps needed to embed essential elements of the matrix process into the school's website and into the school's student-parent handbook and other brochures and documents. It is emphasized again that the school principal approves all of these decisions and actions. Moreover, some of these decisions may need to be authorized at the district or school board levels. Thus, the need for careful planning, scheduling, and sequencing is important, especially as the school gets closer to rolling out the behavioral matrix and accountability process.

Phase 5: With the Entire School Faculty

In Phase 5, the faculty approves the entire Behavioral Matrix document at a formal meeting, and then discusses and organizes the rollout process. Typically, the approval part of the meeting proceeds without controversy as there have been plenty of opportunities to identify and resolve disagreements at the school, grade, and individual staff levels. In most cases, the matrix document is approved by consensus. The most critical message here is the expectation that everyone in the school will consistently support, implement, and evaluate the behavioral matrix and accountability process. Relative to the latter, staff members should understand that the impact of this process will be evaluated on an ongoing monthly basis by the school discipline/PBSS committee, and that there will be periodic opportunities (after the first three months when the matrix is first implemented and biannually thereafter) for the grade-level teams to revisit the distribution of items within their Behavioral Matrix and to debrief behavioral situations that inadvertently were not covered by or anticipated within the matrix.

Specific to the rollout process, a number of decisions must be made relative to when, who, how, and where the matrices will be introduced to the students and when and how the initial impact of the matrix and accountability process will be evaluated. Typically, the matrix rollout occurs after a natural break in the school calendar—for example, immediately after a lengthy vacation or at the beginning of a new marking period or semester.

The initial rollout should be a significant event. Often, it involves class or whole-school assemblies, special programs with guest speakers and student involvement, large and small group student discussions, and training opportunities so that students learn the matrix and its elements. The rollout is especially effective when students and parents are involved in introducing and discussing their involvement in developing the matrix and their commitment to its importance and implementation. At the secondary level, when well-respected students and student groups (e.g., student government, sports, and other representatives) actually present and endorse the matrix, the peer group recognizes its importance and necessity. At the elementary level, when popular and admired role models (e.g., from the high school or community) present and endorse the matrix, similar student commitments result.

Relative to training, the activities initiated during the rollout day should extend through the next two to three weeks. Critically, students need to learn, through direct training and role-play opportunities, every functional facet of the matrix. While many of the classroom expectations should be embedded in the school's social, emotional, and behavioral skills instruction program (see Chapter 5), some of the classroom routines need to be explicitly taught and practiced. Similarly, the expectations and routines for the common areas of the school must be taught and accompanied by walk-throughs and supervised implementation. Finally, some of the more subtle matrix elements need instructional attention. For example, students will need training, practice, and feedback in how to recognize and respond to many of the Intensity 1 corrective responses (e.g., nonverbal redirects and teacher proximity). Moreover, some of the behaviors and emotions related to consequences should be addressed. For example, students will need behavioral instruction in the time-out process before it is ever used (see Chapter 9), and they need emotional instruction in how to accept a consequence without becoming so upset that they make the situation even worse for themselves. All of this training is consistent with the skills, accountability, and consistency foundation of the PBSS (see Chapters 1 and 5). If students are not taught the skills embedded in the matrix process itself, then the potential benefits of the process may never occur.

Finally, classroom and common area posters of the matrix, inserts for students' binders and calendars, bookmarks and refrigerator magnets, and other support materials are helpful in making the matrix a more public, embedded, and conscious part of the schoolwide accountability process. For parents and community partners, the availability of a one-page handout describing the matrix and its place in the school's discipline and behavior management process also is recommended. This paper may also become part of the section included in the school's parent and student handbook for the beginning of each new school year.

Phase 6: With All Faculty and Students

In Phase 6, the Behavioral Matrix is rolled out to the student body. Typically, the rollout involves a first day big splash event. It then moves to a strategic series of implementation events during the following two to three weeks. Eventually, the matrix involves more implicit and embedded daily, hourly, and teachable moment events to the point where the process is self-managed, internalized, and automatic for both students and faculty. Formative and summative evaluations occur throughout the rollout to internalization process—both specific to students' use of the matrix and more broadly to the discipline, behavior management, and self-management outcomes connected to the entire PBSS.

Postscript. The Behavioral Matrix should be developed in a time-efficient way, but the process still must allow enough time for discussion, consensus-building, and commitment both to its underlying principles and to the broader need for consistent, schoolwide accountability policies, procedures, and practices. Critically, the process—between staff, administration, students, and parents—of developing the matrix is as important as the product represented by the document itself. That is, if the document is not accompanied by cross-staff commitment and consistent implementation, then the desired student outcomes will not result.

Significantly, aside from the short, periodic reviews recommended above, an entire behavioral matrix does not need a comprehensive re-examination by a grade-level team for at least three years. Even then, it is rare for a matrix to require substantial rebuilding, and the re-examination typically is accomplished in one meeting. The only exception to this is when there has been a significant change in the makeup (e.g., behaviorally, demographically, or geographically) of the student body or if there has been a sizable turnover of faculty. If either of these occurs at any time, it may be advantageous—relative to content, commitment, and consistency—for the matrix to be largely rebuilt. Thus, under most circumstances, the time invested in initially developing the matrix is distributed across a number of years, resulting in long-term increases in student engagement and self-management, as well as decreases in student disruptions and disciplinary incidents.

SUMMARY

Accountability is defined as "being willing to accept responsibility for one's actions." While it is important for students (and others) to accept responsibility when they have acted inappropriately (socially, emotionally, or behaviorally), from a self-management perspective, it is more important that they plan and prepare to act responsibly before specific interactions. To facilitate this, students need to have a framework that identifies expected positive and prosocial behaviors in different school settings, and different levels of inappropriate behavior so that they understand that some inappropriate behaviors are more serious than others.

The Behavioral Matrix is recommended as the framework of behavioral standards for students and teachers at specific grade levels and across the common areas of a school. When developed and implemented effectively, the Behavioral Matrix increases the consistency across teachers and other staff relative to student expectations, behavior, feedback, and follow-up. This, then, eliminates the dilemmas that occur when (a) there are different sets of behavioral standards across teachers, (b) individual teachers have different sets of standards across students and even when interacting with individual students, and (c) students are expected to adapt to these inequities and inconsistencies.

For teachers who believe that the Behavioral Matrix usurps their autonomy and personal ownership for classroom management, it does not. In fact, the Behavioral Matrix (for behavior) does not differ from the curricular standards or benchmarks (for academics) that all teachers at a specific grade level are expected to cover. For example, all fourth grade teachers are expected to help their students master the same set of academic skills, specified by the state and district, in literacy, math, science, and so on. How they teach these academic standards may vary from teacher to teacher, but they must teach the same skills and proficiencies represented by these standards. Ultimately, students are evaluated on how well they learn and master the material and whether they can demonstrate their proficiency. With the Behavioral Matrix, the academic accountability that has existed for academics for many years now has been extended to include behavioral accountability.

Beyond this, from a school perspective, all students are accountable for their behavior as represented in the Behavioral Matrix. However, when students engage in Intensity III and IV behaviors, functional assessments and strategic or intensive interventions often become necessary, along with a Behavioral Intervention Plan (BIP) or, if the student qualifies, a 504 or Individualized Education Plan (IEP). Relative to the latter group of students, it must be emphasized that *the long-term expectations and standards for student behavior and accountability do not change,* even though the short-term expectations for these individual students *may* be modified. That is, if a student is unable to meet some of the expectations on the Behavioral Matrix due, for example, to a significant skill deficit, disability, or life circumstance, more realistic behavioral goals and expectations are set, and the instructional or intervention services or supports to help the student attain these goals are identified, implemented, and evaluated. However, as these services and supports are successful and as the student makes sufficient progress, the expectations should be accelerated and retargeted such that they progressively become closer and closer to those on the student's grade-level Behavioral Matrix.

This process explicitly addresses an often-stated concern that some (especially challenging) students are not held accountable to the same social, emotional, or behavioral standards as others, and that this undermines the accountability system in the eyes of those other students. Once again, even though specific students may be unable to meet certain behavioral expectations, the expectations still are maintained as an ultimate goal. The challenge is to determine how to implement the intervention programs that help these students to progress such that they can eventually be held fully accountable to all standards. By way of analogy, not every student earns an "A" in every class or meets all of the state's academic standards or benchmark proficiencies. While we want them to, even with intensive instruction and intervention, it does not happen for all students. And yet, by maintaining challenging goals and expectations, most students outperform those whose goals and expectations are significantly modified or minimized.

The point here is that schools and staff need to have high and realistic academic and social, emotional, and behavioral standards and expectations for all students. Moreover, by publicizing, teaching, and holding both students and staff members to these standards (academically through state standards and scope and sequence benchmarks; behaviorally through the Behavioral Matrix), the vast majority of students are successful. Ultimately, the questions for schools and staff are: "Do you have a clear, developmentally appropriate set of explicit behavioral standards?" and "Does your faculty make comparable academic and behavioral efforts to help all students meet the stated competencies in both areas?" With the Behavioral Matrix, the answer to both of these questions should be "Yes."

NOTE

1. Selected sections of this chapter were adapted from an electronic book: Knoff, H. M. (2007). *Developing and implementing the Behavioral Matrix: Establishing school-wide behavioral standards and benchmarks for student accountability.* Little Rock, AR: Project ACHIEVE Press.

5

Teaching Social, Emotional, and Behavioral Skills[1]

> The solution to adult problems tomorrow depends in large part upon the way our children grow up today.
>
> Margaret Mead

**PBSS Implementation Case Study:
Dutch Broadway Elementary School, Elmont, New York**

Dutch Broadway Elementary School is located within a suburban Long Island school district just over the Brooklyn line near New York City. Its enrollment is just over 1,000 prekindergarten through Grade 6 students; 10% of the students receive special education services and 33% receive federally funded meals due to their low socioeconomic status. With a high number of discipline problems in the upper grades and increasing incidents of threats, fights, and other serious offenses, Dutch Broadway began its partnership with Project ACHIEVE after receiving a state-funded Safe Schools grant in 2000.

Under the leadership of its school psychologist and mental health team, Dutch Broadway implemented Project ACHIEVE's Positive Behavioral Support System (PBSS), focusing heavily on the Stop & Think Social Skills Program. More specifically and in collaboration with their classroom teachers, Stop & Think lessons were written during the first three years of the initiative. These lessons were taught on a weekly basis at every grade level, and students with social, emotional, and behavioral challenges were provided additional instruction in intensive small group or individual social skills counseling groups.

While Project ACHIEVE continues to be implemented at Dutch Broadway Elementary School, data were collected as part of the grant report after the 2000 to 2001 and 2001 to 2002 school years (see Kilian, Fish, & Maniago, 2006). The evaluation tools included (a) classroom behavioral checklists, completed by teachers and focusing on the students' social skills, inappropriate behavior and noncompliance with class and school rules, and serious disciplinary offenses; (b) student, teacher, paraprofessional, and parent surveys; (c) office discipline referrals and subsequent consequences, including suspensions; and (d) standardized test scores. A demographically matched comparison school within the district also was used to evaluate the impact of Project ACHIEVE's PBSS.

Behavioral results were documented during the first two years of implementation:

- Consistent decreases in undesirable behaviors occurred across all grades in both classroom and non-classroom settings. For example, bullying behavior decreased from 22 to zero incidents in Grade 3, and by 94.7% in Grade 4, 78.6% in Grade 5, and 82.4% in Grade 6. In the 18 negative student behavior areas tracked, decreased incident rates were noted in 14 of 18 areas in Grade 3 through Grade 5.
- Students at all grade levels improved considerably in the behaviors evaluated within the social skills category.
- Discipline referrals to the principal's office decreased 58% (from 101 during 2000 to 2001 to 42 during 2001 to 2002).
- School suspensions for disciplinary reasons decreased from 15 during 2000 to 2001 to 9 during 2001 to 2002.

Academic results were documented during the first two years of implementation (using the New York State Grade 4 English/Language Arts Test):

- For the Dutch Broadway students, 19% scored at the highest level of the test (scores of 692 to 800) compared with 16% of the comparison school students
- For the Dutch Broadway students, 46% scored at the next level of the test (scores of 645 to 691) compared with 38% of the comparison school students
- For the Dutch Broadway students, 32% scored at the next level of the test (scores of 603 to 644) compared with 23% of the comparison school students
- For the Dutch Broadway students, only 2% scored at the lowest level of the test (scores of 455 to 602) compared with 22% of the comparison school students

INTRODUCTION

If the ultimate goal of PBSS is student social, emotional, and behavioral competency and self-management, then clearly, students need to learn, master, transfer, and apply the specific skills related to this goal. As noted in Chapter 1, on a social level, skills that are important to self-management include listening, communication and conversation, cooperation, negotiation, refusal, help seeking, positive regard, and how to accept responsibility. On an emotional level, important self-management skills include an awareness of one's own and others' feelings, the ability to manage those feelings, and the ability to make the positive self-statements and attributions that support self-esteem, productive expectations, and optimism. Finally, on a behavioral level, important self-management skills include how to follow directions, ignore distractions, and respond to teasing, losing, or rejection; how to acknowledge, apologize, and accept consequences; how to avoid difficult peer or emotionally volatile situations; and how to respond positively and appropriately to peer pressure. In the final analysis, many of the skills in these areas can be organized into interpersonal, social problem-solving, conflict prevention and resolution, and emotional coping beliefs, thoughts, and attributions (i.e., cognitions) and initiations, actions, or responses (i.e., behaviors).

THE IMPORTANCE OF SOCIAL, EMOTIONAL, AND BEHAVIORAL SKILLS INSTRUCTION: REVISITED

Students' positive self-esteem, self-management, and self-efficacy skills and status significantly predict their academic engagement and academic achievement (Goodman & Schaughency, 2001; McNeely, Nonemaker, & Blum, 2002; Payton et al., 2008; Zins, Weissberg, Wang, & Walberg, 2004). Conversely, students' lack of social-emotional competency correlates with them being less interpersonally and behaviorally successful in school and to a progressive decrease in connectedness, from elementary through high school, that negatively affects their academic performance, behavior, and health (Blum & Libbey, 2004). By high school, as many as 40% of students may be chronically disengaged from school (Klem & Connell, 2004). Moreover, in a national survey of almost 150,000 sixth through twelfth graders (Benson, 2006), only 29% to 45% reported that they had such social competencies as empathy, social decision making, and conflict resolution skills.

In Chapter 1, it was noted that research (Payton et al., 2008) reviewing over 200 studies of school-based programs revealed that classroom time spent addressing the social, emotional, and behavioral skills and needs of students helped to increase their academic achievement. In addition, the students involved were better behaved, more positive, and less anxious and earned higher grades and test scores. Critically, updated meta-analyses from this research (Durlak, Weissberg, Dymnicki, Taylor, & Schellinger, 2011) involving 213 school-based social, emotional, and behavioral learning programs and 270,034 kindergarten through high school students indicated that these students demonstrated significantly improved social and emotional skills, attitudes, and behaviors when compared with control students. These students also demonstrated academic gains that reflected an improvement of 11 percentile points.

On a deeper level, this research analyzed the outcomes of the 213 studies across six different student outcomes: (a) social and emotional skills, (b) attitudes toward self and others, (c) positive social behaviors, (d) conduct problems, (e) emotional distress, and (f) academic performance. The studies also were analyzed by their use of social, emotional, and behavioral learning programs that had four research-based training procedures: (a) explicit learning goals, (b) a focus on skill development, (c) a sequenced step-by-step training approach, and (d) active forms of learning (e.g., behavioral rehearsal, cooperative learning).

In the end, the results indicated that the learning programs that used all four recommended training procedures and that were taught by classroom teachers, respectively, were effective in all six outcome areas. The programs taught by teachers or other school staff and that used more than one of the four research-based training procedures were effective in four outcome areas (i.e., attitudes, conduct problems, emotional distress, and academic performance). The programs that did not use all four recommended training procedures and that were taught by nonschool personnel, respectively, were effective in only three outcome areas (i.e., attitudes, conduct problems, and academic performance for the former, and improved social and emotional skills, prosocial attitudes, and fewer conduct problems for the latter). Finally, students' academic performance significantly improved only when the social, emotional, and behavioral learning program was taught by classroom teachers or other school personnel.

A separate meta-analysis of classroomwide programs focused on building and improving the social skills of almost 13,000 general education students (January, Casey, & Paulson, 2011) revealed that the 28 peer-reviewed studies, included in the analyses and conducted between 1981 and 2007, produced small and positive effect sizes. More specifically, the analysis revealed that the social skill programs studied (a) had the greatest effect at the preschool and kindergarten and then the middle school age levels; (b) did not vary according to the socioeconomic (i.e., free lunch) status of the students (although there was a trend toward greater intervention effects in classrooms or schools with higher percentages of free and reduced-price lunch students); (c) demonstrated greater effects when the program was longer in duration and when students had more opportunities to practice and maintain their social skills; and (d) favored programs that used role-playing and other experiential activities, rather than seatwork-based instruction and memorization. As the programs averaged only 25 hours of implementation (i.e., less than one hour per week), it was suggested that programs that infused their skill instruction and practice throughout the school year, embedding them into daily classroom activities and interactions, would show stronger and more lasting effects.

Taken together, all of the research cited above reinforces the impact of social, emotional, and behavioral instruction in the classroom—from elementary through high school; the importance of involving classroom teachers, along with other school personnel; and the impact of learning programs that focus on explicit, skill-based outcomes and active, sequenced learning. Clearly, the connection between students' academic success and their social competency appears to be reciprocal, with difficulties in one precipitating difficulties in the other. Indeed, if a student cannot stay in his or her seat, work independently, or cooperate in a project-based learning group, academic achievement will be more challenging. Conversely, if a student is not academically successful over time, this may result in withdrawal or frustration, or other more serious emotional or behavioral problems.

THE SCIENTIFIC CRITERIA OF AN EFFECTIVE SOCIAL, EMOTIONAL, AND BEHAVIORAL SKILLS PROGRAM

Based on a synthesis of the research above, as well as implementation practice across the country, seven scientific criteria of an effective social, emotional, or behavioral skills program are suggested:

1. Effective social, emotional, or behavioral skills programs teach sensible and pragmatic interpersonal, social problem-solving, conflict prevention and resolution, and emotional coping skills that are needed by today's students and can be applied on a daily basis by preschool through high school students.

2. These effective programs help to address problem situations that frequently occur in classrooms and common areas of the school (Kerr & Nelson, 2010).

3. These programs organize their skills in defined, progressive, yet flexible sequences that are taught across the school year and are integrated into (or become) a district's articulated and scaffolded health, mental health, and wellness program. The skills are sequenced recognizing that some skills are prerequisite to and must be taught and mastered before other more complex skills. Moreover, the calendar that organizes the skill instruction explicitly builds in opportunities for massed versus distributed student practice. This results in enough time for the students to learn, apply, and

master newly taught skills, and later times when specific skills are revisited and reinforced across the school year, providing opportunities for extended and multi-situational practice (Cartledge & Milburn, 1995).

4. These programs use a universal language that is easy for students to learn, facilitates cognitive scripting and mediation, and helps to condition prosocial behaviors and choices leading to progressively more automatic behavior (Ladd & Mize, 1983; Meichenbaum, 1977).

5. These programs use instructional processes based on social learning theory that include teaching, modeling, role-playing, and providing performance feedback (Bandura, 1977; Goldstein, 1988). The programs also overtly plan and systematically transfer students' skill use into different settings, with different people, at different times, and across different situations and circumstances—including those that involve conditions of emotionality (Stokes & Baer, 1977).

6. The programs are an integral part of an evidence-based positive behavioral support system (Dwyer, Osher, & Warger, 1998; Kerr & Nelson, 2010; Knoff, 2000).

7. The programs teach specific cognitive-behavioral skills in explicit and developmentally appropriate ways, and they can be adapted with students from different racial, cultural, language, and socioeconomic backgrounds and with different social, emotional, and behavioral needs (Cartledge & Milburn, 1996).

APPLYING THE SCIENTIFIC CRITERIA USING THE STOP & THINK SOCIAL SKILLS PROGRAM

As noted in Chapter 2, the Stop & Think Social Skills Program (Knoff, 2001) is the social, emotional, and behavioral skills program used by Project ACHIEVE. Based on the cognitive and social learning theory research of Meichenbaum (1977) and Bandura (1977) and the social skills research of Goldstein (1988) and Cartledge and Milburn (1995), the Stop & Think Social Skills Program also is the anchor of Project ACHIEVE's PBSS. Using the Stop & Think program as an exemplar, specific characteristics and components are described below to provide examples of how the scientific criteria above can be applied in a functional way at the classroom and school level.

The Stop & Think Social Skills Program has manuals and materials for both school and home and parent instruction and implementation (Knoff, 2001, 2005b). The program focuses on teaching students interpersonal, social problem-solving, conflict prevention and resolution, emotional coping, academic supporting, and classroom and building routine skills by using classroom or home lessons that involve teaching, modeling, role-play, performance feedback, and transfer of training activities. The Stop & Think school program has four levels: preschool to early elementary (preschool to Grade 1), early to middle elementary school (Grades 2 to 3), middle to late elementary school (Grades 4 to 5), and middle school (Grades 6 to 8). Initially, students are taught the universal Stop & Think language and then the steps for each specific social skill in the third "What are your Choices or Steps?" step. Each manual outlines 10 core and 10 advanced social skills as well as up to 20 additional classroom or building routines. Within a classroom, each social skill is taught in a two-week cycle that includes teaching each social skill's step-by-step scripts and accompanying prosocial behaviors, engaging students in systematic application activities so that they can practice their skills in closer-to-real-life situations, and taking advantage of teachable moments to facilitate skill infusion.

The Stop & Think Social Skills Program was identified with Project ACHIEVE as an evidence-based program by the U.S. Department of Health & Human Services' Substance Abuse and Mental Health Services Administration (U.S. Department of Health and Human Services, SAMHSA, 2010). Below are Stop & Think characteristics or components that exemplify the seven scientific criteria.

Criterion 1. The social, emotional, or behavioral skills program teaches sensible and pragmatic interpersonal, social problem-solving, conflict prevention and resolution, and emotional coping skills that are needed by today's students and that can be applied on a daily basis by preschool through high school students. Social skills are behaviors that students learn—just like they learn academic skills. While educators often focus on what they don't want students to do ("don't fight," "don't talk back," "don't interrupt," "don't tease or taunt other students"), social skills focus on the behaviors that they want students to do. Significantly, when students perform desired behaviors, they rarely perform inappropriate behaviors at the same time.

Because it is organized from preschool through middle school (although the latter manual also is strategically used for specific students at the high school level), and it is part of a schoolwide PBSS, the Stop & Think social skills are taught in all classroom settings in a school by general education teachers. For students with greater need and more challenging behaviors, the social skills also are taught in more targeted social skills training groups by special education, related services, and mental health support professionals.

Some of the core and advanced Stop & Think social skills (some of these skills are taught at the different grade levels) include the following:

The Core Skills:

Listening

Following directions

Asking for help

Ignoring distractions

Dealing with teasing

Contributing to discussions and answering classroom questions

Waiting for an adult's attention—how to interrupt

Dealing with losing

Apologizing

Dealing with consequences

The Advanced Skills:

Deciding what to do

Asking for permission

Joining an activity

Giving or accepting a compliment

Dealing with accusations

Understanding your and others' feelings

Avoiding trouble

Dealing with anger

Dealing with being rejected or left out

Dealing with peer pressure

Walking away from a fight

Criterion 2. The skills program can help to address problem situations that frequently occur in classrooms and common areas of the school (Kerr & Nelson, 2010). The Stop & Think Social Skills Program includes skills to teach classroom and building routines. In the classroom, these routines help students to be prepared and ready to participate in academic activities. Across the common areas of a school, these routines help students to interact positively and safely and to manage their behavior more responsibly and independently. Some of the classroom and building routines in the Stop & Think Social Skills Program include the following:

Entering class

Hanging coats and backpacks

Walking in line

Bathroom behavior

Getting on the bus

Contributing to discussions

Completing seatwork or independent assignments

Bringing the right materials to class

Lining up to leave school

The dismissal skill

Walking safely in the hall

Riding on the bus

Answering questions during lessons

Knowing when to tell an adult about a school safety issue

Criterion 3. The skills program organizes its skills in a defined, progressive, yet flexible sequence (or suggested instructional calendar), recognizing that some skills are prerequisite and must be mastered before other more complex skills are taught. The sequence or calendar has built-in times where specific skills are revisited and reinforced across the school year, providing opportunities for distributed and extended practice (Cartledge & Milburn, 1995). As shown above, the Stop & Think Social Skills Program has a preferred sequence of ten core skills and ten advanced skills that have been field tested. While this sequence is preferred, it is not absolute. As long as teachers are mindful that some social skills are prerequisite to later skills, they can resequence skills to respond to specific behavioral goals, challenging classroom problems, or desired curricular or character education themes.

Beyond this, the Stop & Think Social Skills Program integrates the learning principles of massed and distributed practice into its process by reviewing and revisiting many social skills across the grade levels as well as during a particular school year. In doing this, the program is able to teach the same skill with higher, more developmentally appropriate expectations over time and ensure that the skills are applied in situationally appropriate ways (e.g., at different times of the school year and across different school years).

Criterion 4. The skills program uses a universal language that is easy for students to learn, facilitates cognitive scripting and mediation, and helps to condition prosocial behaviors and choices leading to progressively more automatic behavior (Ladd & Mize, 1983; Meichenbaum, 1977). Social skills in the Stop & Think Social Skills Program are taught using two essential processes: (a) a universal language or set of steps that facilitate the cognitive and physical conditioning of new behavior, and (b) a pedagogical approach that uses behavioral and social learning theory strategies to guide effective instruction.

The Stop & Think Social Skills Program uses a universal five-step language whenever a social skill is taught, reinforced, or implemented:

- Stop and Think!
- Are you going to make a Good Choice or Bad Choice?
- What are your Choices or Steps?
- Do It!
- Good Job!

The Stop and Think step is a self-control, impulse control, and self-management step designed to classically condition (à la Pavlov) students to take the time necessary to calm down and think about how they want to handle different social, emotional, or behavioral situations. The Good Choice or Bad Choice step is an operant conditioning step (à la Skinner) that motivates students to consciously select the choices they make and the behaviors they exhibit. Typically, teachers prompt students, sometimes using the grade-level Behavioral Matrix, as to the positive outcomes or rein-forcements that will result when they make a good choice. Conversely, students are guided to consider the negative outcomes or consequences that will occur if they make a bad choice. These potential positive or negative reinforcements are designed to motivate students to make a good choice.

The What are your Choices or Steps? step uses cognitive-behavioral psychology and mediational learning strategies to help organize, prepare, and guide students to think about steps needed to execute their appropri-ate behavior before enacting it. This is where teachers teach the specific skills scripts for each Stop & Think skill so that students learn and are able to demonstrate (in the fourth step of this process) their good choices—that is, their prosocial behaviors. There are two types of skill scripts—scripts that teach social skills in a step-by-step sequential fashion (step skills) and scripts where students consider and select one of a number of possible good choices (choice skills). For example, the following directions skill script is an example of a step skill because there is only one correct sequence that will result in successful behavior:

1. Listen to the direction.

2. Ask yourself if you understand the direction (if not, ask a question).

3. Repeat the steps of the direction silently to yourself.

4. Get ready to follow the direction.

The dealing with teasing skill script demonstrates the elements of a choice skill where students learn to evaluate different interpersonal situa-tions so that they can strategically select the best choice:

1. Take deep breaths and count to five.

2. Think about your good choices. You can
   a. ignore the teasing,
   b. ask the person to stop in a nice way,
   c. walk away or back away from the teaser, or
   d. find an adult for help.

3. Choose and act out your best choice.

Once students have thought about the good social skill choices or steps needed for a particular situation, they then are prepared to demonstrate them behaviorally.

Thus, in the Do It! step, students behaviorally carry out their plan, implement the social skill chosen, and evaluate whether or not it has worked. With younger elementary school-aged students, teachers may need to repeat the skill steps as their students follow them, and they might even need to physically guide students through some skills. Older students, with prompting, will repeat the Stop & Think steps silently to themselves and perform the prosocial behaviors more independently and automatically over time.

If the Do It! step works, students then are ready to go on to the last step. However, if a step skill doesn't work, students simply go back over the scripts in Step 3 and implement them more carefully. If a choice skill doesn't work, students are prompted to move to another good choice option or identify another social skill that will work. For example, if the ignoring choice does not stop a peer's teasing, then a student might decide to directly ask the peer to stop the teasing, explaining how the teasing is making him or her feel. Once successful, it is on to the last step.

The Good Job! step uses the cognitive-behavioral skill of self-reinforcement such that students reinforce themselves for successfully demonstrating a social skill that helped them respond appropriately to a social, emotional, or behavioral situation. This step is important because students need to learn to self-evaluate and self-reinforce when they make good choices and exhibit prosocial behavior. These skills are also important so that students do not become dependent on adult or peer feedback. Ultimately, from a self-management perspective, students need to learn how to recognize when they are successful and how to reinforce themselves for a job well done.

Criterion 5. The skills program uses instructional processes based on social learning theory that include teaching, modeling, role-playing, and providing performance feedback (Bandura, 1977; Goldstein, 1988). The program also overtly plans and systematically transfers students' skill use into different settings, with different people, at different times, and across different situations and circumstances—including those that involve conditions of emotionality (Stokes & Baer, 1977). The evidence-based behavioral and social learning teaching process used by the Stop & Think Social Skills Program involves five components:

- Teaching the steps of the desired social skill
- Modeling the steps and the social skills language (or script)
- Role-playing the steps and the script with students
- Providing performance feedback to students relative to how accurately they are verbalizing the skill script and how successfully they are behaviorally demonstrating the new skill
- Applying the skill and its steps as much as possible during the day to reinforce the teaching over time, in different settings, with different people, and in different situations

When teaching the steps of a desired social skill, teachers use the Stop & Think Program's universal language. As noted earlier, when they get to the What are your Choices or Steps? step, students are taught the specific choices or steps for the skill they are focusing on.

When modeling a social skill, teachers verbalize the steps to a particular social skill while showing their students how to perform the associated behaviors. Typically, this is done by having teachers re-create an actual classroom or school situation where the particular social skill is needed. For example, in modeling the dealing with teasing social skill, a teacher would have a student tease the teacher in front of the class. The teacher then would talk through the script using the universal Stop & Think language with the skill steps of the dealing with teasing social skill while performing the related behaviors. Thus, during teaching, teachers provide a context for and instruction in performing social skill behaviors. During modeling, teachers show how to implement the skill, verbally and behaviorally, in a simulated situation.

After a teacher models a specific social skill, students are given opportunities to role-play or act out that skill in simulated situations that are relevant both to the classroom and to the social skill itself. Over time, and when appropriate to specific skills, some role-plays will simulate conditions of emotionality so that students learn how to demonstrate their skills when they are feeling tense, pressured, fearful, excited, frustrated, or angry. Role-plays may be done in front of the class or in small or controlled group settings. The teacher, as if directing a scene from a school play, focuses on having students accurately verbalize the social skill script that is being taught and performing the corresponding behaviors during every role-play.

While students are role-playing their social skills, teachers provide performance feedback. This feedback positively reinforces students as they correctly verbalize the social skills steps and demonstrate the appropriate skill or behavior. This feedback also occurs when role-plays get off script. Here, the teacher may freeze the actors, provide corrective feedback to bring students back on script, and resume the scene so that students practice only accurate and appropriate behavior. Finally, after successfully completing a role-play, teachers provide additional performance feedback by debriefing the scene and reviewing students' performance of the social skill script and behavior.

After the modeling, role-play, and performance feedback steps, teachers place students into as many classroom situations as possible where they need to apply or transfer the social skills training. These transfer of training opportunities simulate real-life school situations, along with the emotional conditions that may be present, so that students can experience and master their skills at a more realistic level. This step involves teachers setting up situations in the classroom that require students to apply, under controlled and supervised conditions, their new social skills. It also occurs as teachers prompt, as appropriate and needed, the use (or infusion) of different social skills during pivotal moments in the classroom.

Over time, this pedagogical process involving teaching, practice, application, and infusion helps students to understand the importance of using specific social skills and to learn, master, and use their prosocial skills at more automatic and independent levels over time. In summary,

When teaching and modeling, teachers need to make sure that students

- have the prerequisite skills to be successful,
- are taught using language that they can understand,
- are taught in simple steps that ensure success, and
- hear the social skills script as the social skills behavior is demonstrated.

When practicing or role-playing, teachers need to make sure that students

- verbalize (or repeat or hear) the steps to a particular social skill as they demonstrate its appropriate behavior,
- practice only the positive or appropriate social skill behavior,
- receive ongoing and consistent practice opportunities,
- use relevant practice situations that simulate the emotional intensity of the real situations so that they can fully master their social skills and be able to demonstrate them under conditions of emotionality, and
- practice the skills at a developmental level that they can handle.

When giving performance feedback, teachers need to make sure that the feedback is

- specific and descriptive,
- focused on reinforcing students' successful use of the social skill, or on correcting an inaccurate or incomplete social skills demonstration, and
- positive—emphasizing what was done well and what can be done well (or better) next time.

When transferring or applying social skills after instruction, teachers need to make sure that they reinforce students' prosocial skills steps and behavior when students

- have successfully demonstrated an appropriate social skill,
- have made a bad choice, demonstrating an inappropriate social skill,
- are faced with a problem or situation but have not committed to, nor demonstrated, a prosocial skill, or
- must use the skill in situations that are somewhat different from those used when the skill was originally taught and practiced.

Criterion 6. The skills program is an integral part of an evidence-based positive behavioral support system (Dwyer et al., 1998; Kerr & Nelson, 2010; Knoff, 2000). As discussed in Chapters 1 and 2, the Stop & Think Social Skills Program is the anchor of Project ACHIEVE's PBSS. When implemented effectively, three levels of self-management are accomplished: (a) students learn the self-management skills (at appropriate developmental levels) that they need for self-control and independent learning; (b) school staff learn the self-management skills that they need to run positive, effective, and well-organized classrooms; and (c) schools or districts organize and execute the self-management processes that help them to identify their resources, build their capacity, and sustain successful buildingwide systems of prevention, strategic intervention, and intensive need services for all students, especially those with behavioral or mental health concerns.

Criterion 7. The skills program teaches specific cognitive-behavioral skills in explicit and developmentally appropriate ways, and they can be adapted with students from different racial, cultural, language, and socioeconomic backgrounds, and with different social, emotional, and behavioral needs (Cartledge & Milburn, 1996). The Stop & Think Social Skills Program has been successfully implemented in rural, urban, and suburban schools, at preschool through high school levels across the country. It has been implemented in schools with diverse, multicultural and multinational groups of students, in a range of communities with students from significant levels of poverty to high levels of affluence and in schools where a majority of the students do not speak English as their primary language (the Stop & Think signs are printed in both English and Spanish). The program also has been used in many Native American reservation schools (e.g., Navajo, Shoshoni, Arapaho, Alaskan native) by incorporating each native culture's teachings on positive social, emotional, and behavioral values and expectations and translating the Stop & Think steps and materials bilingually. These accomplishments have occurred because school personnel have successfully applied the seven scientific criteria discussed in this chapter to the individual histories, backgrounds, and needs of their students, staff, and communities. These successes also have occurred, in some instances, because the schools and districts recognized the need to move away from previously adopted character education programs to an evidence-based social skills program.

Character Education Versus Social Skills Programs. In contrast with the seven criteria or characteristics of an evidence-based social skills program, most character education programs either are not evidence-based or do not adhere to a large number of these criteria (Knoff, 2005a).

Indeed, most character education programs talk about (rather than teach and practice) social, emotional, or behavioral skills. They discuss constructs of behavior (e.g., respect, responsibility, cooperation) rather than teach specific behaviors, and they present these constructs at times (especially at the preschool and elementary school levels) when students do not have the higher order thinking skills to understand either the constructs or their associated behaviors. Many character education curricula do not modify their instruction for different age levels of students or for diverse learners or learners with special education needs. Finally, most character education programs are not integrated into a schoolwide PBSS.

While states that have statutes or requirements in this area consider social skills programs as character education programs, it is important to note that most character education programs are not designed as social skills programs. At the very least (see the last section in this chapter), if a school or district is thinking about adopting a character education program for its PBSS, its selection committee should compare and contrast the program with the evidence-based criteria above as well as against one or two evidence-based social skills programs.

Summary. An evidence-based social, emotional, or behavioral skills program provides an important, necessary foundation to a schoolwide PBSS program that has student self-management as a primary goal. From an instructional perspective, a social skills program teaches its skills in pedagogically sound ways so that students learn, master, and can apply their skills in a variety of real-life situations, including those that involve conditions of emotionality. Effective social skills programs also can be modified and adapted to students who learn in different ways, and they include practical skills that help students to succeed in both classroom and school settings. Finally, a social skills program should include skills that students can use to prevent or respond to situations involving teasing, taunting, bullying, harassment, hazing, and physical aggression.

A BRIEF REVIEW OF SOME NOTABLE SOCIAL, EMOTIONAL, AND BEHAVIORAL SKILLS PROGRAMS

There are literally hundreds of social, emotional, and behavioral skill programs or curricula on the market today, and yet the vast majority of them are not evidence-based. An evidence-based program has (a) demonstrated consistent positive, data-based outcomes across multiple settings, students, circumstances, implementations, and implementers; (b) demonstrated its effectiveness under controlled and comparison conditions; and (c) been externally and independently evaluated by an expert panel that typically is convened by a federal agency or its designee. Some non-evidence-based programs identify themselves as research-based, but there are no set criteria as to what represents quality research, and anyone can claim that their research is sound and that it validates their program. Indeed, some programs do not acknowledge that their research was conducted by the program's developer using small, unrepresentative, non-randomly selected samples of convenience, and that their outcomes were not blindly and independently evaluated by outside experts using objective criteria.

A review of existing evidence-based or well-researched social, emotional, or behavioral skills programs (Arkansas Department of Education, 2009) identified eight published programs that meet most, if not all, of the scientific criteria discussed earlier in this chapter: Lion's Quest, Positive Action, Second Step, Providing Alternative Thinking Strategies, Life Skills Training, Boys Town, Skillstreaming, and the Stop & Think Social Skills Program. Six of these programs are listed on the National Registry of Evidence-based Programs and Practices (NREPP) website sponsored by the U.S. Department of Health and Human Services' Substance Abuse and Mental Health Services Administration (U.S. Department of Health and Human Services, SAMHSA, 2010). Two of these programs (Boys Town, Skillstreaming) have a substantial degree of research evidence in refereed journals and high levels of implementation nationwide. All of these programs have been implemented extensively in schools and classrooms nationwide.

These eight published programs can be organized along a continuum that ranges from a social-emotional learning focus to a behavioral, social skills instruction focus (see Figure 5.1). Below, the eight programs are briefly reviewed along this social-emotional learning to behavioral skills instruction continuum.

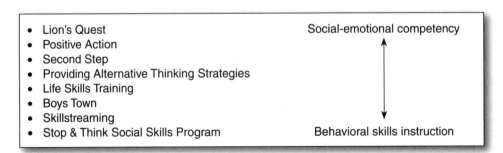

Figure 5.1 Evidence-Based Social, Emotional, and Behavioral Programs

- Lion's Quest
- Positive Action
- Second Step
- Providing Alternative Thinking Strategies
- Life Skills Training
- Boys Town
- Skillstreaming
- Stop & Think Social Skills Program

Social-emotional competency

Behavioral skills instruction

Source: Project ACHIEVE Press. Dr. Howie Knoff (author).

Lion's Quest (published by Lions Clubs International Foundation; website: www.lions-quest.org). This Kindergarten through Grade 12 curriculum is divided into three levels: K to Grade 5, Grades 6 to 8, and Grades 9 to 12. The K through Grade 5 curriculum focuses on character education, social and emotional learning, and service learning using six topics and 24 skill-building lessons. The Grade 6 to 8 program focuses on character development, communication and decision-making skills, and service learning, guiding young people toward healthy choices and drug- and violence-free lifestyles. This curriculum contains eight topical units and 102 skill-building lessons. The Grade 9 to 12 level focuses on cultural awareness, interpersonal communication, personal management and responsibility, and study and writing skills through more than 100 life skills lesson plans organized in four-year, one-semester, or nine-week program options.

Positive Action (published by Positive Action, Inc.; website: www .positiveaction.net). This program consists of five components in a K through 12 curriculum: self-concept, physical and intellectual positive actions, and social and emotional positive actions. Each kit contains an instructor's manual with scripted 15-minute lessons along with prepared materials. Included are student activity booklets, journals (for Grade 4 to 12), and other hands-on materials for 30 students. The lessons contain activities that address academic standards, and some lessons are aligned with states' standards.

Positive Action is based on the concept that positive thoughts lead to positive actions, positive actions lead to positive feelings about yourself, and positive feelings lead to more positive thoughts. Its goal is to teach positive actions for the physical, intellectual, social, and emotional areas of the self.

Second Step (published by Committee for Children; website: www .cfchildren.org). Second Step is a violence prevention program that teaches social skills such as empathy, emotion management, problem solving, and cooperation. It is divided into three sections: preschool to kindergarten, Grades 1 to 5, and middle school. For the two younger groups, the program uses lesson cards with photographs that prompt discussions about real-life situations. These lesson cards include objectives, scripts, discussion questions, role-plays, and other activities. The preschool to kindergarten level also incorporates puppets and songs on a CD. The Grades 1 to 5 level has an accompanying video. For middle school students, a DVD provides informational video clips, dramatic vignettes, skill-practice demonstrations, and interviews with real students as teachers use fully scripted lessons that incorporate group discussion; individual, partner, and group activities; and interactive exercises, games, and skill practice. There is a separate parent program available, with some materials available in Spanish.

Providing Alternative Thinking Strategies (PATHS; published by Channing Bete Company; website: www.channing-bete.com/prevention -programs/paths/paths.html). The PATHS curriculum is a program for educators and counselors that is designed to facilitate the development of self-control, emotional awareness, and interpersonal problem-solving skills. The curriculum consists of an instructional manual; six volumes of lessons, pictures, and photographs; and additional materials. A research book is also available. PATHS is designed for use with elementary school-aged children. The purpose of the PATHS Curriculum is to enhance the social competence and social understanding of children as well as to facilitate educational processes in the classroom.

Life Skills Training (published by Princeton Health Press; website: www.lifeskillstraining.com). Promoted as a program to help elementary, middle, and high school students develop skills to reduce tobacco, drug and alcohol abuse, and violence, Life Skills Training focuses on three primary learning objectives: drug resistance skills, personal self-management skills, and general social skills. The program begins at Grade 3 and extends into high school. The entire elementary section (Grades 3 to 4, 4 to 5, 5 to 6) features 24 sessions that are 30 to 35 minutes in length. For the middle school, there are 30 sessions divided between Grades 6 to 9, and the high school section consists of ten sessions that are 40 to 45 minutes in length for Grades 9 and 10.

Life Skills Training is classroom based and features lecture, discussion, coaching, and practice as instructional methods. The curriculum sets include a teacher's manual and 30 student guides. An elementary-level sample lesson is available online, providing a large number of worksheets. It features a decision-making model called the "Stop-Think-Go" method. There is a parent guide and DVD (available in Spanish) and a workshop kit available for parent trainers. It addresses adolescent drug use and the development of student personal self-management and social skills.

Tools for Teaching Social Skills in Schools (published by Boys Town Press; website: www.boystownpress.org). This workbook is a series of instructional lesson plans for teaching 28 social skills including following instructions, staying on task, working with others, accepting criticism, listening, ignoring distractions, making a good choice, sharing, and showing respect. Lesson plans have activities that use discussion, activities, journaling, role-play, and reading. The workbook also includes reproducible skill pages, techniques to blend social skills into academic lessons, ideas for bulletin board displays and student motivators, and strategies for increasing parent support. The book also has chapters explaining the role of social skills in the classroom, how to task-analyze skills, how to set behavioral expectations for students, and how to use consequences to teach social skills.

Skillstreaming (published by Research Press; website: www.research press.com, www.skillstreaming.com). Skillstreaming is a prosocial skills training program available for three instructional levels: early childhood—preschool through Grade 1, elementary school—Grades 2 to 5, and adolescent—Grades 6 to 12. It focuses on addressing the social skill needs of students who display aggression, immaturity, withdrawal, or other problem behaviors. It is designed to help youngsters develop competence in dealing with interpersonal conflicts, learn to use self-control, and contribute to a positive classroom atmosphere. The program uses a four-part training approach involving teacher modeling, student role-playing, group performance feedback, and transfer of training (practicing the skills at home and in the community). Two video training programs are available for staff training.

The Stop & Think Social Skills Program has been discussed earlier in this chapter (School materials published by Cambium Learning/Sopris West Educational Services: www.projectachieve.info/productsandresources/thestopthinksocialskillsprogramschool.html; Home/Parent materials published by Project ACHIEVE Press: www.projectachieve.info/productsand resources/parentstopthinkbook.html).

SELECTING A SKILLS PROGRAM AT THE DISTRICT LEVEL

As part of a prekindergarten through high school health, mental health, and wellness curriculum (see Chapter 2) that is committed to teaching social, emotional, and behavioral skills to all of its students, the choice of an appropriate program or curriculum should be a district-level decision. That is, rather than having, for example, different elementary schools in the same district make independent (and, likely, different) choices on a social, emotional, or behavioral program, districts should form a selection committee made up of district and school representatives who review a number of possible programs and choose the best one. While a different program or curriculum may be chosen at the elementary versus secondary level, the district's selection and use of a single program (a) helps to maintain instructional consistency and integrity especially when there are high mobility rates of students and staff across different schools within the same district; (b) makes purchasing materials easier and more cost-effective; and (c) facilitates consistent districtwide training, support, implementation, and evaluation.

While the recommendation for the district-level selection of a social, emotional, or behavioral skills program may seem unprecedented or unusual, it is consistent with the way most districts choose their literacy, mathematics, and other academic curricula. Indeed, when choosing a new academic curriculum, especially at the elementary level, most districts form a selection committee that is charged with identifying the needs, goals, and desired outcomes of all of its students while assessing the strengths and weaknesses of the current curriculum. The committee then reviews recent research that is relevant to the targeted academic area, agrees on the criteria that will guide the selection process, and identifies an initial pool of programs or curricula that meet most of the criteria. After narrowing the pool, the committee examines review copies of the top three to five curricula, interviews teachers from other districts who have used the curricula, and listens to formal presentations from the authors or publishers of the highest rated curricula. Finally, the committee makes a final recommendation of one or more (perhaps, in rank-ordered fashion) curricula to the superintendent or school board, and a final decision is made. This same process is recommended when selecting a social, emotional, or behavioral program or curriculum, especially given the importance of these skills to positive school and classroom climates, academic engagement, prosocial success, and academic achievement (see the introduction sections of this chapter).

Selecting a Social, Emotional, and Behavioral Skills Program at the Secondary Level. At the secondary level, the selection of a social, emotional, and behavioral skills program follows a somewhat different track. First, it is important to recognize that state legislatures or departments of education often require that students receive coursework in different health, mental health, and wellness areas at the secondary level. Typically, this coursework involves information and skills training in areas related to physical and emotional health, drugs and alcohol, sexual health and relationships, cultural and racial sensitivity, gender differences and interactions, career exploration and job skills, bullying and harassment, and tolerance as related to social justice and discrimination. Based on our experience, the units related to these course areas often are not logically organized into or presented as an articulated, scaffolded health, mental health, and wellness curriculum with an integrated scope and sequence, coordinated curricula and instruction, and staff members who meet periodically to ensure that desired student outcomes are accomplished. Thus, the skills instruction across these units often is inconsistent, disjointed, redundant, and sometimes even contradictory.

Given this, the selection of a social, emotional, and behavioral skills program at a district's secondary level may begin with a health, mental health, and wellness summit where all of the middle and high school staff who oversee, teach, or are interested in these areas meet together to plan. The goal of the meeting is to form a task force (that includes students and parents) that (a) analyzes the goals and outcomes of the required or existing coursework units; (b) identifies additional needed or desired instruction; and (c) develops an articulated and scaffolded outline and sequence of course content that is connected with descriptions of the staff expertise needed to teach each unit. The task force also evaluates existing curricula to identify specific social, emotional, and behavioral skill gaps and to determine if there are areas of potential inconsistency or contradiction. Based on this latter evaluation, there may be no need for an additional or specialized social, emotional, or behavioral skills program as discussed in this chapter. That is, the skills that the secondary level students need to learn may already be present within the existing health, mental health, and wellness curricula. At this point, task force members need to make sure that the skills are being taught in a logical sequence—from grade to grade and unit to unit, and that the instruction consistently conforms to the seven scientific criteria of an effective skills program discussed in this chapter.

Eventually, the task force should integrate the secondary level's newly designed health, mental health, and wellness program and process with the one at the elementary level.

After completing its work, the task force should give way to the staff who teach the health, mental health, and wellness units that have been established. These staff should meet periodically to oversee the implementation of the program, evaluating its effectiveness and outcomes at staff, student, and community levels.

SUMMARY

In order to effectively teach social, emotional, and behavioral self-management skills, it is necessary to teach the cognitive-behavioral skills and scripts using a teach-model-role-play-performance-feedback-transfer of training format that is embedded in a progressive teach-apply-infuse process. The initial goal is to provide enough positive practice opportunities so that students learn targeted skills and scripts. The broader goal is to transfer the training, providing students with additional application and infusion opportunities such that they learn to independently use their skills in different situations and settings with different people and personalities and under different conditions of emotionality. When done with high levels of consistency, this facilitates both skill mastery and skill transfer. When the consistency extends across students, staff, settings, situations, and circumstances, a schoolwide impact can be seen.

This chapter focuses on evidence-based ways to teach students skills that facilitate social, emotional, and behavioral self-management. Emphasizing cognitive-behavioral instruction, mastery, application, and automaticity through the seven scientific criteria of an effective skills program, eight specific programs were reviewed with a recommendation that programs be chosen at the district, rather than individual school, level. The Stop & Think Social Skills Program is used to exemplify the functional implementation of the seven criteria and to demonstrate the impact of a skills program on students' interpersonal, social problem-solving, conflict prevention and intervention, and emotional coping skills and interactions. Chapter 7 extends this conversation, showing how to apply the social skills process to address the skill deficits or needs of students involved in teasing, taunting, bullying, harassment, hazing, and physical aggression.

NOTE

1. Selected sections of this chapter were adapted from a technical assistance paper: Arkansas Department of Education, State Personnel Development Grant. (2009, October). *School-wide discipline, behavior management, and student self-management: Focusing on social skills instruction and selecting an evidence-based social skills program.* Little Rock, AR: Author.

6

School Safety and Crisis Prevention, Intervention, and Response

It's never too late to be what you might have been.

George Elliot

PBSS Implementation Case Study:
Cleveland Elementary School, Tampa, Florida

Project ACHIEVE's partnership with Cleveland Elementary School in Tampa, Florida, began during the 1993 to 1994 school year. Demographically, during five years of on-site implementation, Cleveland Elementary' s enrollment averaged 500 students per year with an approximate racial makeup of 20% Caucasian, 62% African American, 17% Hispanic, and less than 1% other minority students. Cleveland Elementary also had an average mobility rate of new and withdrawn students of 66% and a poverty level that encompassed 97% of its student body.

At the time of implementation, Cleveland Elementary drew its students from a neighborhood of public housing complexes in one of the most dangerous sections of Tampa. In fact, it was in this area where a series of serious racial disturbances occurred in 1987. Given this background and the need to reach out to parents and other stakeholders in the community, Project ACHIEVE was awarded a Metropolitan Life Foundation "Positive Choices: Youth Anti-Violence Initiatives" grant in 1995 to create Stop & Think neighborhoods and communities. Working with parents, the leadership councils from the local public housing complexes, the business community, and other agencies and support groups, a safe community and safe school partnership was created to benefit all of the students attending Cleveland Elementary.

Recognizing that school reform often takes up to five years to accomplish, the outcome data from the initiative were analyzed by clustering the first five years (1993 to 1998) of Project ACHIEVE implementation together and then comparing them to the last two years (1998 to 2000) of continued implementation. The results were notable:

Behavioral Outcomes

- Total discipline referrals to the principal's office dropped from an average of 45.0 referrals per 100 students for the two years prior to project implementation, to 34.5 referrals per 100 students for the next five years (approximately one referral per school day over an entire year), to 21.3 referrals per 100 students for the last two years (approximately one referral every two school days over the year).
- In-school suspensions dropped from an average of 21.0 suspensions per 100 students for the two years prior to project implementation to 16.4 suspensions per 100 students for the next five years to 11.0 suspensions per 100 students for the last two years.
- Out-of-school suspensions dropped from an average of 5.9 suspensions per 100 students for the two years prior to project implementation to 4.3 suspensions per 100 students for the next five years to 1.8 suspensions per 100 students for the last two years.

Academic Outcomes

- Grades 2 through 5 students taking the Scholastic Aptitude Test (SAT-8) reading section between 1993 and 1995 scored, on average, at the 22nd percentile; the Grades 2 through 5 students taking the SAT-9 from 1995 to 1999 had a median percentile rank at the 43rd percentile—indicating significant academic improvements.
- Grades 2 through 5 students taking the same test during the 1999 to 2000 school year also had a median percentile rank at the 43rd percentile—thus sustaining these academic improvements.
- In math, students taking the SAT-8 between 1993 and 1995 scored, on average, at the 29th percentile; the students taking the SAT-9 from 1995 to

1999 had a median percentile rank at the 51st percentile, and the students taking the same test during 1999 to 2000 had a median percentile rank at the 52nd percentile—the latter two cohorts both scoring above the national average and significantly higher than the 1993 to 1995 cohort.

Special Education Outcomes

- Special education placements averaged 2.5 placements per 100 students for the first five years versus 1.6 placements per 100 students for the next two years.

INTRODUCTION

Two special situations were introduced in Chapter 1 during the discussion outlining the primary components of the Positive Behavioral Support System (PBSS): setting-specific situations that occur in the common areas of the school (i.e., the cafeteria, hallways, bathrooms, buses, playgrounds, or gathering areas) and student-specific situations that involve teasing, taunting, bullying, harassment, hazing, and physical aggression. Relative to the first special situation, students' social competency and self-management skills clearly contribute to the positive climate and safe interactions in the common areas of a school. This, in turn, helps students to positively and successfully enter their classrooms, settle in, and academically engage with their teachers and the learning process. Students' social competency in the common areas also helps to minimize the negative peer interactions that form the foundation of teasing, taunting, bullying, harassment, hazing, and physical aggression—the second special situation (Knoff, 2009a).

While special situations still tend to focus on student behavior, as noted in Chapter 1, they are special situations because there are other ecological factors that significantly contribute to positive and safe common school areas: the absence of teasing, taunting, bullying, harassment, hazing, and physical aggression and the presence of prosocial interactions and social competence. These domains are used to complete Special Situation Analyses—analyses that help to create the conditions that result in safe common school areas and peer interactions and that are used to systematically determine why a special situation problem is occurring so that strategic interventions can be identified, prepared, and implemented. These domains involve the following areas: (a) how students behave and interact together, and the degree of negative versus positive peer pressure (student characteristics, issues, and factors); (b) how staff interact with students (and each other), and the quality and quantity of staff supervision (teacher and staff characteristics, issues, and factors); (c) the physical plant of the school or a specific school area, the logistics of how students and staff physically interact and move from setting to setting, and how the school schedule impacts the logistics, number, and mix of students in specific school areas (environmental characteristics, issues, and factors); (d) the incentives and consequences in different common school areas relative to appropriate versus inappropriate student behavior, respectively; and (e) the availability and effective use of school resources to facilitate positive interactions, student management, and group self-management (resources and resource utilization).

This chapter focuses on setting-specific special situations at the prevention, problem solving, and crisis management levels (see Chapter 7 for the student-specific special situations). Relative to prevention, ways to organize schools, staff, and students such that common areas of the school are safe, secure, and prosocial are presented. Relative to problem solving, we review ways to conduct Special Situation Analyses that evaluate unsuccessful or unsafe common areas so that strategic or intensive interventions are identified and implemented. Relative to crisis management, the necessary components of an effective crisis management process are outlined. Within this chapter, ways to conduct safety audits, complete common school area screenings, and conceptualize an Emergency Operations Plan (EOP) also are addressed.

THE FIVE SETTING-SPECIFIC COMMON SCHOOL DOMAINS: PREVENTION

The ultimate goal in this area is to have consistently safe and secure common school areas where students and staff interact in positive, prosocial, and proactive ways. In a preventative sense, this occurs when elements within the five special situation domains described below work interdependently in effective ways.

Student Characteristics, Issues, and Factors. Students demonstrate effective interpersonal, social problem-solving, conflict prevention and resolution, and emotional coping skills when the behavioral expectations for each common school area are explicit, specific, and consistent across all grade levels (see Chapter 4, which discusses the identification of these expectations within the context of the Behavioral Matrix). These skills then need to be behaviorally taught to mastery (just like a social skill; see Chapter 5) to all students at the very beginning of the school year, and they need to be infused and reinforced throughout the year by individual students, different peer groups, and staff.

At some point, these common school area skills become automatic for most students and, depending on their developmental maturation, they are prompted by their presence (e.g., "when I am in the bathroom, I need to . . ."), the task demands (e.g., "when I am done with my lunch, I need to . . ."), or the people (e.g., "when the whistle blows at the end of recess, I need to . . .") in the respective settings. As they are demonstrated, appropriate skills and behaviors need to be positively acknowledged or reinforced (by the students themselves, the peer group, and the staff), and inappropriate skills and behaviors, in contrast, need to be corrected (or self-corrected). At times, depending on how serious the inappropriate behavior is, the response may involve consequences and reteaching or administrative involvement and action.

Ultimately, all of this is done consistently across students, staff, settings, and situations. This involves consistent behavioral expectations and instruction; consistent peer, staff, or setting prompts and cues; and consistent positive, corrective, or administrative responses. This instruction and response continuum was introduced as part of the ten scientific principles discussed in Chapter 1 (see Figure 1.3, Chapter 1).

Relative to identifying the logistical and behavioral expectations in the different common areas of the school, a functional and task analytic approach is recommended. That is, staff members need to determine the different phases of student movement within each setting and what they want students to do within each phase. Below are the typical phases within a number of common school areas. Critically, for each of these settings, staff members (and students) need to determine the behavioral expectations for the typical or routine circumstances and situations within each phase, the skills or behaviors that students should be taught to prevent or quickly resolve mild conflict or challenging situations, and what staff prompts and student responses are needed when extreme conflict or emergency situations occur.

Hallway Phases:

1. Lining up and exiting the classroom or other setting

2. Walking down the hallway and interacting with peers or staff

3. Entering the next classroom or setting

Bathroom Phases:

1. Lining up and entering the bathroom

2. Using the facilities

3. Washing and drying hands and throwing away towels (if needed)

4. Exiting the bathroom and returning to class or another setting

Bus Phases:

1. Appropriate behavior and interactions at the bus stop

2. Lining up and entering the bus

3. Walking within and sitting down in the bus

4. In-seat behavior and interactions

5. Leaving the seat and walking to the bus exit

6. Exiting the bus and walking to the next setting (e.g., the playground, into the school, back home)

Playground Phases:

1. Approaching and entering the playground

2. Selecting a playground area, game, or apparatus

3. Playing or interacting in that area, during that game, or on that apparatus

4. Leaving and entering a new area, game, or apparatus

5. Getting called in and lining up at the end of the playground period

6. Exiting the playground and walking to the next setting

Cafeteria Phases:

1. Lining up and entering the serving area

2. Getting food and interacting with staff in the serving area

3. Exiting the serving area and proceeding to and sitting down at a table

4. Table manners, eating, and interacting with peers and staff

5. Cleaning up, leaving the table, throwing away trash, and returning utensils

6. Exiting the cafeteria and walking to the next setting

Relative to the skills and behaviors required within each common school area phase, these are best taught using the same script and skill and social learning theory (i.e., teach, model, role-play, performance feedback, transfer of training) approaches discussed for the social skills training in Chapter 5. While the scripts may differ and the instruction may be modified for students at different grade or maturational levels, some sample scripts for different common school areas are shown below (Knoff, 2007e).

Lining Up to Leave the Classroom:

1. Wait for the teacher's direction

2. Stand up and put your chair under the desk

3. Walk quietly to the door of the classroom and get into the line

4. Keep your eyes toward the front of the line, your hands by your side, your mouth quiet, and the space between yourself and the person in front of you

5. Wait for your teacher's direction to leave the classroom

Walking in Line in the Building:

1. Keep your eyes on the line leader (pilot)

2. Walk to the right and keep your distance (space) from the student in front of you

3. Keep your hands by your side

4. Keep your voice quiet

5. Keep your feet quiet but moving

Bathroom Behaviors:

1. Go into the bathroom silently, stop and count the number of students

2. When a space is open, walk to and use the facility

3. Flush once when done, and walk to the sinks

4. Wash your hands—one person at a time

5. Dry your hands with one paper towel and put it in the wastebasket

6. Walk out of the bathroom and get into line

Riding on the Bus:

1. Sit down, facing forward

2. Keep your hands in your lap

3. Keep your feet in front of you or on the floor

4. Use an inside voice

Playing Games at Recess on the Playground:

1. As a group, agree on the rules and decide how to begin the game

2. Make sure that everybody takes a turn

3. Thank everyone for playing—be a good winner and loser

Busing Food and Tables in the Cafeteria:

1. Stand up

2. Check to see what needs to be cleaned in your area

3. Pick up any things on the table or floor that need to be taken care of

4. Walk to the throwaway area

5. Put everything in the proper places (recycling, trash, silverware, trays, etc.)

6. Walk to your dismissal line

Teacher and Staff Characteristics, Issues, and Factors. Like the students, staff members (instructional, support, paraprofessional, administrative, and others) need to know, learn, and consistently demonstrate effective interpersonal, social problem-solving, conflict prevention and resolution, and emotional coping skills in the common areas of the school. Indeed, they need to know how to teach, prompt, and reinforce the behavioral expectations discussed above as well as the skills or behaviors that students are taught to prevent or quickly resolve conflicts or to respond to during extreme conflict or emergency situations. Critically, staff members need training in these important areas, and the training should use the same teach, model, role-play, performance feedback, and transfer of training approaches used with the students. Ultimately, staff members and students should be able to demonstrate the skills and behaviors when different circumstances occur and conditions of emotionality exist. Beyond this, students should be consistently held accountable for their appropriate and inappropriate behavior, respectfully, regardless of whether the staff person is known or unknown, instructional or paraprofessional. Moreover, specific policies and procedures should exist that describe staff members' responsibilities for monitoring and supervising students in the common areas of the school, and they should be continuously evaluated and held accountable to these policies.

Environmental Characteristics, Issues, and Factors. Safe and secure common school areas result most often when there is a comprehensive process to continuously plan, implement, and evaluate the safety and security of the entire school. This occurs when schools conduct scheduled school safety audits, remediate identified weaknesses or gaps, and update their practices when, for example, more effective procedures or new technologies become available. These audits also help to prevent crisis situations, and they establish the protocols for an effective first response system when crises actually occur (see section below). A comprehensive school safety audit typically addresses specific broad areas (Texas School Safety Center, 2008; Trump, 2011; Virginia Department of Education, 2000):

- The development and use of policies and procedural documents relevant to school, staff, student, parent, law enforcement, and outside personnel
- The development of school prevention, intervention, and crisis management and response plans and processes (see later section below) and how they are implemented and evaluated
- The security of the school grounds, classrooms, and common areas by school administrators and staff, school security staff, and police before, during, and after school hours
- The physical plant of the school, including its lighting, monitoring or surveillance, and alarm systems; its scheduling and traffic patterns for students in common school areas; its staff supervision and deployment patterns and responsibilities; and its classroom organization, cleanliness, and safety and security characteristics
- The involvement of students, parents, and relevant community stakeholders in school safety processes; the professional development and training of staff members; and the use (with students) of school drills and simulations
- The response times of school or district security and law enforcement personnel, along with other first responders during drill and actual emergency situations
- How information and data are collected that formatively and summatively evaluate all processes and procedures

Specific to the common areas of a school, the school safety audit analyzes the presence of certain critical factors (Texas School Safety Center, 2008; Trump, 2011; Virginia Department of Education, 2000):

School Exterior and Play or Gathering Areas

- School grounds and play or gathering areas are fenced and secure
- Staff, visitor, and student parking areas have been designated, have appropriate signage, and are secure
- There is one clearly marked and designated entrance for visitors
- Signs are posted for visitors to report to the main office through a designated entrance
- Restricted areas are clearly marked
- All exterior doors are numbered on the outside, and these numbers are clearly visible from the street
- Exterior doors, unless designated for entry, lack exterior hardware and are keyed to allow re-entry

- All areas of the school grounds and buildings are accessible to patrolling security and emergency vehicles
- Bus loading and drop-off zones are clearly defined
- Fire zones are clearly marked
- Access to the bus loading area is restricted to other vehicles during loading and unloading
- Staff are assigned to bus loading and drop-off areas
- Parent drop-off and pickup areas are clearly defined
- There is adequate lighting around the building
- Lighting is evident and working at entrances and other points of possible intrusion
- Parking lots are lighted properly, and all lights are functioning
- There is visual surveillance of play areas, bicycle racks, and other exterior areas
- Visual surveillance of parking lots from the main office is possible
- The perimeter of the school building is clear of debris, obstructions, and safety hazards
- Shrubs and foliage are trimmed to allow for good sight lines (3'-0"/ 8'-0" rule), and to prevent people from hiding behind them
- Ground floor windows have no broken panes, and the locking hardware is in working order
- Basement windows are protected with grills or well covers that are secure and locked
- Access to the roof is restricted with no climbable plantings, trees, or architecture
- The school grounds are free from trash or debris
- The school's exterior walls and other surfaces are free of graffiti

School Interiors: Classroom, Common, and Staff Areas

- There is a central alarm system in the school
- All doors have working locks, and classroom doors have locks that can be activated from the inside
- High-risk areas are protected by high security locks and an alarm system
- Doors accessing internal courtyards are securely locked from the inside
- Mechanical rooms and hazardous storage areas are locked
- Classrooms are numbered with reflective material over and at the bottom of each door and on exterior windows
- All interior doors have small break-resistant windows
- Convex mirrors (as needed) are in place to see around corners in hallways and up and down stairwells
- The main entrance is visible from the main office
- All entries to the building are controlled and supervised

- Signs directing visitors to the main office are clearly posted immediately outside and inside the school
- Visitors are required to sign in and are issued identification cards or badges
- All full-time, part-time, and visiting staff (including bus drivers) are issued identification badges that are worn and visible
- Exit signs are clearly visible and point in the correct (and alternative) directions
- Hallways, bathrooms, stairwells, common areas, and classrooms are properly lit
- Locker areas are well lit and unassigned lockers are secured
- Emergency and fire drill procedures are posted
- There is adequate access to fire extinguishers, first aid supplies, and cardiac defibrillators
- Emergency lighting is properly installed and functioning
- Bathroom and other school walls are free of graffiti
- Hallways, bathrooms, and other common areas are appropriately supervised by staff
- There is a telephone or two-way communication system between the main office and classrooms, staff rooms, relevant common school areas, and relevant outside school areas (including bus and drop-off areas)
- There is a public address system that works properly, can be accessed from several areas in the school, and can be heard and understood both inside and outside of the school

Beyond the school safety audits, other environmental characteristics, issues, and factors include the physical layout of the different common school areas, the traffic patterns within each setting, the formal and informal scheduling that results in different numbers of students in these settings at different times of the day, and the scheduling and physical deployment of staff members relative to presence and supervision.

Incentives and Consequences. This domain involves the incentives and consequences that motivate individual students, peer groups of students, and staff members to demonstrate the interpersonal, social problem-solving, conflict prevention and resolution, and emotional coping skills that result in positive, safe, and secure common school areas. To be effective, most of these incentives and consequences should be delivered in the actual settings where the behavior or interactions occur, and, as students get older, the best incentives and consequences come from the peer group or from the students themselves. At times, however, prosocial behavior in the common areas of the school is strengthened when there also are teacher- or classroom-based incentives or consequences. That is, some students demonstrate more appropriate common school area behavior when classroom teachers hold them accountable in these settings through classroom-delivered incentives and consequences.

The impact and selection of incentives and consequences was discussed from a scientific perspective in Chapter 1 and from a student accountability perspective in the context of the Behavioral Matrix in Chapter 4. Expanding briefly on the latter, there are times when a Behavioral Matrix for a specific common school area is strategically important or useful. Typically developed to address persistent misbehavior on a school bus or in the cafeteria, these more specialized matrices are recommended as a result of data-based special situation analyses (see section below). Thus, common school area matrices are not generally needed or recommended at the Tier 1 prevention level. They are discussed here to provide examples of appropriate incentives and consequences that are contingent on students' common school area behavior.

A school bus Behavioral Matrix developed by a real school is shown in Figure 6.1. Created jointly by the school discipline/PBSS committee with a representative group of their bus drivers and the district's director of transportation, this matrix has the same structure as a classroom-focused grade-level matrix. That is, the committee explicitly identified the expected behaviors on every bus for the school, connecting them to meaningful student incentives and rewards delivered by the bus drivers themselves. The Behavioral Matrix, which was discussed and taught to all students on the first day of school by the students' teachers and at least one bus driver, identified a continuum of increasingly more inappropriate or serious bus behaviors connected to corrective responses, consequences, or administrative actions. The corrective responses and most consequences were delivered by the bus drivers at the time or on the day when the inappropriate behavior occurred. At times, the consequences also involved a student's classroom teacher (sometimes with his or her parents). Finally, for the most serious offenses, the school principal took responsibility after a direct referral from a bus driver and after validating the concern and the involvement of an individual student or multiple students.

As with a grade-level matrix, a common school area matrix identifies the behaviors expected of students in a specific setting and how staff will consistently respond to both appropriate and different intensity levels of inappropriate student behavior. This is especially helpful in a cafeteria when supervision often is shared by different staff members on a rotating basis, by paraprofessionals who may not command the same respect from the students as the instructional staff, or by one or two administrators who are depending on students to largely manage their own behavior. This is similarly helpful on school buses that (a) transport different age-groups of students (b) using drivers who need to develop personal relationships with students, and yet, who often feel that they lack the incentives or consequences to motivate appropriate behavior, (c) in a setting that students often do not see as the first and last school setting of their school day.

Figure 6.1 Sample of a School Bus Common School Area Behavioral Matrix

on the Bus

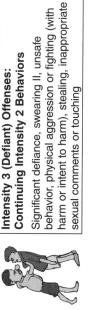

Expected Bus Behaviors:

Listening and following driver's directions, walking in and walking out, sitting immediately in assigned seat, always staying in seat in listening position with book bag on lap, quiet inside voices, positive words and voices always, treating property with respect

Incentives and Rewards:

Praise, smile, positive statement to student, special seat privileges, happy notes to teacher or home, treat at lunch for all bus riders, playing special CD or song on bus, additional points to classroom point system

Intensity 1 (Annoying) Offenses:

Not listening or following directions, leaving or falling out of seat or seat jumping, pushing or shoving I, loud or disruptive noises, talking back to driver, eating or drinking on bus, swearing I

Corrective Responses:

Stop & Think prompt, nonverbal prompt (increasing or decreasing volume on CD), verbal warning (on PA), informing student of potential loss of points or privileges, move student to another seat next ride

Intensity 2 (Disruptive) Offenses: Continuing Intensity 1 Behaviors

Excessive arguing or defiance (talking back or refusal to follow driver's directions, teasing, name-calling, bullying or threatening other students, pushing or shoving II or inappropriate physical contact (no injury, non-sexual), swearing I, excessively loud noise

Corrective Responses and Consequences:

Loss of incentive or reward from above, note or phone call or discussion with parent or teacher, loss of preferred seat or immediate reseating to front of bus (at stop sign or for next bus ride), loss of points for bus or school or class reward

Intensity 3 (Defiant) Offenses: Continuing Intensity 2 Behaviors

Significant defiance, swearing II, unsafe behavior, physical aggression or fighting (with harm or intent to harm), stealing, inappropriate sexual comments or touching

Consequences:

Referral to principal, conference with parent and driver, bus suspension, community service (on bus/with driver), school-based consequence, role-playing incident with counselor or other adult

Intensity 4 (Dangerous) Offenses or Continuing Intensity 3 Behaviors

District or school code of conduct offense

Administrative Responses:

Follow school district rights and responsibilities code of conduct procedures and guidelines, expulsion from bus

Source: Project ACHIEVE Press. Dr. Howie Knoff (author).

Resources and Resource Utilization. In a preventative sense, when conducting their comprehensive needs assessments and resource analyses (see Chapter 2), schools need to consider how the resources identified can help them in their common school areas. In a creative sense, schools need to look beyond what they can (or cannot) buy and the staff members that they can (or cannot) use to discover ways to find and use other people, products, technologies, or innovative practices to create and sustain positive common school area settings. For example, some secondary schools have held contests where students have generated cost-effective solutions for common school area dilemmas. Significantly, when these solutions were implemented, not only were they effective, but the student body was more committed to ensuring their success.

Other schools have used parents, the Parent-Teacher Association (PTA), community or business partners, local and state foundations, and other out-of-district clubs or organizations to enhance their resources. This has resulted, for example, in the use of (a) a successful university cafeteria program in a public school's cafeteria, (b) dogs in a local police unit's K-9 division to reinforce positive playground behavior, and (c) a group of grandparents at a nearby church as check-in buddies for students coming into school each morning. Still other schools have involved high school students needing community service credits in their middle schools as hallway, library, and computer lab assistants.

Beyond the generation of new resources, schools also need to look at how they are using existing resources. For example, even when there are enough individuals to supervise, for example, a cafeteria, playground, or hallway, it is how they are deployed that really matters. Indeed, if the four supervisors on a playground are all huddled and talking together on a corner of the blacktop, the intended impact of their presence is not achieved. Instead, the playground could be zoned into three areas, and three of the four supervisors could be designated as zone captains who are responsible for constantly sweeping among, interacting with, and positively reinforcing or constructively correcting the students in their zone. The fourth supervisor could be designated as a free safety, responsible for moving randomly across all three zones when things are going well and for moving strategically to back up a specific zone captain when a challenging situation requiring more than 45 seconds to resolve occurs. In this latter role, the zone captain moves to directly address the situation in his or her zone, and the free safety replaces the captain by taking over the sweeping duties within the zone. The success of this approach is further enhanced when the staff members and students have both been trained and have practiced these maneuvers during the few weeks of every new school year, and when they know the specific prompts needed to vacate a zone if a prolonged or serious event occurs.

In the cafeteria, resources are enhanced when the food service and custodial staff become part of the behavior management team. In the hallways and bathrooms, supervision and safety are enhanced when students are an integral part of the process—motivating and reinforcing their peers for prosocial interactions, while discouraging or reporting inappropriate behaviors.

Summary. In the end, when schools take the preventative steps, across the student, teacher and staff, environmental, incentive and consequence, and resource and resource utilization domains, to build and sustain effective common school area procedures and interactions, the number of challenging behaviors and the intensity of the critical events that do occur are minimized. This results in fewer situations to address and debrief and less need to formally analyze why certain problems are occurring. At the same time, school staff members need to be trained and skilled in conducting Special Situation Analyses so that they can analyze and resolve, typically through the school discipline/PBSS committee, serious or persistent common school area problems. The next section of this chapter briefly outlines this analysis process using the five special situation domains above.

THE FIVE SETTING-SPECIFIC COMMON SCHOOL DOMAINS: PROBLEM SOLVING

When frequent, escalating, or significant problems are occurring in a common school area, a setting-specific Special Situation Analysis is needed. This problem-solving process involves a data-based, functional assessment to determine why the problem is occurring, strategically linking the results to interventions and solutions that solve the problem. Described in detail in Chapter 8, this process involves seven interactive steps that result in (a) the identification, clarification, and specification of the problem concern or situation; (b) the functional assessment and analysis of why the problem is occurring; (c) the planning, preparation, and implementation of the interventions needed to resolve the problem; and (d) the evaluation of the intervention's implementation integrity, intensity, and success. As noted above, setting-specific Special Situation Analyses focus on all five of the special situation domains, eventually identifying which ones are contributing to the identified problem.

To begin, after specifying and clarifying the special situation problem and the common school area where it is occurring (problem identification), the reasons underlying the problem are analyzed across the five special situation domains (problem analysis) along with the existing strengths, resources, and other factors that are periodically preventing the problem, or preventing the problem from being more serious. Typically, given the ecological and interactive nature of most common school areas, the underlying reasons for a specific challenge or concern often involve two or more domains. Once the sources of the problem are validated, an intervention plan is devised, implemented, and evaluated (intervention and evaluation). Critically, while fewer than five domains may be responsible for the problem, all five domains generally are involved in the intervention.

Below are descriptions of the most important areas to investigate during problem analysis for each of the five special situation domains. In order to best understand this information, it might be important to read and then re-read this section after reading the problem analysis section in Chapter 7 and all of Chapter 8.

Student Characteristics, Issues, and Factors. The problem analysis process here evaluates the who, what, when, where, why, and how conditions that exist when the problem situation occurs and does not occur and that result from or follow its occurrence or nonoccurrence. This analysis is completed for four related groups of students:

- The students who are exhibiting the problem
- The students who are contributing to the problem but are not the primary offenders
- The students who are not part of the problem but are bystanders observing the problem
- The students who are trying to prevent or minimize the impact of the problem and who might be involved in the long-term intervention or resolution of the problem

For the students who are exhibiting or contributing to the problem, the functional assessment analyzes the gap between the interpersonal, social problem-solving, conflict prevention and resolution, and emotional coping skills that these students have but are not demonstrating and the skills that they need to behave appropriately in the common school area. From this, the analysis determines the reasons for the gap. For example, do the students have (a) skill deficits, where they lack the needed skills because they have not been taught, learned, or mastered them; (b) performance or motivational deficits where they have mastered these skills but refuse to demonstrate them, or choose to demonstrate inappropriate behaviors; (c) skill or performance deficits due to inconsistent instruction or inconsistently delivered incentives or consequences; or (d) a combination of the above conditions.

Beyond this, the analysis also should investigate the demographic (e.g., gender, grade level, race or cultural background) and situational (e.g., number of years in the school, current teachers, academic or peer group status) characteristics of the four groups of students and whether these characteristics are impacting how they are interacting in the school area of concern. These analyses help uncover important dynamics that may be contributing to the problem—for example, racial issues or situations where a senior class or a group of student athletes are using their status to cause problems and intimidate other students in a specific common school area.

By way of example, when functionally analyzing the hallway behavior in a middle school, and the degree of running, pushing, and shoving that occurs in between most periods, there are student questions that need to be answered:

- Are there specific students, groups of students, or grade levels of students who are the primary offenders? Are there specific students who are the typical victims? Are there specific students who consistently reinforce the inappropriate behavior? Are there specific students whose presence or actions result either in less inappropriate behavior by the primary offenders or more appropriate student behavior in general?
- Do the different groups above vary by gender, race or culture, socioeconomic status, or where they live in the community? Do they differ by the elementary schools that they attended, by their grade point average (GPA), or by the teachers whose classes they attend?
- Are there certain times or events during the school day, places in the school, or other characteristics or conditions present when the running, pushing, and shoving largely occurs? Are there other times, places, or conditions present when students pass through the hallways in safe and appropriate ways?
- When it exists, why does the inappropriate behavior occur, and why do the offending students behave appropriately when that happens? When they behave appropriately in the halls, are there specific reasons why or conditions that are present? Do the offending students choose to behave appropriately versus inappropriately at different times or due to different conditions? Does the presence of or the response from specific peers or staff members increase the offending students' appropriate behavior, and does the presence of or response from other peers increase these students' inappropriate behavior?
- How long has the inappropriate behavior been occurring? Is this a historical pattern of concern, or has the inappropriate behavior just recently begun?
- What are the strengths, skills, and assets of the different groups of students noted above, what are the attitudes of the latter three groups toward the students demonstrating the inappropriate behavior, and what is their commitment to seeing the behavior change?

Teacher and Staff Characteristics, Issues, and Factors. The problem analysis process here specifically analyzes the who, what, where, when, why, and how of the administrators, staff, and other adults who are present in the common school area of concern, and other teachers or staff who are not in these settings but are, nonetheless, influencing students' common school area behavior—positively or negatively. Mirroring the functional assessments within the student domain, the problem-solving process here investigates (a) who the administrators, staff, and other adults are in the school—demographically, experientially, and situationally; (b) what they are contributing—positively, negatively, or not at all—to the problem situation relative to their interactions and responses, their lack of responses, or their physical absence from the setting; and (c) how their strengths and weaknesses, skills and abilities, beliefs or expectations, and motivation or resistance relate to the problem situation, or its absence, prevention, or resolution.

Revisiting the running, pushing, and shoving scenario in the middle school hallways, certain staff questions need to be answered:

- Are there specific staff members whom (different groups of) students respond to more positively or negatively, and does their presence in the hallway predict when running and pushing occurs or does not occur, respectively?
- Do staff members consistently teach (in advance) and prepare or remind students of the hallway expectations before they enter the hallways? How (and how quickly, directly, and consistently) do they reinforce or correct students (if they do) for appropriate versus inappropriate hallway behavior as it occurs?
- Are there enough staff members in the hallway throughout the school day, are they present from the beginning to the end of the passing period, and are they effectively positioned along the hallways to maximize their impact?
- Do the different student groups, especially those who are exhibiting the problem behaviors, respond appropriately and similarly to every staff member, or are there differences in their responses?
- If present, why are there differences in how students respond to certain staff members? Does this relate to gender, race, culture, experience, role, status, responsibility, or other differences between the specific staff members and students involved?
- Does the presence or the response from specific staff members increase or decrease students' appropriate versus inappropriate behavior?
- Is the running, pushing, and shoving a historical or a recent pattern of behavior? Does it relate to the characteristics or student management approaches of the school's administrators or changes in one or more administrators over time?
- What is the commitment of the staff members and other adults in the school to change the behaviors of concern?

Environmental Characteristics, Issues, and Factors—Physical Plant and Logistics. In general, the problem analysis process here specifically investigates the settings where the inappropriate student behavior is largely occurring, the dynamics and conditions (both positive and negative) within those settings or environments, the logistics whereby students and staff members enter and exit the settings, and how these conditions are contributing to or causing different facets of the problem. Depending on the common school area, this assessment could involve analyses of (a) the physical dimensions, layout, and condition of the setting and the organization of any furniture or equipment; (b) how and how many students and others move into, out of, and within the setting during specific time periods; (c) how students and adults are clustered or organized within the setting, and how many different types (e.g., grade levels) of students are present at different points in time; (d) how quickly students must enter and exit the setting; (e) the student to staff ratios and how supervising staff are organized or deployed within the setting; and (f) other related and relevant factors. Once again, this information is merged with the data from the other domains resulting in a profile of strengths and resources and weaknesses and liabilities within the setting, to go along with the analyses of the reasons for the targeted concerns.

All of the physical plant and logistical characteristics and factors above relate, potentially, to the running, pushing, and shoving problem in our middle school hallway. For example, does the inappropriate behavior occur in hallways that are furthest from the office or instructional (as opposed to elective) classrooms? Does it occur in hallways that are more narrow or crowded than others; that have more disorganized two-way traffic patterns than others; that are closer to different school exits or have more blind turns or corners than others; or that are longer or shorter than others? Clearly, these and other questions try to correlate specific physical plant or logistic factors to the running, pushing, and shoving in the hallway. If the inappropriate behavior occurs regardless of these factors, then the analysis will focus on the other four special situation domains. If the inappropriate behavior occurs in certain parts of the school or due to specific logistical conditions, then these factors need to be addressed during the intervention process.

Incentives and Consequences. Within this domain, it is important to analyze the incentives and consequences that motivate, or could motivate, students and staff to demonstrate appropriate behavior and interactions in the common area of concern or those that reinforce inappropriate behavior. This analysis is done at the individual, group (both peer and adult), and student body and whole-staff levels. It also focuses on the motivational conditions that exist when the problem is occurring or does not occur and that need to exist to resolve and replace the problem in the future.

At the prevention level (see the first section of this chapter), the ultimate question is: "Who or what will motivate everyone in the school to create and sustain a positive, nurturing, supportive environment where everyone interacts in the common areas of the school in tolerant, prosocial, and proactive ways?" At the problem-solving level, the ultimate question (if this domain is contributing to the problem) is, "Who and what is reinforcing the appropriate versus the inappropriate student (or staff) behavior occurring in a specific common school area?"

To answer this latter question, the functional assessment should look at the groups of students delineated above, the administration, staff, and other adults in the school, and other individuals (e.g., older siblings, parents, peers attending other schools) to determine how they might be motivating or reinforcing, consciously or inadvertently, the inappropriate behavior that is occurring. Often, the assessment looks at the antecedent conditions (i.e., the situations that exist or what happens before the inappropriate behavior), the characteristics of the inappropriate behavior that results, and the outcomes or consequences that follow as a result of the inappropriate behavior. Periodically, these analyses produce confounded or what appear to be contradictory results. For example, there are times when the adults are positively reinforcing appropriate common area behavior, while the peer group is positively reinforcing the inappropriate behavior and negatively reinforcing students who are complying with the adults' expectations. At other times, staff members appear to be holding students accountable for their inappropriate behavior, but they occasionally let students get away with inappropriate behavior, which ends up strengthening this inappropriate behavior over time. Finally, when a group of students, or an entire student body, receives consequences for the inappropriate behavior of a small number of students whom they cannot influence (e.g., having an assembly cancelled when a few students are unruly), the larger group of students may themselves demonstrate higher levels of inappropriate behavior because of their frustration or to protest the inequity (from their perspective) of the consequence.

Relative to the running, pushing, and shoving in the middle school hallway example, it is important to integrate the questions within the incentives and consequences domain with the other special situation domains to determine why inappropriate behaviors are occurring in the hallway:

- The staff members have not consistently taught, practiced (under conditions of emotionality), transferred, and held students accountable for (through consistently delivered incentives and consequences) the skill of excusing yourself when students are in a crowded hallway and need to get to their next destination quickly.
- The students exhibiting these behaviors know that certain teachers, who are supervising the hallways on specific days, will not stop and hold them accountable because (a) they need to start their own classes on time, (b) they do not want to waste or lose the time writing up students who are pushing in the hallway, (c) they know that

nothing will happen to these students if they send them to the principal's office, or (d) they know that they will need to supervise the students after school if the principal gives them after-school detention after the write-up.

- The administration has not allotted sufficient time for students to pass in the hallway, and those students with the furthest physical distance between their respective classrooms during certain periods feel that they need to push through other students in order to make it to the next class without a detention for being late.

- Specific students know that the hallway near the school's gym area is unsupervised on those early afternoons when the coaches and sports teams are traveling to away games (and the hallway supervision has not been modified) such that they can get away with the inappropriate behavior most of the time.

Once again, in completing these data-based analyses, the outcomes may result in a conclusion that motivational factors are irrelevant to the inappropriate hallway behavior, or that these factors are secondary to other, more-primary conditions and domains. At the same time, it is important to note that, even when they are not primary or secondary causal factors, motivational factors still are important during the intervention process, for example, to motivate staff to implement the intervention with integrity, or to motivate the different groups of students to become involved in the intervention and its short- and long-term success.

Resources and Resource Utilization. In the context of explaining the presence of, or preparing to resolve, a common school area concern, the problem analysis process here specifically focuses on whether the problem relates to a lack of needed resources. The deeper analysis determines whether the school (a) has identified and is utilizing existing resources; (b) is ineffectively or inappropriately using its existing resources; or (c) has resource gaps that can be closed by using other school, district, or community resources, or by purchasing the needed resources. In a school, the breadth of potential resources includes money and finances; facilities and physical plant; materials (e.g., books, videos, equipment) and activities; time, scheduling, deployment, and logistics; people and professional development; technology; and creativity and hard work (Knoff, 2007a; Knoff, 2009b). Table 6.1 outlines specific resources in each of these areas that may be used to address situations (a) and (c) above. Relative to the people resources, this may involve individual and groups of students, staff, administrators, and others inside and outside of the school. This includes individuals who have special expertise in conducting sophisticated multifactored Special Situation Analyses or in linking their results to effective intervention plans or individuals who are needed to implement the actual intervention.

Table 6.1	Conducting a Resource Analysis of a School: Possible Resources to Consider

Money/Finances

Possible Areas to Investigate:

- Federal, state, and district funding
- Discretionary money controlled by the school due to site-based management
- Grant or foundation money
- Business or other local donations

Facilities and Physical Plant

Possible Areas to Investigate:

- Areas of the school available before and after school, during evenings, during weekends
- Rooms whose space is underutilized due to low student enrollments or that could be better utilized with more efficient student and staff scheduling
- Empty or unused rooms
- More effective use of computer, media, physical education, and cafeteria space
- More effective use of hallways for more effective traffic and transition patterns

Materials and Activities

Possible Areas to Investigate:

- More effective use of art, physical education, computer, media, and textbook materials
- More effective use of audiovisual and other technological equipment
- Sharing, from teacher to teacher, of curriculum-specific or instructional activities to support classroom learning
- Sharing, from parents, businesses in the community, or other community resources, relevant activities to support classroom learning
- Accessing donations of support materials (e.g., software, books, equipment) for school or classroom use

Time/Scheduling/Deployment/Logistics

Possible Areas to Investigate:

- Block and other more effective approaches to scheduling
- More efficient student and staff transitions when moving from outside to inside a classroom and when moving from one subject area to other subject areas within the same classroom

- More efficient use of grade-level, committee, and whole staff meeting times
- Amount of out-of-class interruptions of classroom instruction (e.g., due to PA announcements, students going to pull-out groups) that decrease academic engagement
- Amount of in-class interruptions of classroom instruction (e.g., due to discipline problems, off-task behavior, lack of preparation) that decrease academic engagement
- Amount of staff absenteeism requiring the use of substitute teachers
- Degree and level of student tardiness

People/Professional Development

Possible Areas to Investigate:

- Knowledge and use of existing student, staff, and parent skills and talents for those within or currently interacting with the school
- Knowledge and use of existing district-level staff who could become available to the school
- Knowledge and use of community-based resource people who could become available to the school
- Knowledge and use of resource people, accessed through the internet or other technological means, who could become available to the school

Technology

Possible Areas to Investigate:

- Hardware and software programs or other advances
- Web-based and cloud computing advances
- Audiovisual, instructional, and telecommunication advances
- Distance learning and assistive support advances

Creativity and Hard Work

Possible Areas to Investigate:

- Levels of and approaches to facilitate staff communication, cooperation, motivation, and innovation
- Survey for and completion of a staff resource directory
- Available rewards and incentives to staff and students for and to motivate them toward exceptional accomplishments
- Opportunities to celebrate exceptional accomplishments for staff and students

Source: Project ACHIEVE Press. Dr. Howie Knoff (author).

Relative to (b) above, the problem analysis should investigate whether, for example, the school has effectively prioritized and efficiently expended its money; identified and remediated the flaws in its facilities or physical plant; bought and used equipment, other materials, and technology correctly; maximized the skills, capacity, and creativity of its students, staff, and administration; and planned its time, schedule, and logistics to prevent or address common school area concerns. Applying this analysis to the running, pushing, and shoving in the middle school hallway, below are some examples of a few ineffective resource decisions or directions with their possible, more effective alternatives:

- Rather than spending money on hidden cameras in the hallways to catch students' inappropriate behavior, the money may be better spent on professional development that teaches the school discipline/ PBSS committee how to conduct Special Situation Analyses and on the release time needed to implement the identified interventions (money and finances).
- Rather than significantly increasing the staff supervision in the hallways, the situation might be better served by making some hallways one-way, putting rugs or rumble strips on the floors in identified problem areas, or painting or tiling selected floors or walls in ways that cue students to slow down to safe speeds (facilities and physical plant).
- Rather than putting a lot of time and effort into delivering consequences to students who have already run or pushed in the hallway, the problem might be solved by putting posters up on the walls in strategic places reminding students of the hallway expectations, and possible incentives and consequences (materials and activities).
- Rather than allow students to crowd some hallways because they need to visit their lockers to retrieve books and other materials, the students' lockers might be strategically separated across and within grade levels across the school, grade-level students might be allowed to visit their lockers during alternating periods during the day, or classrooms might be reorganized to decrease the amount of travel for students between classes and to increase the presence and proximity of their own teachers during passage (time, scheduling, deployment, and logistics).
- Rather than only use school staff to patrol the hallways, the school might train and use students from different clubs or organizations to take turns being hallway helpers to remind their peers to demonstrate appropriate behavior (people and professional development).
- Rather than pool the monthly data on all of the students sent to the principal's office for hallway offenses, the administration might reprogram its database and adapt its office referral forms and process to track the specific hallways with the highest number of offenses so that the problem analysis can isolate the right hallways, students, times of the day, and staff for intervention (technology).

In summary, it takes knowledge, skills, collaboration, motivation, and effort to conduct a Special Situation Analysis. However, when done by staff members who have the expertise, the time and resources, and the commitment and cooperation of their administration and colleagues, the return on investment has a strong upside in that existing problems can be solved, and the solutions can be sustained over long periods of time. To best accomplish this, it is recommended that a subcommittee of the school discipline/PBSS committee be trained and responsible for a school's Special Situation Analysis process. When needed, it is important that this subcommittee have permission to use out-of-school experts from other schools, or at the district, community, region, state, or national levels. Finally, it is essential that subcommittee members understand the differences between interventions that stabilize a special situation and those that resolve it.

Relative to this latter point, in most special situations, stability typically is needed before intervention can succeed. That is, if there is so much physical, social, emotional, behavioral, or organizational chaos in or around a common school area, this needs to be resolved so that the Special Situation Analysis and intervention can be effectively and efficiently executed. This is because the chaos may make an accurate analysis of the special situation difficult or even impossible—masking or confounding the real problems and reasons underlying the problem. This will then result in an unsuccessful intervention plan and outcomes that may exacerbate the problem or dishearten the staff. The chaos may also be increasing the severity or emotionality of the situation—making the common area problem worse or seem worse than it actually is. Thus, once again, decreasing or eliminating the chaos allows the problem-solving process to address a more accurate version of the actual problem.

Revisiting running, pushing, and shoving in the middle school hallway one last time, it may be that the number of students involved and the frequency and severity of the misbehavior is so extreme that the hallways are out of control war zones. Given this, a number of different stabilization activities, organized across the special situation continuum, may be appropriate.

Possible Student Stabilization Activities. Try controlling the number of students present in the hallways at any one time by limiting the number of hallway passes allowed during class time, staggering (with enhanced staff presence and supervision) the number of students passing through the hall in between class periods, or keeping the students in single classrooms during the school day and having their teachers rotate to them after each class period (until the situation is stabilized and interventions can be implemented).

Possible Teacher/Staff Stabilization Activities. In addition to having all teachers participate in the student activities above, ensure that every adult in the school is actively present in the hallways in between every class period and before and after school, that the most problematic hallways have more staff presence during the times or periods when previous problem situations have most typically occurred, and that some staff are assigned to escort the most problematic students through the hallways either before or after the rest of the students have passed.

Possible Environmental/Logistical Stabilization Activities. Close off certain hallways and restrict or rearrange the traffic patterns in others, increase the lighting or signage in the most problematic hallways, and install overhead cameras and flat screen monitors that show students how they are being observed.

Possible Incentive/Consequence Stabilization Activities. Strengthen the frequency, duration, immediacy, or significance of individual and peer group incentives and consequences that are delivered by teachers, staff, administrators, parents, and others for appropriate and inappropriate hallway and related behavior and open or expand the availability of intensive intervention or treatment settings in the school where students demonstrating the most significant inappropriate behavior can be placed to stabilize the situation and motivate and facilitate future behavioral change.

Possible Resource Stabilization Activities. Increase the number, degree, significance, or specialization of the professionals brought into the school to plan, facilitate, or directly participate in the stabilization process, including Special Situation Analysis experts, district security and law enforcement experts and personnel, parents, and community leaders.

CRISIS MANAGEMENT AND EMERGENCY OPERATIONS PLANS AND PROCESSES

As the discussions above have provided numerous examples of common school area interventions, this section focuses on crisis management planning and the responses needed during times of emergency. Emergency situations often involve one or more common areas of the school. While a school's clear goal is to prevent emergencies and crises from occurring, the reality is that unpredictable, unplanned, or uncontrollable crises always can occur, and schools must be prepared. Thus, school staff members, through their school discipline/PBSS committee, need to identify possible emergency or crisis situations (e.g., extreme weather conditions, racial harassment, gang fights, a student or faculty member's death, a hostage event) and complete the analyses and preparations that establish the procedures, training, and resources necessary to stop and stabilize these crises as they are developing or occurring (Trump, 2011). Schools and districts also need to prepare the crisis response services, supports, and strategies needed to address the security and social, emotional, and behavioral needs of everyone directly or indirectly involved or impacted by the crisis once it is over (e.g., Brock et al., 2009; Dwyer & Osher, 2000; Dwyer, Osher, & Warger, 1998).

Every school or district should have a written crisis management plan or EOP that summarizes all of its crisis preparation, intervention, and response system needs and efforts. Eventually, all of the preparation, training, and response protocols, with their related policies, procedures, and activities, should be compiled into an emergency operations handbook for use at the district and school levels. Some of the most important characteristics or elements of the plan and the handbook are listed below.

The Plan or Handbook

- Is developed by a district team that includes representatives of its school discipline/PBSS committees or by an individual school discipline/PBSS committee
- Is reviewed and updated on an annual basis
- Is consistent with district, local, and state laws, policies, and procedures
- Establishes a well-coordinated emergency response process developed with and involving law enforcement, district and local emergency management personnel, fire and medical, and other first- and crisis-response agencies and entities
- Prepares the school to respond to natural disasters; transportation and other on-site accidents; acts of violence—especially those involving casualties and fatalities; power outage, fire, chemical, or biohazard incidents; bomb threats, hostage takings, and other intrusions; and other emergency events or circumstances
- Establishes lockdown, lockout, central location assembly, building and site evacuation (including reverse evacuation—outside-in), and weather-related (e.g., drop and cover, tornado, earthquake) procedures that are reviewed or practiced with staff and, as needed, by students on a quarterly basis
- Establishes additional crisis management or emergency training protocols and schedules for students, staff, school and district administrators, and community partnership, as desired or needed
- Includes, in the procedures immediately above, the designation of primary and alternative evacuation sites, confidential reunification sites for students and parents that are out of sight from parents, a plan for student-parent reunification, and a plan for sustaining school occupants in the school or at on-site evacuation locations for at least 72 hours

- Includes, in the procedures above, procedures and provisions for individuals with limited mobility or special health (and other) needs
- Includes in the training above all staff—including custodial, secretarial, food service, transportation, and other maintenance staff; and permanent substitute teachers, if possible
- Includes an updated map—shared with law enforcement, fire, hazardous material, and other community partners as needed—of the school's layout with room numbers, evacuation routes, mechanical rooms and utility shutoffs, hazardous storage areas, telephones and other communication systems, locations of first aid kits, and other site-specific information as relevant
- Establishes a traffic control plan to coordinate on-site emergency and other vehicles and personnel and the student-parent reunification process
- Establishes an incident command and responsibility structure and organization that includes a chain of command for when the principal or other administrators are not present during the emergency
- Concurrent with the command structure, designates on-site and backup command posts, located in line of sight of the campus, for use during emergencies
- Identifies (through or with the district's permission) a communications liaison as part of the command structure—an individual who will coordinate communications during and after the crisis with parents, the community, the local press, and others
- Identifies (through or with the district's permission) a parent casualty liaison as part of the command structure—one or more individuals who communicate with parents to notify them about student injuries, arrests, casualties, or deaths
- Ensures that there are easy-to-understand briefing cards or checklists outlining the most essential components or procedures above in critical locations in the school (especially at all command and communication posts), at central assembly locations, and with district or community support personnel
- Establishes an evaluation and debriefing process (sometimes called an after-action review) that occurs after each emergency event to determine the effectiveness and efficiency of the multifaceted response systems and to make recommendations (as needed) for changes or improvements in these processes—including the need for additional prevention or response training, resources, activities, or elements
- Establishes and prepares a post-crisis response process that addresses the immediate student, staff, family, and community post-crisis needs and activities as well as their needs and activities for the first weeks, month, quarter, half year, and full year as well as anniversary dates post-crisis

There are three types of crises for schools to plan for: a crisis with advanced notice, one with minimal notice, and one with no notice. A crisis with advanced notice is one that is impending and that a school or district has one or more hours to prepare for. For example, a tornado watch occurs when weather conditions exist that may result in tornados, and this advanced notice status gives schools time to send students home early, secure students in safe areas, or remind them about tornado signals and procedures. A crisis with minimal notice is one that is imminent and typically cannot be avoided and that a school or district has less than an hour to prepare for. For example, a tornado warning occurs when funnel clouds have been observed by eyewitnesses or on Doppler radar, and this notice results in immediate evacuations of students and staff into secure areas and emergency-related announcements or notifications to parents and others. A crisis with no notification is one that occurs without warning, for example, when a major earthquake demolishes a town leaving significant, widespread damage and a high number of fatalities. This calls for the full implementation of all school and community emergency procedures, including those related to stabilization, security, triage, casualty, fatality, off-school site evacuation, and parental or family reunification.

In the end, while schools need to incorporate crisis prevention into their PBSS planning, procedures, and activities, crises do occur. Given this, schools and districts need to prepare for the different categories of and specific crises that may occur and factor in the needed procedures when they occur with advanced, minimal, or no notice. During a crisis, the ultimate goals are (a) to minimize the impact of the crisis for those directly and indirectly involved; (b) to stabilize the situation as quickly as possible after the crisis has passed; and (c) to provide physical and emotional services and support in the aftermath. Relative to this latter point, schools, districts, and communities need to implement post-crisis responses as quickly as possible. This should address the immediate post-crisis needs of students, staff, and their families as well as these individuals' needs in the days, weeks, months, and years (e.g., on the anniversary dates) to follow.

SUMMARY

This chapter focuses on setting-specific special situations at the prevention, problem-solving, and crisis management levels. Relative to prevention, ways to organize schools, staff, and students such that common school areas are positive, safe, and secure were presented. This included attention to five specific Special Situation domains—the student, teacher and staff, environmental, incentive and consequence, and resource and resource utilization domains—and the goals of building and sustaining effective common school area interactions and minimizing the number of challenging behaviors and the intensity of critical events in those areas. Relative to problem solving, ways to conduct Special Situation Analyses were discussed, emphasizing the importance of analyzing why certain special situations are occurring so that successful, multifaceted strategic or intensive interventions are identified and implemented. Relative to crisis management, the necessary components of an effective crisis management process and plan were outlined.

This chapter also addressed ways to conduct safety audits, complete common school area screenings, and organize an EOP. Finally, the importance of involving students, parents, and community stakeholders and partners in special situation planning and preparation was highlighted.

7

Teasing, Taunting, Bullying, Harassment, Hazing, and Physical Aggression[1]

> Not everything that is faced can be changed. But nothing
> can be changed unless it is faced.
>
> James Baldwin

PBSS Implementation Case Study:
Baltimore City Schools, Baltimore, Maryland

On April 20, 1999, I was in Baltimore, Maryland, working with the Baltimore City Schools as part of a three-year, three-city federal dissemination grant awarded to Project ACHIEVE from the U.S. Department of Education's Office of Special Education Programs in 1998. On that day, two high school seniors killed twelve students, one teacher, and themselves at Columbine High School in Littleton, Colorado, setting off a wave of concern in every community that "anything can happen at any time and in any place."

> Once news of the shootings became public, a school psychologist employed by the school district in Baltimore and I immediately notified the superintendent's office that we were available to assist. Specifically, we recommended that the superintendent hold a news conference as soon as possible to assure his community that his schools and students were safe and to inform them of how such acts could be prevented in Baltimore.
>
> At ten o'clock the next day, the superintendent and I participated in a press conference where we addressed the local media to deliver our message. While Baltimore is no stranger to violence, we felt that our quick response to the devastating events at Columbine was necessary, stabilizing, and helpful to the climate of the schools during a difficult and emotional time.

INTRODUCTION

The issue and impact of teasing, taunting, bullying, harassment, hazing, and physical aggression (TTBHHPA) on students' feelings of safety and security in their schools, their academic engagement in the classroom, and—for some—their academic achievement and graduation has been well-chronicled over the past 25 years or more (Batsche & Knoff, 1994; Cook, Williams, Guerra, Kim, & Sadek, 2010; Espelage & Holt, 2001; Glew, Fan, Katon, Rivara, & Kernic, 2005; Swearer, Espelage, Vaillancourt, & Hymel, 2010). While many different legal and other definitions exist for these acts (U.S. Department of Education, Office of Planning, Evaluation and Policy Development, Policy and Program Studies Service, 2011), it is not always clear when teasing becomes taunting, taunting becomes bullying, bullying becomes hazing, and hazing becomes harassment. For this reason, we conceptualize these special situation acts along this loose continuum, suggesting that the severity or intensity of the offense increases from teasing through physical aggression. At the same time, we recognize that the social, emotional, and behavioral impact of TTBHHPA is unique to each person. Regardless, whether students experience a mild or a severe reaction to one of these acts, every school's Positive Behavioral Support System (PBSS) needs to be dedicated (a) to the prevention of acts of TTBHHPA (by both students and staff); (b) to their analysis when they do occur; and (c) to the strategic responses and interventions that eliminate them in the future.

The beginning of the preventative process relative to TTBHHPA is the development of district and school policies that outline and clearly state that these acts are inappropriate and, in many cases, against state department of education regulation or state law. Indeed, most states now have laws, policies, or regulations that specifically address one or more of these acts. For example, as of February 2012, 48 states, including the District of Columbia, have state laws or policies that relate to bullying in schools, with 14 of these states including cyberbullying in these statutes, and 38 of these states including electronic harassment. In addition, 48 states, including the District of Columbia, have state laws or policies that require a school policy that relates to cyberbullying, and 42 of these states require school sanctions (Hinduja & Patchin, 2012). Thus, all students need to be informed of district and school TTBHHPA policies at the beginning of every school year, programs to educate and train both students and staff in ways to prevent, identify, and respond to these situations should follow (see the relevant sections in this chapter), and active school-home-community efforts should be included as part of a planned, coordinated, and ongoing public relations and social marketing campaign.

To facilitate this entire process, this chapter builds on the information discussed in Chapter 6 on setting-specific special situations. Specifically, Chapter 6 described (a) five special situation domains; (b) the importance of focusing on special situation prevention; and (c) the importance of using a data-based, functional assessment problem-solving process to identify strategic or intensive intervention directions. This chapter extends this information, highlighting bullying as an exemplar for the behaviors represented along the TTBHHPA continuum.

Given the significant amount of research and practice focused on bullying over at least the past decade, we now know a great deal about its dimensions and dynamics—at the prevention, strategic intervention, and intensive need or crisis management levels (Bender & Losel, 2011; Cook et al., 2010; Leff & Crick, 2010; Swearer et al., 2010; Ttofi & Farrington, 2009; Vreeman & Carroll, 2007; Zins, Elias, & Maher, 2007). While we strongly encourage educational and mental health professionals to maintain their research and practice currency in the bullying and other special situation areas, we believe that the bullying research and practice areas provide a good blueprint to inform the broader student-specific special situation process. At the same time, it will soon become apparent that bullying rarely needs a formal, packaged bullying program or a specialized curriculum. Below, we describe a logical, defensible, and effective bullying program that is embedded in Project ACHIEVE's comprehensive PBSS approach.

Bullying: Definitions, Impacts, and Approaches

Relative to the schools, bullying is defined as a form of repeated aggression where one or more students socially, psychologically or emotionally, physically or behaviorally, or sexually harass or harm other students (a) to a significant degree during one or more incidents, or (b) repeatedly over a period of time. More specifically, bullying can include physical aggression; verbal aggression—including persistent teasing, taunting, and threats; virtual aggression—such as through cyberbullying; the more subtle or indirect aggression that results in social exclusion; or aggression that is sexual, sexually motivated, or gender or gender identity (e.g., gay, lesbian, gender confused) related. Typically, acts of bullying are unprovoked, and the bully is perceived as stronger or as having more power than the victim (Card & Hodges, 2008; Knoff, 2007h, 2009a; Nansel et al., 2001; Pöyhönen, Juvonen, & Salmivalli, 2010). While the research continues to validate and differentiate this area, we have a reasonably clear picture of the (a) characteristics of bullies; (b) developmental patterns of bullying; (c) relationships between victims and bullies; and (d) interventions needed for bullies and to address bullying.

Based on a meta-analysis of 153 studies from a pool of 1,622 studies published since 1970 (Cook et al., 2010), research investigating the predictors of bullying and victimization during childhood and adolescence has identified separate groups of students who are bullies versus bully-victims (who are both victims of bullies and bullies themselves). Pooling this research with other studies (Craig, Pepler, & Atlas, 2000; Espelage & Holt, 2001; Glew et al., 2005; Huesmann & Reynolds, 2001; Leff & Crick, 2010; Nansel et al., 2001; Swearer & Doll, 2001; Swearer, Espelage, & Napolitano, 2009; Swearer et al., 2010; Tolan, Gorman-Smith, & Loeber, 2000; Zins et al., 2007), empirically based characteristics and developmental patterns of bullying appear:

Bullies

- Bullying occurs along a spectrum from teasing and gossiping, to taunting and bullying, to harassment and verbal threats or intimidation, to physical aggression and violence. Some associate bullying with a lack of tolerance for diversity.
- Boys are generally found to be bullies more frequently than girls, although this may be due to researchers' focus on the more overt forms of bullying which boys tend to engage in more than girls.
- Bullying appears to peak during the transition years from elementary to middle school (i.e., around age 11 or 12), occurring most frequently from sixth to eighth grade. Although bullies appear to be rejected and isolated during their elementary school years, they may become more accepted and liked by peers during middle school.
- Bullying has been correlated with indicators of anger, depression, impulsivity, anxiety, and attitudes that support violence. Bullies often have both social competence and academic challenges; negative expectations, attitudes, or beliefs about themselves, about school, and about others; and difficulties resolving problems with others. Bullies tend to be negatively influenced by their peers.
- Bullies tend to come from homes characterized by conflict and poor parental supervision, and they are influenced by negative community factors.
- Bullying occurs very often in unstructured school settings or common areas of the school (e.g., the playground). Bullying, however, does not correlate with school or class size.

Bully-victims

- Bully-victims are rejected and isolated by their peers as they also exhibit their own bullying behavior. Bully-victims have more risk factors than either bullies or victims, and they are in greater need of prevention and intervention programs.
- Bully-victims typically exhibit both externalizing (e.g., acting out) and internalizing (e.g., anxiety, withdrawal, depression) difficulties.
- Bully-victims have significantly negative expectations, attitudes, or beliefs for themselves, and they demonstrate academic difficulties.
- Bully-victims lack social competence and social problem-solving skills, and they are negatively influenced by peers.

Victims

- Boys are more likely to be victims of bullying than girls. Girls tend to be bullied more through personal or relational attacks, while boys experience more physical or aggressive attacks. Bullying sometimes occurs due to relationship variables between the bully and victim and not just as a function of initiation by a bully.
- Students from preschool through age 16 respond to bullying through a range of negative emotions or reactions: anger, revenge, self-pity, confusion, loneliness, physical and psychological distress, depression, anxiety, somatic symptoms, and lowered self-esteem. These reactions result in these students sometimes feeling abandoned, afraid of school, and worried at school. Victims also are lonelier and have more difficulty making friends. All of this potentially results in school avoidance or absences, difficulties concentrating while at school, and poor school performance.
- Victims of bullies are more prone to suicidal ideation, severe depression, or extreme acts of hostility or aggression.
- Victims are likely to demonstrate internalizing (e.g., anxiety, withdrawal, depression) difficulties and to lack social and social problem-solving skills. They often are noticeably rejected and isolated by their peers.

Comparisons

- Having negative attitudes and beliefs about others significantly predicts whether a student will be a bully or bully-victim.
- Having negative attitudes about oneself significantly predicts whether a student will be a victim. However, the strongest predictors of becoming a victim include poor social competence skills and an inability to establish and maintain satisfactory interpersonal relationships with others.

- While both groups are weak in their social competence skills, bullies have relatively better skills than victims. Bully-victims, however, have the most difficulties in the area of social competence.

When considering school-level and individual interventions for bullying and bullies, the research recognizes key factors related to intervention:

- Adults are generally unaware of or underestimate the extent of bullying that occurs in schools, and they may not intervene even when aware of bullying. While this is changing as many states enact legislation in this area, this suggests that adult involvement is critical to preventing and responding to bullying situations and behavior.
- The peer group needs to be included in any intervention program as some students have become desensitized to bullying over time due to its frequency in some schools. Students must recognize bullying when it occurs and be willing to intervene and stop it.
- Relative to bullies, comprehensive, multifaceted programs that include social cognitive interventions that include social skills, social-cognitive problem solving, and aggression reduction and replacement training have the strongest empirical support.

Beyond the research summarized above, very few studies, at least in the United States, have addressed or fully validated research-proven ways to decrease or prevent bullying as part of a schoolwide initiative (Doll & Swearer, 2006; Leff & Crick, 2010; Merrell, Gueldner, Ross, & Isava, 2008; Swearer et al., 2010; Ttofi & Farrington, 2009; Vreeman & Carroll, 2007). This is partly because many bullying programs have focused narrowly on decreasing or eliminating bullying rather than also increasing and strengthening students' social competency and emotional and behavioral self-management skills. In addition, many bullying programs are stand-alone programs, implemented in the absence of an evidence-based, multi-tiered PBSS. Indeed, it is suggested that when the skill, accountability, consistency, and special situation components of Project ACHIEVE's Tier 1 PBSS are implemented with integrity and intensity, low or minimal levels of TTBHHPA result. Hence, the TTBHHPA incidents that remain are successfully addressed through small group or individual student analyses and interventions, rather than additional schoolwide approaches. Thus, in this scenario, there is no need for a specialized, formal, or packaged bullying program (e.g., Olweus, Bully-Proofing)—the multi-tiered PBSS is the bullying program.

At the same time, if high levels of TTBHHPA exist despite the presence of an effectively implemented Tier 1 PBSS, a Special Situation Analysis should be completed and linked to explicit intervention directions and approaches. Based on these analyses, a more formal published and packaged bullying program may be needed.

THE SPECIAL SITUATION DOMAINS FOR TEASING, TAUNTING, BULLYING, HARASSMENT, HAZING, AND PHYSICAL AGGRESSION

In Chapter 6, five special situation domains (i.e., the student, teacher and staff, environmental, incentive and consequence, and resource and resource utilization domains) were described at the prevention, problem solving, and crisis management levels. Relative to TTBHHPA, a sixth peer group characteristics, issues, and factors domain is now added. Embedded in Chapter 6's problem-solving discussion of the student characteristics, issues, and factors domain, this new domain is needed given research establishing that peers directly or actively reinforce (by being antagonists) or indirectly or inadvertently reinforce (by observing, but being uninvolved bystanders) others' bullying behavior (e.g., Bosworth, Espelage, & Simon, 1999; Pellegrini, Bartini, & Brooks, 1999; Rigby, 2000, 2001, 2002).

Below, these six domains are used to organize the student-specific special situations discussion at the prevention, problem-solving, and crisis management levels. The prevention level focuses on promoting prosocial student and staff interactions, minimizing students' TTBHHPA interactions, and decreasing or eliminating these negative interactions when they occur at low or mild levels. The problem-solving level focuses on determining why these behaviors occur at moderate or high frequency or significant or extreme levels in a school and linking the results of these special situation analyses to strategic intervention approaches. The crisis management level revisits the Chapter 6 discussion in this area, extending it to student-specific special situations.

Student-Specific Special Situations—Prevention. Student-specific special situation prevention activities involve schoolwide processes that result in (a) empowered students who are tolerant, have sound interpersonal, social problem-solving, and conflict prevention and resolution skills, can disarm or discourage TTBHHPA attempts, and feel comfortable reporting bullying incidents in a safe and confidential manner; (b) prosocial and supportive classroom settings that teach and reinforce appropriate interpersonal interactions between students and between students and adults; (c) safe and secure common areas of the school (e.g., hallways, cafeteria, buses) where peer groups demonstrate and reinforce prosocial interactions and actively deter TTBHHPA; and (d) involved parents and community partners who collaborate such that everyone is aware of and engaged in reinforcing a prosocial and no tolerance for antisocial behavior school culture. From a student perspective, the focus is on promoting students' self-management and social competency skills, knowing that these skills typically prevent TTBHHPA. Indeed, throughout this book, discussions have emphasized the importance of teaching students interpersonal, social problem-solving, conflict prevention and resolution, and emotional coping skills (Chapter 5); motivating and holding them accountable for using these prosocial skills (Chapter 4); maintaining consistency relative to behavioral expectations, instruction, and accountability; and applying or reinforcing appropriate student and staff behavior in the common areas of the school (Chapter 6).

While not yet emphasized, most of the components above also help students and staff to respond to mild levels of TTBHHPA such that these incidents are immediately addressed, discouraged, and quickly eliminated. More specifically, a closer look at the sample Stop & Think social skills in Chapter 5 reveals that students are routinely taught a number of TTBHHPA response skills (e.g., responding to teasing, to peer pressure, to being rejected or left out; understanding others' feelings; walking away from a fight). These skills can help victims and bystanders to respond effectively to those who, for example, tease, taunt, or bully; and, when used, these responses might discourage or eliminate future inappropriate interactions.

A closer look at the sample Behavioral Matrices in Chapter 4 reveals that there are corrective responses, consequences, and administrative actions suggested for staff when they observe different intensity levels of TTBHHPA. Beyond this, when the Behavioral Matrix is taught to and used consistently with students, and when the Matrix consequences for TTB-HHPA are explicitly outlined at the beginning of the school year, this training often becomes its own disincentive as students understand that they will be held accountable for TTBHHPA behavior.

Finally, a closer look at the factors that contribute to positive and safe common school areas (see Chapter 6) reveals that both students and teachers need to understand how to create and sustain these positive school settings and learn how to respond to different intensity levels of TTB-HHPA which, as noted above, occur most often in these common school areas. Once again, the presence of these processes in a school's crisis management or Emergency Operations Plan (EOP) and the training and discussions related to that plan communicate to everyone that prosocial behaviors are expected and will be reinforced, and that there will be consequences and accountability for acts of TTBHHPA. This message is especially powerful when it is communicated, highlighted, and owned by the students across their various peer groups.

While Chapter 6's setting-specific discussion of the first five special situation domains is easily adapted to the TTBHHPA student-specific context here, some additional prevention activities within the peer group domain are recommended. For example, staff and students need to

- Understand the similarities and differences across the different cohorts and peer groups in the school so that (as developmentally appropriate) discussions within and across these peer groups can be facilitated about issues of communication and collaboration, tolerance and individual differences, and conflict prevention and resolution as they especially relate to TTBHHPA. These discussions could focus on how student differences or stereotypes (e.g., involving gender, socioeconomic status, race and culture, academic proficiency, extracurricular activities) sometimes contribute to TTBHHPA, and how everyone needs to understand, tolerate, and celebrate these differences and diversities.

- Understand the short-term, long-term, and generational (if present) student, peer, school, and community TTBHHPA histories among different peer groups as students enter each school year, and how to strengthen positive student interactions and prevent (continued) negative interactions. This is particularly important as students from different elementary schools merge into single middle schools and students from different middle schools merge into single high schools.

- Organize and empower different student groups across the school (e.g., student government leaders, athletes, performing arts students at the high school level) to take the lead in preventing and responding to TTBHHPA such that students are holding their peers accountable for prosocial interactions.

- Involve (as appropriate) representatives from different peer groups in special situation analyses when incident levels of TTBHHPA are increasing or to help debrief TTBHHPA situations that are significant or pervasive.

- Maintain and sustain a week-to-week and month-to-month schoolwide focus on evaluating, communicating, and celebrating student group successes in this area and systematically transferring those successes from year to year to build a strong prosocial and anti-TTBHHPA culture.

Student-Specific Special Situations—Problem Solving. A number of TTBHHPA situations might trigger the need for the special situations problem-solving process. These include situations that involve frequent, long-standing, or particularly intense levels of TTBHHPA where one or more students are victimized by individual or groups of students who are (a) supported or reinforced by specific or large groups of peers or bystanders; (b) avoided, ignored, or allowed by staff to commit these acts; or (c) supported or reinforced by parents or other adults outside of the school. As noted in Chapter 6, Special Situation Analyses typically involve all or part of the school discipline/PBSS committee, and they evaluate the who, what, when, where, why, and how conditions that exist, predict, and result when TTBHHPA does and does not occur. This entire problem-solving process is completed by identifying the individuals responsible for the TTBHHPA, analyzing these dynamics and underlying reasons for these acts across the six special situation domains, and then linking the results to strategic or intensive interventions that individually and systemically resolve the problem immediately and into the future. If the

TTBHHPA occurs most often in a common school area, the Special Situation Analysis and intervention process combines both setting- and student-specific elements.

As noted earlier, there is considerable overlap between the setting-specific and student-specific special situation analyses for four of the five domains discussed in Chapter 6 (i.e., the teacher and staff, environmental, incentive and consequence, and resource and resource utilization domains). Thus, this chapter and section focuses on the student and peer group domains and on understanding and intervening with those whom we will now call the aggressors (or aggressor-victims), the victims, and the negatively contributing or uninvolved bystanders.

From a research and problem-solving perspective, there are numerous reasons why some students are TTBHHPA aggressors (or aggressor-victims), victims, or negatively contributing or uninvolved bystanders—both on an individual and on a group level. We have organized these student-specific reasons throughout this book along a skills, motivation and accountability, and consistency continuum and will use that same functional structure here.

Skills. Relative to skills, TTBHHPA aggressors and negative bystanders are most often involved in their respective activities because they have not learned or mastered relationship skills, emotional control skills, or consequence and response skills. Consistent with the research summarized above (e.g., Cook et al., 2010), examples of these skill gaps or skill deficits include the following:

1. Relationship Skills:

Listening or following directions

Asking for help

Ignoring (distractions)

Apologizing

Dealing with peer pressure

Beginning and ending a conversation

Giving and accepting a compliment

Being a good leader

2. Emotional Control Skills:

Setting a goal

Evaluating yourself

Understanding your feelings

Understanding others' feelings

Dealing with anger

Walking away from a fight

Standing up for your rights

Avoiding trouble

3. Consequence/Response Skills:

Dealing with consequences

Dealing with peer pressure

Dealing with accusations

Dealing with fear

Dealing with teasing, being rejected, or being left out

Responding to failure

Dealing with another person's anger

Students are most often victimized because they have not learned or mastered prevention skills, problem-solving skills, or protection skills:

1. Prevention Skills:

Listening and following directions

Setting a goal

Avoiding trouble

Evaluating yourself

2. Problem-Solving Skills:

Asking for help

Understanding your feelings

Understanding others' feelings

Dealing with peer pressure

3. Protection Skills:

Dealing with teasing, being rejected, or being left out

Dealing with accusations

Dealing with fear

Dealing with another person's anger

Standing up for your rights

Walking away from a fight

Finally, students are most often uninvolved bystanders because they have not learned or mastered recognition skills, response skills, and resolution skills:

1. Recognition Skills:

Listening and following directions

Understanding your feelings

Understanding others' feelings

Evaluating yourself

Beginning and ending a conversation

Standing up for your rights

2. Response Skills:

Being a good leader

Dealing with fear

Dealing with another person's anger

Dealing with peer pressure

3. Resolution Skills:

Providing emotional support or empathy

Setting a goal

Problem solving

Dealing with consequences

Dealing with teasing, being rejected, or being left out

Being assertive

Asking for help

Critically (see Chapters 8 and 9), there are four related skill instruc-tion areas where these four student groups might be having difficulties—individually or as part of a group: (a) they may not have been taught or mastered these skills, (b) they may be learning or mastering these skills at a slower rate than their peers, (c) they may not have learned or mastered the ability to transfer or apply these skills in real-life situations, or (d) they may not have learned or mastered the ability to use these skills under highly (for them) emotional conditions. Clearly, if the problem analysis confirms one or more of these as the direct (for the aggressors) or indirect (for the other three student groups) reasons for the TTBHHPA, the inter-vention plan will need to include skill instruction. This may occur, as needed, on an individual student or on a group instruction level, and the instruction should follow the principles and practices already described in the Stop & Think skills chapter (see Chapter 5).

Relative to skill instruction, role-playing and performance feedback are essential elements. Once the TTBHHPA situations have been analyzed and specific social, emotional, or behavioral skills identified, the teaching, scripting, and role-playing process can begin. For example, a Stop & Think skills script to teach a student how to deal with bullying might include the following in a role-play situation between an actual bully and a previously victimized student, or between a student playing a bully and the victimized student:

> Here comes Jason. He's always picking on me. Oh no—he saw me! [Jason starts to bully . . .] I need to Stop and Think. Am I going to make a good choice or a bad choice? If I make a bad choice, Jason will think that I'm afraid of him, and he'll bully me for the rest of the year. I need to make a good choice. What are my choices or steps? Well, first I need to take a deep breath, stand up straight, and look right at Jason. Next, I need to tell him in a firm voice that I don't want any trouble with him and that I am going to walk away from him. Last, I need to keep my eyes on him, back off him, and then walk away as soon as I am a safe distance away. OK—I'm ready to just do it. Here I go. Great—I did a good job. Hopefully, he'll stay away from me from now on.

Critically, the role-plays should focus first on teaching the student the skill scripts and behaviors to mastery; then on facilitating the transfer or application of the skill in different settings and situations, and with differ-ent aggressor and bystander behaviors; and then on practicing the skill under conditions of emotionality so that the student can execute the skill in real life when these conditions exist. Beyond this, when the Stop & Think skill is role-played by a past bully and his or her victim, both parties need to learn how to both prosocially interact in and proactively disengage from future situations that may lead to renewed bullying. In this way, the bully and the victim learn (and, hopefully, practice) the prosocial interactions that prevent future bullying, the disengagement interactions that deter the early stages of bullying, and the response interactions to successfully resolve a situation if bullying reoccurs.

Motivation/Accountability. Beyond the skill areas, some students may be aggressors, victims, or bystanders, respectively, because either there are incentives or consequences motivating their TTBHHPA-related behaviors or they are not held accountable (e.g., by themselves, staff, peers, or parents) for appropriate behavior. While these motivation and accountability areas are embedded in the teacher and staff and incentive and consequence special situation domains (see Chapter 6), analyses need to identify whether these areas are contributing to the TTBHHPA behavior on an individual or student group level. That is, for example, a bully (bully-victim) may be motivated to bully because he or she wants attention, control, power, or revenge. A negative bystander may be motivated to support bullying because he or she wants the attention, social support, or validation of the bully (or someone else), or to avenge a previous situation where the victim got him or her into trouble at school or at home. A group of negative bystanders may be motivated because they represent a gang that is in conflict with the gang represented by the victims. During a TTBHHPA incident, an uninvolved bystander may be motivated, for example, by the fear of recriminations from either the bully or the negative bystanders or because there are insufficient school or adult incentives to get involved or consequences if they remain uninvolved.

In the end, the Special Situation Analysis needs to consider the impact of competing or conflicting motivational and accountability dynamics across the four student groups described. Whether on an individual or group basis, if these dynamics are present, the intervention plan needs to address them by unpacking the conflicting dynamics (e.g., where recriminations from the negative bystanders for trying to stop a TTBHHPA incident are more compelling than the incentives from the adults for getting involved), and repacking the dynamics so that they are positive, consistent, and reinforced across all of the groups involved.

Consistency. Relative to the consistency, students may be TTBHHPA aggressors (or aggressor-victims), victims, or negatively contributing or uninvolved bystanders when the expectations, instruction, incentives and consequences, or accountability responses that encourage prosocial interactions and discourage TTBHHPA interactions are inconsistent across people, time, situations, settings, and circumstances. When inconsistency occurs,

- TTBHHPA occurs more in the settings where the expectations appear to allow these incidents,
- students who have learned effective avoidance and response skills are victimized less than those who have not been taught these skills,

- negative student bystanders become more active when there are no consequences for their inappropriate behavior, and
- uninvolved student bystanders remain inactive when they know they will not be held accountable by other peers or adults.

Critically, inconsistency can occur at a student, peer group, or staff level in a school, it might involve mixed or contradictory messages across schools in the same district, or it could occur between parents and school officials, or between school and community constituencies.

As discussed previously, consistency is a process, and the source, target, degree, setting, time frame, and impact of inconsistency needs to be analyzed before interventions can be planned and implemented. Given all of the individual and groups of students and adults, respectively, who could be contributing to any existing inconsistencies, the problem analysis process here can become quite complex. This complexity, nonetheless, needs to be tackled, because avoidance might ensure continued or escalating levels of TTBHHPA. Ultimately, interventions focused on re-establishing consistency need to be implemented with high levels of integrity and intensity and past the history or previous levels of inconsistency (see Chapters 8 and 9). They need to reduce and remove future inconsistency, rebuild and reinforce preventative and prosocial interactions, and decrease and eliminate any negative or inappropriate interactions that were established or strengthened by the previous inconsistency.

A Third Special Situation. The last two chapters focused on setting-specific and student-specific special situations, respectively. A third special situation, introduced for the first time here (and revisited in Chapter 9), involves the more personal or idiosyncratic circumstances in students' past or current lives that impact them in pervasive, and often devastating, ways. These circumstances might include current or past life events or crises, traumatic experiences or chronic stresses, or physical or emotional conditions or disabilities. More explicitly, these may involve parental divorce or long-term unemployment, the loss of a parent or sibling, being homeless or adopted, having a physical or learning disability, physical or sexual abuse, or adjusting to a chronic or acute physiological or medical condition. These relate to TTBHHPA behavior in that they may help to explain some of the prevailing conditions that relate directly or indirectly to the behavior of students who are aggressors, victims, or negative or uninvolved bystanders. For example, the anger or rage that some students feel due to excessive levels of past taunting, bullying, or harassment that they experienced may help to explain their own current taunting, bullying, or harassment behavior as directed to others. Conversely, the anxiety or emotional trauma that some students feel due to excessive levels of past taunting, bullying, or harassment may help to explain their complete emotional and behavioral paralysis and inability to escape from the continued or additional victimizations. Critically, these circumstances may explain a student's current state of TTBHHPA affairs as well as why some students are unable to respond to strategic or intensive interventions—though they are the best ones under the circumstances.

Relative to intervention, for the more personal special situations that impact a student's social, emotional, or behavioral status or interactions and that cannot be undone (e.g., a student's past emotional or sexual abuse), instruction and interventions that teach the student cognitive-behavioral coping skills and processes must be included in the plan. In addition, for those circumstances that are situational in nature and that can be addressed or resolved (e.g., being homeless, not having positive role models, not having appropriate clothing), the plan should include the needed services, supports, resources, and implementation steps to resolve the situation and then the approaches needed to help the student cope with any physical, social, emotional, or behavioral effects of the situation. Critically, while resolution and coping interventions are necessary, they may not fully resolve all of the social-emotional impact of previous traumas, life circumstances, or other unique special situations. Indeed, some individuals live with the effects of these traumas throughout their lives. At the same time, the lack of complete healing does not invalidate the need for these important interventions.

Analyzing Fights. Across the TTBHHPA continuum and as a subset of physical aggression, fighting is somewhat unique in its level of emotional intensity and interpersonal conflict. At the same time, it is another excellent example of why this continuum is considered a special situation and why it includes the peer group as its own domain. Moreover, consistent with this section on problem solving, the need to analyze the dynamics underlying any fight once again demonstrates the important link between problem analysis and the strategic interventions that will prevent its reoccurrence.

In analyzing most in-school fights, staff and students typically agree that certain characteristics typically are present:

- Most fights occur in a common area of the school—in a hallway or bathroom, in the cafeteria, or on the playground.
- Most fights do not occur through spontaneous combustion. Typically, there is a period of increasing tension and disagreement between the two students prior to the fight; the fight may have actually been planned, or there is advanced warning that it might occur; and there is some posturing and verbal confrontation between the two students immediately prior to the fight.
- Usually, there is some level of mutual resignation or a tacit, or even explicit, agreement between the two students that the fight will occur. While some fights do involve a clear aggressor and victim, these fights are rare and one-sided, and they involve bullying and taunting (given the nonaggressive reaction of the victim) more than fighting.

- While they often occur in a common area of the school, most fights are staged as far away as possible from any staff members who are in that area. At the same time, the buildup to the fight often attracts most of the other students in the vicinity, and they often form a circle (which we call the ring of terror) around the possible combatants. In some schools, the students in the ring of terror lock arms to increase the difficulty of adult intercession. During the buildup to the fight, these students also are often encouraging or exhorting the fight to occur.
- If one of the two involved students wants to walk away from the fight, either the ring of terror does not break (with some students pushing the student back into the ring), or it breaks, but then the escaping student is teased or taunted—perhaps for the rest of his or her school year.

While there may be other, relevant variables in the other special situation domains to fully explain the fight situation (e.g., not enough adult supervision, the absence of a preventative PBSS, mixed messages on fighting between school and home), the peer dynamics described above virtually compel the fight. Indeed, when faced with a peer group that increases the emotionality of the prefight situation, and that either does not allow one or both students to physically walk away or ridicules any student who does walk away, the chances that the fight will occur (unless stopped by the adults) are almost assured. Given this, in linking assessment to intervention, it is necessary to develop strategies, including consequences, tailored to both the students involved in the fight and the peers in the ring of terror.

Relative to strategies, when a fight actually occurs, school administrations typically use their district's code of conduct, which often recommends a multi-day school suspension for the students directly involved. Just prior to the suspension, however, the administrators need to ask a critical question: "Will this suspension, while required as an administrative response on the code of conduct (and on the school's Behavioral Matrix—see Chapter 4), also act as an intervention by eliminating future fights between these students once they return?" If the answer is "No," then the administrators should initiate the steps needed to determine why the fight occurred and what services, supports, strategies, or programs are needed to prevent future fights. To accomplish this, the administrators may assemble selected members of their school discipline/PBSS committee or building-level School Prevention, Review, and Intervention Team (SPRINT; see Chapter 3) to begin the analysis process—even during the suspensions. In fact, before the suspended students leave the school with their parents, an administrator may inform them that they are required, under the conditions of the suspension, to show up at the district office where, for example, a school psychologist, counselor, or social worker will meet with them (students and parents) to debrief, discuss, and analyze the history, prevailing conditions, and underlying reasons for the fight.

During this meeting or series of meetings, more formal individual student assessments may be conducted, and more formal mediation sessions may be required involving both students and parents. In addition, the students may be required to role-play, with each other and in the presence of their parents, ways (a) to prosocially interact, (b) to prevent future escalations of disagreements or tensions, (c) to diffuse higher levels of tension or conflict, and (d) to disengage from the highest levels of conflict that again may result in a physical altercation.

Eventually, another meeting—with an administrator from the school and selected others—should occur to discuss how the students will re-enter the school and handle the first day back after the suspension. If ready and needed, part of this meeting also may involve the preparation of a longer-term intervention plan with the involved students and their parents. Critically, when the suspension is over, the actual re-entry process should begin where both students, individually or together, meet in the principal's office (or with someone who has been predesignated) as soon as the students walk onto campus and before they proceed to their homeroom or first class.

Relative to the peer group involved in the fight, specific strategies also are needed. However, consistent with the discussions earlier in this chapter and in Chapter 7, these interventions should be linked to the underlying reasons why the peers either actively promoted the fight or were unable to or did not help to prevent, disengage, or resolve the fight. If students in the ring of terror were consciously motivated to induce the fight, there should be consequences, followed up with practice sessions (following the "If you consequate, you must educate" principle; see Chapter 1) where they are required to role-play prevention, disengagement, and resolution behaviors. These role-plays should occur in the same location where the most recent fight occurred, and they should simulate the same interpersonal, emotional, and conflictual conditions to a positive resolution.

At an extreme level, consequences for selected students in the ring of terror might have to parallel those for the students involved in the actual fight—especially if these students explicitly compelled the fight. For example, if the latter students receive a three-day suspension for actually fighting, the former students receive a one-day suspension for their involvement. While this may seem surprising, the one-day suspension is consistent with the analysis that the peer group contributed important dynamics to the eventual fight, that these students behaved with clear intent to encourage the fight, and that these students must be held accountable for their behavior. Naturally, consequences at this level (i.e., Intensity IV on the school's Behavioral Matrix) need to be communicated to all students at the beginning of the school year. Significantly, in our experience, when these consequences are clear and implemented consistently, they do decrease this inappropriate peer and bystander behavior with a concomitant decrease in student fights.

As noted above, additional characteristics and conditions in one or more of the other five student-specific special situation domains often also contribute to the existence of student fights. These are summarized in Table 7.1 along with different strategies to stop and stabilize a fight situation, and to intervene such that future fights are prevented.

Table 7.1 Student-Specific Special Situations Interventions: Fighting Example

Domain	Stabilization Strategy	Intervention Strategy
Students:		
Aggressor(s):	Immediate separation of students involved Transport of aggressor to secure place in school Interview, collect information Call parents/arrange transport home	Determine if administrative action will prevent repeat of inappropriate behavior If not, complete functional assessments and develop intervention plan Begin plan implementation
Victim(s):	Immediate separation of students involved Transport of victim to secure place in school Interview, collect information Call parents/arrange transport home	Determine if administrative action will prevent repeat of inappropriate behavior If not, complete functional assessments and develop intervention plan Begin plan implementation
Peers/ Bystanders:	Immediate separation of students involved Transport of peers to secure place in school Interview, collect information Determine their contribution to the problem	Determine if administrative action will prevent repeat of inappropriate behavior If not, complete functional assessments and develop intervention plan Begin plan implementation
Adults:		
Administrators	Implementation of relevant crisis intervention plan(s)	Planning meeting with relevant administrative, security, mental health, and other school and community resources to develop action plan
Teachers/Staff	Lockdown of building with noninvolved students	Implementation of developed action plan
Parents	Notified of incident and its resolution via communication sent home with all students	Involvement in community problem-solving and action meetings
Community	Notified as needed through district public information officer	Involvement in community problem-solving and action meetings along with other outreach and intervention initiatives

Domain	Stabilization Strategy	Intervention Strategy
Adults:		
Physical Plant/ Logistics:	Immediate lockdown of building, supervised release of students at end of the day	Increased security/adult supervision in hallways, staggered passing of students between periods
Accountability:	Immediate delivery of district-set consequences for involved students and peer groups	Discussion of incentives and consequences with entire student body
Resources:	District/community resources (police, others) involved as needed to gain control of the building and situation	Priority use of building, district, and community resources to implement action plan as designed

Source: Project ACHIEVE Press. Dr. Howie Knoff (author).

To summarize, based on completed special situation analyses, TTB-HHPA interventions may target (a) students, negatively involved or uninvolved peers, and victims; (b) staff, parents, or others outside of the school; (c) specific school settings, situations, degrees of supervision, or other logistical circumstances; (d) student, peer group, staff, parental, or community incentives or consequences; and (e) the lack of or the use of existing resources. Intervention may focus on students who have previously exhibited TTBHHPA behavior or who demonstrate a high probability of engaging in such behaviors; students who are victimized due to behaviors that trigger TTBHHPA or to behavioral responses (or the lack of effective responses) that reinforce TTBHHPA; peer groups that facilitate, support, or reinforce these students' inappropriate (or appropriate) behavior; school settings where these acts most frequently occur; and parents whose children and adolescents are directly or indirectly involved. These interventions also may target those students who have previously been involved in TTBHHPA, teaching them successful ways to avoid these situations in the future, and how to respond if the conditions reoccur. Finally, these interventions may include other adults in the school, helping them to successfully recognize and respond to TTBHHPA incidents, or motivating them and holding them accountable for these responses now and in the future.

Student-Specific Special Situations—Crisis Management. The special situation discussion thus far has paralleled our multi-tiered approach to schoolwide PBSS. Summarizing briefly, the core PBSS components, involving social skills instruction, developmentally sensitive motivation and accountability systems, staff and student consistency, and preventative setting- and student-specific special situation activities, form the foundation of a schoolwide process that minimizes or quickly addresses the vast majority of a school's TTBHHPA status or concerns. At the secondary prevention level, these evidence-based components help organize a problem-solving schema that is used to functionally determine the reasons why a school has continuing or persistent TTBHHPA problems. The confirmed reasons, generated through this analysis, then are linked to effective and efficient strategic interventions that eliminate future TTBHHPA incidents, replacing them with prosocial interactions and processes. Finally, at the tertiary, crisis-management level, the focus is on the students, peers, staff, or parents who demonstrate or support high levels of serious, persistent, and resistant TTBHHPA behavior; or on schools that have toxic climates or settings where TTBHHPA behavior is pervasive and out of control. Here, crisis management or intensive services, supports, strategies, or programs are needed. Crisis management focuses largely on stopping and stabilizing the current crisis situations, while the intensive interventions focus on helping everyone to debrief and cope with the aftermath of the situations, and to prevent new or renewed crises in the future.

Ways to analyze and address crisis management concerns in the five core special situation domains were discussed in Chapter 6. In the sixth peer group characteristics, issues, and factors domain, a number of problem analysis and intervention approaches have been presented in this chapter. To complete this discussion, the stabilizing and crisis-management strategies for a sample situation that could easily escalate to a crisis level are briefly outlined. The situation involves racially motivated taunting, and the strategies, organized across the special situation domains, are presented in Table 7.2.

Table 7.2 Stabilizing and Crisis Management Responses to Racially Motivated Taunting Across the Special Situation Domains

Domain	Stabilization Strategy	Crisis Management Strategy
Students:		
Aggressor	Immediate suspension	Evaluation, treatment, behavioral intervention plan, possible alternative school or setting placement
Victim	Removal to principal's office, counseling support, call and debriefing conference with parents	Social skills training, mediation sessions with bully and others in the peer group
Peers	Separation into different rooms of the school for debriefing, separate and joint meetings with parents	Sensitivity or tolerance training, behavioral contract

Domain	Stabilization Strategy	Crisis Management Strategy
Adults:		
Administrators	Implementation of relevant crisis intervention plans	Planning meeting with relevant administrative, security, mental health, and other district, school, and community resources to develop plan of action
Teachers/Staff	Lockdown of building with students not involved in incident	Implementation of developed action plan
Parents	Notified of incident and its resolution via communication sent home with all students	Involvement in community problem-solving and action meetings
Community	Notified as needed through district public information officer	Involvement in community problem-solving and action meetings, social marketing and outreach initiative on tolerance and no tolerance for bullying
Physical Plant/ Logistics:	Immediate lockdown of building, supervised release of students at end of the day	Increased security and adult supervision in hallways, staggered passing of students between periods
Accountability:	Immediate delivery of district-set consequences for involved students and peers relative to tolerance and bullying	Discussion of incentives and consequences with entire peer group
Resources:	Police or other district resources involved as needed to gain control of the building and situation	Priority use of building, district, and community resources to implement action plan as designed

Source: Project ACHIEVE Press. Dr. Howie Knoff (author).

A SPECIAL NOTE ABOUT CYBERBULLYING AND HAZING

Cyberbullying has been defined as the willful and repeated harm that is inflicted on a student through the use of computers, cell phones, and other electronic devices (Hinduja & Patchin, 2010; Morris, 2011). Cyberbullying includes e-mails, texts, blogs, social networking posts, videos and pictures, and other electronic messages that are intended to embarrass, ostracize, humiliate, bully, threaten, or harass one or more students. As noted in the introduction to this chapter, even though it occurs largely off campus, the vast majority of states have cyberbullying laws or policies that focus on school-aged students and that require a written school policy and school sanctions. This has occurred in response to a number of cyberbullying suicides and research linking cyberbullying to low self-esteem, suicidal thoughts, academic problems, school violence, delinquent behavior, and family problems.

While involving elements of teasing, taunting, bullying, and harassment, cyberbullying is somewhat unique because (a) the victims often do not know who the bully is or why they have been targeted; (b) an incident can involve entire schools, communities, states, and countries if the story, picture, or post goes viral; (c) the bullying may be easier—especially when the bully does not receive negative feedback, for example, from a group of bystanders; and (d) the bullying may be unintentionally more harmful given that the impact on a victim is not immediately visible. As noted earlier, districts and schools should discuss their policies with students and parents at the beginning of every school year, and follow-up training should occur in the areas of prevention, problem solving, and crisis response. Students must understand the potential effects of cyberbullying, that they will be held accountable if it occurs, and that they need to inform an appropriate adult if they know it does occur. While the ultimate goal is to prevent cyberbullying, schools still need to prepare a continuum of responses to deal with it strategically and definitively if preventative activities are not successful.

Hazing also has some similarities with bullying, except that some incidents have involved permanent physical damage, lifelong emotional traumas, and even death. Commonly associated with college-level students, hazing has increasingly crept into the high school culture. Hazing refers to "any activity expected of someone joining a group (or to maintain full status in a group) that humiliates, degrades, or risks emotional and/or physical harm, regardless of the person's willingness to participate" (www.stophazing.org), and research has suggested that well over 40% of college students report experiencing hazing in high school (Allan & Madden, 2008). Examples of hazing include personal servitude or public abductions or kidnappings; sleep deprivation or restrictions on personal hygiene; yelling at, swearing at, and insulting new members or rookies; being forced to wear embarrassing or humiliating attire in public or to be publicly naked; consumption of vile substances or smearing them on one's skin; burnings, brandings, or physical beatings; binge drinking, drinking games, or forced alcoholic (or water) consumption; and sexual simulation and sexual assault. At least 45 states have laws or legislation that specifically address hazing.

Given the group dynamics, the social pressure, and the institutional history within some organizations, clubs, or teams, hazing is distinctly different from teasing, taunting, bullying, harassment, and physical aggression. And yet, it clearly fits within the context of the student-specific special situation discussions in this chapter. In the end, many of the prevention-oriented recommendations outlined above are applicable to hazing. From a problem-solving perspective, the generational history of hazing within some groups will need to be added to the analysis and to the intervention. At a crisis-management level, students (and the adults supervising them) need to recognize that no amount of physical or emotional harm is worth a membership into any organization or club. Every year, there are too many incidents of the damage experienced by students due to hazing. Hazing, like teasing, taunting, bullying, cyberbullying, harassment, and physical aggression, must be integrated into schoolwide PBSS approaches.

SUMMARY

This chapter focuses on the student-specific special situations of TTBHHPA at the prevention, problem solving, and crisis management levels. Relative to these levels, a sixth peer group characteristics, issues, and factors domain was added to the five special situation domains (i.e., the student, teacher and staff, environmental, incentive and consequence, and resource and resource utilization domains) described in Chapter 6. This domain is needed given research establishing that peers directly or actively reinforce (by being antagonists) or indirectly or inadvertently reinforce (by observing, but being uninvolved bystanders) others' bullying behavior.

The prevention discussion focused on ways to promote prosocial student and staff interactions; to minimize students' TTBHHPA interactions; and to decrease or eliminate these negative interactions when they occur at low or mild levels. The problem-solving discussion focused on determining why these behaviors occur at moderate or high frequency or significant or extreme levels and linking the special-situation analysis results to strategic intervention approaches. The crisis-management discussion revisited the Chapter 6 discussion, extending it to student-specific special situations.

At all levels, it is critical to involve parents and community stakeholders and partners. Relative to the home, outreach activities help reinforce parents' support of schools' comprehensive school safety and discipline programs, and they may involve training so that parents can use the same social skill and (adapted) accountability approaches as the school. Relative to the community, outreach might involve police, social service and community mental health agencies, government and juvenile justice personnel, the business and faith communities, and formal and informal neighborhood networks and associations. At the prevention level, the ultimate goal is to have parents and community agents universally recognize that TTBHHPA are unacceptable and preventable. At the strategic intervention level, community resources might provide the pivotal components that decrease the potential for continuing incidents among at-risk groups of students. Finally, at the crisis-management level, parents and community agents must collaborate to stop extreme or persistent TTBHHPA behavior or critical incidents even if they have occurred just one time.

NOTE

1. Selected sections of this chapter were adapted, with permission, from Knoff, H. M. (2007). Teasing, taunting, bullying, harassment, and aggression: A school-wide approach to prevention, strategic intervention, and crisis management. In Zins, J., Elias, M., & Maher, C. (Eds.), *Bullying, victimization, and peer harassment: Handbook of prevention and intervention in peer harassment, victimization, and bullying.* New York: Haworth Press; and Knoff, H. M. (2009). *Implementing effective school-wide student discipline and behavior management systems: Increasing academic engagement and achievement, decreasing teasing and bullying, and keeping your school and common areas safe.* Little Rock, AR: Project ACHIEVE Press.

8

Functional Assessment and Why Students Become Behaviorally Challenging[1]

> Sometimes the road less traveled is less traveled for a reason.
>
> Jerry Seinfeld

PBSS Implementation Case Study:
Jesse Keen Elementary School, Lakeland, Florida

Project ACHIEVE was conceived and first implemented at Jesse Keen Elementary School during the 1990 to 1991 school year as part of a partnership with the Polk County School District. Jesse Keen was a full-service school, a Chapter I schoolwide school, and it established and staffed a parent drop-in center that provided parent training and outreach services during the 1990s. Supported over 10 years through six U.S. Department of Education, Office of Special Education Program grants, Jesse Keen's staff received training in every component of Project ACHIEVE largely over a five-year period of time.

Jesse Keen, located in an inner city warehouse district, had a fairly stable enrollment during the 10 years of on-site Project ACHIEVE implementation. During this time, the school's enrollment averaged 650 students, approximately 60% of whom were Caucasian, 30% African American, and 10% from other minority backgrounds. Jesse Keen's mobility rate of new and withdrawn students also averaged 72%, and 87% of the student body received federally funded meals due to family poverty.

While the Project ACHIEVE partnership resulted in many significant outcomes in the school climate, staff development, student discipline and behavior management, academic achievement and intervention, and parent involvement areas (Knoff & Batsche, 1995), the results below are due most to the data-based problem solving process discussed in this chapter and instituted during the very first year of the project. Analyzing and averaging outcome data across ten years of implementation and using 1989 to 1990 data as a baseline, there were many significant results:

- There was a drop in the number of special education referrals from 10 referrals per 100 students in the school to an average of 3.9 referrals per 100 students (a 61% decrease) over ten years.
- Special education referrals averaged 3.68 referrals per 100 students for the first five years of the project (1990 to 1995) and increased only slightly to 4.10 referrals per 100 students during the next five years (1995 to 2000).
- There was a decrease in special education placements from 6 placements per 100 students during the baseline year to an average of 2.6 placements per 100 students (a 57% decrease) over ten years.
- Special education placements averaged 2.52 placements per 100 students for the first five years of the project and 2.73 placements per 100 students for the next five years.
- There was a 16% decrease in the number of office discipline referrals for students with disabilities from 73 referrals per 100 students to an average of 61 referrals per 100 students.
- Grade retentions decreased from 6 retentions per 100 students to an average of 3.6 retentions per 100 students over the ten-year implementation period (a 47% decrease).

INTRODUCTION

When students exhibit ongoing, persistent, or intensive social, emotional, or behavioral challenges in a classroom or school, and they resist or do not respond to effective classroom instruction and preventative Positive Behavioral Support System (PBSS) approaches (see Chapters 1, 4, and 5), the reasons underlying the challenges must be determined so that strategic or intensive instructional or intervention services, supports, strategies, or programs can be successfully implemented. In order to accomplish this, a data-based, functional assessment problem-solving process needs to be embedded in the multi-tiered system of instructional and intervention approaches that range in intensity and focus. The problem-solving process must ecologically assess the different factors in a classroom, school, district, home, or community, and how they are causing or contributing to the challenging situation. In addition, the process needs to evaluate students' responses to the prevention, strategic, or intensive instructional or intervention approaches implemented to determine their success.

This chapter discusses challenging student behavior in the context of a multi-tiered Response-to-Instruction and Intervention (RTI^2) process that guides Project ACHIEVE's School Prevention, Review, and Intervention Team (SPRINT) process. After defining RTI^2, the data-based, functional assessment problem-solving process is outlined along with its most essential problem identification and problem analysis procedures. Seven high-hit reasons why students do not develop or demonstrate needed social competency and self-management skills and behaviors then are described. The chapter concludes by setting the stage for Chapter 9 where functional assessment results are linked with specific services, supports, strategies, or programs.

DESCRIBING RTI^2

While practiced for decades within the health and mental health communities, the importance of evaluating students' responsiveness to scientifically based intervention was legislatively introduced to education as part of the 2004 reauthorization of the Individuals with Disabilities Education Act (IDEA). Initially focused on services to students with possible learning disabilities, this process has been increasingly applied to approaching all students' academic and social, emotional, and behavioral outcomes. Functionally, Response-to-Intervention also has been combined with Response-to-Instruction (hence, RTI^2) in recognition that some students need modified, different, or more intensive instructional approaches in order to be academically or behaviorally successful, while other students need targeted, strategic, or intensive interventions in order to be successful (Knoff, 2009b; Knoff & Dyer, 2010).

RTI^2, then, involves evaluating the degree to which students (a) master academic material in response to effective instruction and (b) demonstrate appropriate prosocial behavior in response to effective behavioral instruction and classroom management. It begins in the general education classroom with evidence-based curricula taught by highly qualified teachers using effective instructional practices. When students do not academically or behaviorally progress or respond to effective instructional conditions, RTI^2 relies on a functional assessment problem-solving process to determine the reasons for the lack of progress or success, linking them to strategic or intensive instructional or interventional approaches that facilitate specific outcomes and student progress, achievement, and proficiency.

Depending on the severity of the problem (e.g., based on frequency, duration, or intensity) or the intensity or complexity of the needed services and supports, the problem-solving process is completed by an individual classroom teacher (with or without consultative support) or through the grade-level or building-level SPRINT team, respectively (see Chapter 3). The focus, ultimately, is on early, responsive, and strategic instruction or intervention that is delivered and evaluated, to the greatest degree possible, in the general education classroom resulting in student learning, mastery, and proficiency on state- and district-identified academic and social, emotional, and behavioral outcomes.

Because some students' social, emotional, or behavioral challenges directly relate to their academic failure and frustration, the RTI² problem-solving process always considers this possibility from the beginning, analyzing students in the context of their Instructional Environments. As briefly discussed in Chapter 1, the Instructional Environment (see Figure 8.1) consists of the teacher or instructional, curricular, and student factors that help students to succeed, that explain why they do not succeed, or that are included in the instructional or intervention plan to help turn the student around to success. The possible interplay between students' academic status and their behavioral challenges explains why Project ACHIEVE's effective schools model (see Chapter 1, Figure 8.1) emphasizes the interdependency (i.e., the overlap) between academic and behavioral instruction and intervention through the Positive Academic Supports and Services (PASS) and PBSS models, respectively.

Figure 8.1   The Three Components of Students' Instructional Environments

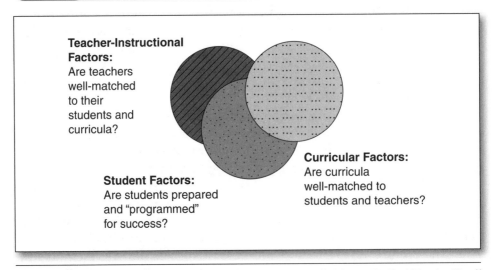

Source: Project ACHIEVE Press (as adapted from Rosenfield, 1987). Dr. Howie Knoff (author).

When implemented with integrity, the RTI^2 process provides information and data that promote quality decisions regarding effective school and schooling practices and a cascade of approaches to address the academic or behavioral needs of At-Risk, underachieving, unresponsive, and unsuccessful students. The timing of when and where to pursue consultation and the data-based problem-solving process, however, is another critical decision. That is, at what level of risk, underachievement, unresponsiveness, or lack of success does a teacher begin the problem-solving process, and what criteria determine when to involve other consultants, the grade-level SPRINT team, or the building-level SPRINT team? Three principles help answer these questions:

1. Teachers (and other staff) should begin the problem-solving process (see Step 1 in the section below) as soon as they have academic or social, emotional, or behavioral concerns about a student. Early, successful intervention is important for all students when needed.

2. Teachers (and other staff) should ask for collegial support or consultative assistance whenever effective classroom instruction or behavioral management approaches have not produced expected academic or social, emotional, or behavioral outcomes and after they have implemented instructional modifications or classroom interventions, within their areas of expertise and with integrity and needed intensity, that have not helped their students to progress.

3. When needing consultative assistance, teachers (and other staff) should request the level of support (for example, a one-on-one consultation, support from the grade-level or building-level SPRINT team, respectively) that they feel is warranted by the severity of the problem (e.g., based on frequency, duration, or intensity) or the anticipated intensity or complexity of the needed services and supports.

Said differently, teachers should not implement instructional or intervention approaches in the classroom when they are unfamiliar, untrained, or inexperienced with them. Indeed, teachers should not implement unfamiliar approaches on their own simply because (a) they are embarrassed to ask for consultative assistance, (b) the school culture views these requests as a sign of incompetence, or (c) the school's RTI^2 process requires teachers to implement a certain number of interventions independently even though teachers are randomly selecting these interventions and, thus, they have low probabilities of success.

These principles also reinforce the importance of accessing the level of problem-solving expertise needed for a student situation as quickly as possible. More specifically, the RTI^2 process is not a lockstep process. That is, students should not have to fail at the classroom and grade-level

SPRINT levels of problem analysis and intervention in order to receive building-level SPRINT assessment or intervention services. If the severity of the problem or the intensity of the services warrant it—even, for example, on a student's first day of school—then the building-level SPRINT team should be immediately involved.

As reflected above, the service delivery approaches embedded in the RTI² process involve problem solving, consultation, and intervention. Below, the data-based, functional assessment problem-solving process is described in more detail.

THE DATA-BASED, FUNCTIONAL ASSESSMENT, PROBLEM-SOLVING PROCESS

Data-based problem solving is the hub that connects all of the spokes of the RTI² process, and it is vital that all instructional, related services and support, and administrative staff in a school are collaboratively trained and competent in its implementation. While somewhat sequential, data-based problem solving is still a fluid, flexible, and strategic process involving four inherent elements: (a) problem identification, clarification, and specification; (b) problem analysis and functional assessment; (c) intervention planning, preparation, and implementation; and (d) evaluation of implementation integrity, intensity, and success. These essential elements are expanded into seven interdependent steps below.

Step 1: Reviewing Existing Data, Records, and Student History

When a teacher has concerns about a student's social, emotional, or behavioral progress or status, the first formal steps in the RTI² process include

- examining all of the existing cumulative, attendance, assessment, and intervention records on the student that are present in or available to the school, and documenting all essential information;
- determining, with help if needed, the student's current functional skill level in all academic and behavioral areas, and how much progress the student has made on an annual basis;
- ensuring that the student's hearing and vision, at the very least, have been checked and approved by the school nurse, while collecting any additional medically related information known by the school;
- contacting the parents to discuss the initial concerns, while also gathering pertinent information from them;
- interviewing previous teachers (and others) who have taught or worked with the student; and
- determining the need for classroom observations by someone skilled in that area.

All instructional and support staff in a school need to be trained to complete these steps and activities during the professional development process that should precede the implementation of a schoolwide RTI^2 process. At the same time, any staff person could still request assistance (e.g., from a school nurse in the medical area, from a counselor or social worker in the parent interview area) at any time in any of the areas above.

Once the information above has been collected, the teacher should better understand (a) the frequency, duration, or intensity of the current concerns, and whether they are occurring across time, people, settings, and situations; (b) whether the concerns about the student are new and shared by other current staff members; (c) if other colleagues have expressed similar concerns about the student in the past; and (d) what instructional or intervention services, supports, strategies, or programs the student has received in the past, and whether or not they were successful. More specifically, in determining the current functional status of the student, the teacher will identify and validate the student's social, emotional, and behavioral skills, assets, and abilities, and the student's behavioral progress and learning patterns over time. In collaborating with medical personnel, the presence or absence of relevant physical or physiological, chemical or biochemical, hormonal or genetic, neurological or cognitive, or other circumstances or events can be discerned or discounted. In meeting with the parents, the teacher can share his or her concerns; solicit information, perceptions, and assistance from them; and begin to build the strong, collaborative relationship that needs to be sustained throughout the problem-solving process. In addition, as appropriate, the teacher (or attending related services professional) can get parent permission to obtain relevant, out-of-district educational, medical, mental health, or other records, and to contact and discuss other professionals' past or present involvement or treatment with the student.

Step 2: Completing a Gap Analysis

As noted, if justified by the severity, intensity, or complexity of a student's problems, the classroom teacher presents the case to the building-level SPRINT team. After systematically outlining the most relevant information collected during Step 1 of this process, the teacher responds to questions from the members of this multidisciplinary team, and other known and unknown information is discussed. If the team decides that the primary concerns are clear enough, and that there is enough valid information to proceed, it chooses the best assessment or intervention consultant to continue the problem-solving process with the teacher in the settings where the concerns exist. If there are too many unanswered questions, the discussion in the team meeting eventually is suspended, different individuals are asked to obtain the answers to these questions, and the discussion is continued at a future, reconvened meeting once the needed information is available.

The decision on the best consultant to work with the classroom teacher on a case is the primary goal of the initial building-level SPRINT meeting. Given the typical complexity of most cases at this level, it is rare that the reasons underlying a student's difficulties are so clear that, sight unseen, the instructional or intervention services, supports, strategies, or programs can be accurately determined at the meeting itself and readied for implementation. Thus, virtually all Step 2 gap analyses—especially for the most challenging social, emotional, or behavioral cases brought to the building-level SPRINT team—are completed collaboratively in the field by the identified SPRINT team consultant, the classroom teacher, and others (including the student him- or herself) who are relevant to the identified concerns. At this stage, these analyses involve (a) identifying the gap between the student's current versus expected (or desired) level of functioning, (b) identifying the replacement behaviors that become the goals of the intervention plan and process, and (c) quantifying the gap to the greatest degree possible. Once again, a problem-solving, consultation, intervention approach is used throughout the RTI^2 service delivery process.

A student's skill gap is determined by contrasting the social, emotional, and behavioral self-management skills that he or she has mastered (regardless of age level) with the skills that he or she should have mastered, given developmental and maturational expectations. One way to organize these skills is to assess and analyze a student's personal self-management (e.g., attention control, emotional control, and self-concept/self-esteem) skills; interpersonal (e.g., engagement and response, problem-solving, and conflict prevention and resolution) skills; and environmental or situational (e.g., school, classroom, academic supporting, and extracurricular) skills. After contrasting a student's current with expected social, emotional, and behavioral skills, the skill gap most typically results in a need to (a) increase the frequency of existing behaviors or establish new behaviors; (b) decrease the frequency of, or eliminate, inappropriate behaviors; (c) increase the duration of appropriate behaviors or decrease the duration of inappropriate behaviors; (d) decrease the latency time relative to the appearance, or initiation, of appropriate behaviors; or (e) increase the intensity of appropriate behaviors or decrease the intensity of inappropriate behaviors.

Even when there is a need to decrease or eliminate inappropriate behavior, the problem-solving process should concurrently focus on increasing or establishing appropriate replacement behaviors. Replacement behaviors describe the positive, proactive, or prosocial emotional or behavioral competencies or self-management skills that teachers and others want the student to demonstrate. These skills are never described using the words *not, stop,* or *don't.* While some teachers intuitively believe that the primary goal of a behavioral intervention is to stop an inappropriate behavior (e.g., running, swearing, bullying), they need to understand that many challenging students will replace one inappropriate behavior for another if the intervention does not also focus on true replacement behaviors (i.e., walking, appropriate conversation, positive or neutral social interactions).

The next activity in this step is to quantify the gap. This is especially important because these numbers help to set short-term progress monitoring goals and long-term intervention goals. In most cases, the quantification reflects a behavior's frequency, duration, intensity, or latency. If the problem involves some type of assessment instrument or tool, the gap may relate to the test's norm-referenced standard score or t score. Finally, as some social or interaction problems or replacement behaviors may be more descriptive in nature, they may require a more qualitative or process-oriented gap analysis approach.

The last activity in Step 2 is to prioritize the clarified concerns and replacement behaviors. As very few students have only one academic or behavioral concern, prioritization is necessary in order for the data-based, functional assessment problem-solving process to move effectively and efficiently toward intervention success. Simplistically, intervention priorities can be determined by rank ordering the student concerns or targets for change by (a) intensity or severity, (b) interdependency or overlap, or (c) ease of success. When concerns are arranged by intensity, the teacher and consultant organize them from the most troubling, intense, problematic, or serious to the least. When arranged by interdependency, the concerns are prioritized by first targeting those that, if successfully resolved, would simultaneously help resolve other listed concerns. For example, interventions that increase students' in-seat behavior may also resolve the same students' negative peer interactions when they are out of their seats, their non-completion of academic work at their seat, their defiance when teachers direct them to reseat themselves, and their lack of academic skill mastery when they miss work due to the out-of-seat behavior.

Finally, the listed concerns or replacement behaviors can be arranged by how quickly or effortlessly they can be changed. Targeting intervention goals by ease of success often is done (a) to show teachers (or others, including the students themselves) that success is possible, especially when they are convinced that the student can never change, or (b) when there is a need for a strategic early victory that will help build the momentum for later more sustained success. While this approach often does not resolve the most pressing or pivotal student concerns, it can help establish the positive attitudes and beliefs that change can occur—attributions that are needed to eventually address the more complex or intense issues of concern.

The Functional Assessment Process. As the gap analysis proceeds and transitions into Step 3 (i.e., the development of hypotheses to explain the gap), the functional assessment process has actually begun. Whether a functional assessment is performed individually by a classroom teacher or with a colleague or consultant from the grade- or building-level SPRINT team, respectively, there are a series of common academic and behavioral assessment questions that help to guide this process. These questions are best organized into the three interdependent domains of the Instructional Environment (see Table 8.1 and, once again, Figure 8.1)—the teacher or instructional factors, curricula factors, and student factors.

Table 8.1	Important Functional Assessment Questions in the Instructional Environment

Student Characteristics and Conditions involve characteristics and conditions that relate primarily to a student's cognitive and academic ability, attitudes toward schooling, and readiness for academic and social, emotional, and behavioral learning. These characteristics directly relate to those behaviors that support learning, progress, and achievement. These characteristics and conditions also involve student behaviors that directly support academic and social learning and progress, such as self-competence skills, social skills, and the effective use of the teacher and teacher time.

When students are referred for academic difficulties, these relevant questions should be considered:

- Does the student have the prerequisite skills for the required or desired tasks?
- Does the student have the prior learning strategies to facilitate the advanced learning desired?
- Does the student have the self-competency, cognitive or metacognitive, motivational, social and interactive, and other learning-supporting skills needed to be successfully involved in the desired task?
- Does the student have and use the appropriate learning styles and approaches needed to successfully complete the desired tasks?

When students have behavioral difficulties, these relevant questions should be considered:

- Can the referral source (e.g., the teacher) adequately describe the referral concern (and other student liabilities) in behavioral terms or are there only vague descriptions of concerns (e.g., "the child has a problem with defiance")?
- What occurs before, during, and after the behavior of concern?
- What are the student's strengths across domains relevant to the referral problems, across domains that might be used in an intervention program for the referral problem, and across other domains that do not necessarily relate to the referral problem?
- Where does the problem occur least often? Is the problem occurring more or less often than (a) last week, (b) last month, (c) the beginning of the year, or (d) at the onset of the problem? When did the problem

behavior first occur? What is the teacher's preferred approach in solving the problem?

- What is the function of the behavior for the student, for other students, and for the teacher? What is the teacher's style, skill, and investment in dealing with the problem?
- Is the problem a skill, performance, or self-management deficit for the student? Is the problem a skill, performance, or self-management deficit for the teacher?
- How often can the behavior occur and still be tolerable for the teacher? How do (or should) other students behave, when the problem behavior is occurring, such that their behavior or reaction is appropriate? If the challenging student were unable to engage in the problem behavior, what other problem behaviors might occur in substitution?
- What interventions have been tried before? What were the goals and characteristics of these interventions, how were they implemented, and what were the outcomes for the student and for the teacher, parents, and significant others?
- What would motivate the teacher to work on this problem in the classroom setting? How would solving the problem behavior make the teacher's day easier? What is the teacher's commitment to work on the problem?

Teacher Characteristics, Performance, Effectiveness, and Conditions involve characteristics and conditions that teachers bring to the classroom that ultimately translate into the effective instructional skills and behaviors that maximize student learning. Also involved here are those school and schooling skills, activities, and interactions that teachers perform that make their instructional approaches effective.

When students are not learning or making sufficient progress in a classroom or when they are referred for academic difficulties, questions related to a teacher's instructional approach or other related instructional factors should be considered:

- Does the Instructional Environment support the learning process?
- Is the teacher being effective with the student?
- Is the teacher adapting the curriculum such that there is an appropriate student-curriculum match?
- Is instruction programmed for student success?
- When special academic interventions are necessary, does the teacher have the knowledge, skill, confidence, objectivity, or interactional skills needed to maximize success?
- When special academic interventions are necessary, are there appropriate resources, support materials, and staff available to the teacher to maximize success?
- When special academic interventions are necessary, is a problem-solving process used that links assessment directly to intervention?

(Continued)

Table 8.1 (Continued)

> - When special academic interventions are necessary, are the interventions acceptable to the teacher, socially valid, and effectively implemented?
>
> *Curricular Characteristics and Conditions* involve characteristics and conditions of the academic curricula being used (or that were previously used) in a classroom and include a curriculum's content and materials as well as the processes that are used to ensure student learning and mastery.
>
> When considering the curriculum within the context of students referred for academic difficulties, these relevant questions should be considered:
>
> - Does the curriculum specify the particular objectives that the student is expected to master for each instructional unit?
> - Does the curriculum specify the particular skills that the student must possess as a prerequisite to meeting the instructional objectives for each unit?
> - Does the curriculum task analyze specific skills, when appropriate, such that sequential and mastery-oriented learning results for all students?
> - Does the curriculum provide a range of levels to accommodate the different cognitive and language levels that might exist within an integrated classroom?
> - Does the curriculum introduce new skills such that students have a high probability of success, and provide sufficient positive practice opportunities for students to attain mastery?
> - Does the curriculum have built-in opportunities for students to transfer new training to other academic situations, applications, and contexts?
> - Does the curriculum have horizontal skill books and other materials available for students who need extra instruction or practice to attain mastery?
> - Does the curriculum follow research-based methods of instruction relative to student mastery and other relevant outcomes?

Critically, these questions, and the data-based ways to answer them, are integrated into the schoolwide problem-solving training needed and noted earlier in this chapter, and they are used consciously and explicitly during the early implementation of the RTI^2/SPRINT process. Indeed, when everyone is trained and uses these question-oriented protocols, it results in earlier and higher-level data collection and problem analysis, especially by classroom teachers at the beginning of the process, and it increases the potential that these teachers will solve some of their own student problems more independently over time. Even if the latter result does not occur, the quality and integrity of the data that teachers bring to and present to the grade- or building-level SPRINT teams, respectively, increase the effectiveness and efficiency of the SPRINT meetings themselves because teachers already have the answers to some questions or have the data that other team members can use to answer the more complex case-related questions.

Given the fluid nature of problem solving, these questions cut across Step 2 and Step 3. Once again, because some students' social, emotional, or behavioral problems may have academic roots, Table 8.1 presents some of the most important functional assessment questions, at this stage of the problem-solving process, in both areas. Clearly, not all of the questions are relevant to every student concern, and some essential questions may need to be added given the unique nature of some students' challenges.

Step 3: The Development of Hypotheses

The RTI²'s data-based, functional assessment problem-solving process basically applies the scientific method to student and other concerns. That is, the process involves generating hypotheses to explain why certain student situations are occurring, conducting assessments to confirm or reject the hypotheses, linking strategic instructional or intervention services, supports, strategies, or programs to the confirmed hypotheses, and evaluating whether the implemented approaches facilitated a positive change and/or desired outcomes.

Hypotheses, quite simply, are organized in the following format:

"The (describe here) problem behavior is occurring because (generate hypothesis here)."

The first part of the statement is a behaviorally specific description of the student concern or the identified gap. The second part of the statement specifies the hypothesized reason for the concern or gap based on all of the information collected during the first steps of the problem-solving process. An example of a hypothesis might be, "Jason is throwing chairs because the math work is too hard for him and he gets frustrated."

In Step 3, hypotheses are generated in up to six domains: the three domains within the Instructional Environment, and the classroom or peer, school or district, and home or community domains, respectively. Critically, hypotheses related to the Instructional Environment address reasons that tend to cause a student's difficulties. For example, students may demonstrate poor or nonexistent social skills because (a) the school does not use a social skills curriculum or require teachers to teach these skills (curriculum domain); (b) teachers are not teaching social skills effectively because they have never been appropriately trained (teacher or instructional domain); or (c) the students are not learning, mastering, or applying the social skills that are being taught (student domain). If these hypotheses are confirmed, then the intervention approaches that result should directly resolve the social skills problem. That is, the students of concern should begin demonstrating prosocial skills when the school acquires a social skills curriculum, trains and holds teachers accountable for its implementation, and ensures that students learn the different social skills to mastery, respectively.

Hypotheses in the latter three areas address factors that contribute to or correlate with student difficulties, but do not cause them. For example, a student may be demonstrating poor or nonexistent social skills because (a) the peer group is reinforcing his inappropriate behavior (classroom or peer domain); (b) he has difficulty in crowded common school areas where his teachers are not present (school or district domain); or (c) he is upset because his parents are getting a divorce (home or community domain). While intervening with the peer group and the crowding in the common school areas, respectively, may temporarily change the student's behavior, the student still needs to learn and demonstrate appropriate behavior when other peer groups reinforce his inappropriate behavior in the future or when crowding occurs in other schools during other school years. Thus, the more permanent solution to this problem would be to teach and motivate the student to ignore or resist social pressure from the current and future peer groups and to transfer the social skills that he demonstrates in his classroom into any common school setting that has large numbers of students and no teacher supervision.

Relative to the divorce, the intervention is not to encourage the parents to reconcile but to teach the student how to emotionally cope with the divorce so that he is able to demonstrate his prosocial skills in different settings even when he is upset about his parents and current family situation. Thus, while the divorce is contributing to and triggering the student's emotionality, the direct resolution of the problem (i.e., the emotionality that is impacting his social skill behavior) is to teach and motivate the student to learn and use emotional coping skills.

Relative to analyzing the peer, school setting, and home conditions in the case example above and linking them to respective interventions, then, the student's lack of or inability to demonstrate existing social skills is the primary cause of the student's difficulties. While a comprehensive intervention plan would still move to eliminate the inappropriate peer reinforcement, the overcrowded common school areas, and any acrimony between the parents during and after the divorce, replacing them with positive peer interactions, safer and more organized common school areas, and parents who are consciously minimizing the emotional impact of the divorce on their son, the intervention plan also would include the cognitive-behavioral training or therapy needed to teach the student how to control his thoughts, emotions, physiological reactions, and behavioral responses to these challenging conditions. Once again, while a change in the triggering conditions might help the student in the short term, successful cognitive and emotional control training will have a broader and more generalized effect in the long term.

High-Hit Instructional Environment Hypotheses. While teachers and consultants should investigate possible hypotheses in all six of the problem analysis domains above, the remainder of this section focuses on the most typical high-hit hypotheses present within the Instructional Environment (see Figures 8.2, 8.3, and 8.4). While outlined separately, please recall the interdependent nature of these three domains, and the fact that many of the related questions in Table 8.1 are hypotheses that also need to be considered and tested.

The teacher or instructional characteristics and factors domain involves effective instructional and classroom management skills and strategies that maximize student learning, achievement, and self-management. Also involved here are the instructional remediations, accommodations, and modifications that effective teachers make to help all students to learn (see the PASS blueprint in Chapter 1).

At times, students are not learning, mastering, or demonstrating appropriate social, emotional, or behavioral skills in the classroom because of teacher or instructional factors. When this occurs, it is usually because the teacher does not know or is not demonstrating effective

Figure 8.2 Problem Analysis: Possible Reasons for Teachers' Lack of Success on Behalf of Their Students

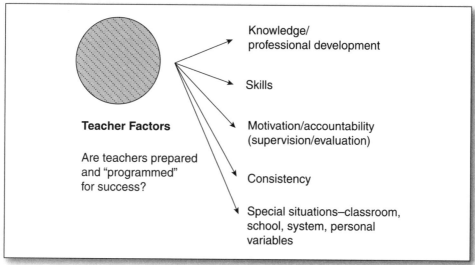

Teacher Factors

Are teachers prepared and "programmed" for success?

- Knowledge/ professional development
- Skills
- Motivation/accountability (supervision/evaluation)
- Consistency
- Special situations–classroom, school, system, personal variables

Source: Project ACHIEVE Press. Dr. Howie Knoff (author).

Figure 8.3 Problem Analysis: Possible Curricular Reasons for Teachers' and Students' Lack of Success

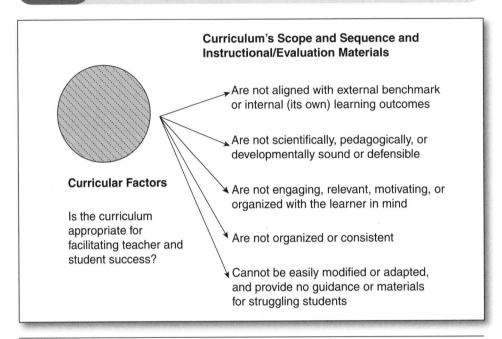

Source: Project ACHIEVE Press. Dr. Howie Knoff (author).

Figure 8.4 Problem Analysis: Possible Reasons for Students' Lack of Self-Management Progress or Success

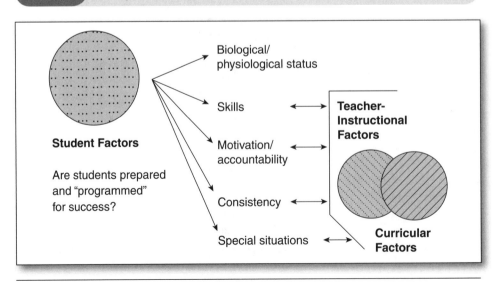

Source: Project ACHIEVE Press. Dr. Howie Knoff (author).

instructional interactions or because of ineffective instructional interactions. Both of these possibilities could involve interactions that are generalized across all of the students in a classroom, or that are specific to just the challenging students. Moreover, the ineffective instruction may have occurred in previous years or in other settings. That is, this year's teachers may have inherited a problem that originated with other colleagues or at an earlier time.

When teacher or instructional factors are directly impacting a student's challenging behavior, there are five high-hit areas or reasons to explore and analyze (see Figure 8.2): (a) the teacher does not have the information, knowledge, or understanding of how to work with the student(s) (knowledge or professional development); (b) the teacher has the knowledge but is not able to transfer it into actual skill or behavior in the classroom (skills); (c) the teacher is not motivated to learn the needed information or demonstrate the appropriate behavior or is not held accountable for these actions by supervisors or administrators in the school or district (motivation or accountability); (d) the teacher has the knowledge, skills, and motivation but demonstrates them inconsistently during classroom interactions with the students (inconsistency); and (e) there are unique situations or circumstances affecting the teacher's ability to appropriately or successfully interact with the students (special situations). Below are some specific examples or hypotheses in these high-hit areas.

- *Knowledge or Professional Development and Skills.* Teachers may not have the information or skills to effectively organize their classrooms and teaching schedules; to teach social, emotional, and behavioral skills and classroom routines; to identify meaningful incentives and consequences, and use them consistently; to differentially respond to challenging student behavior as on the Behavioral Matrix; or to implement classroom-based interventions based on data and classroom-oriented functional assessments.

- *Skills.* In addition to the circumstances above, teachers may not have their own emotional control skills, helping them to maintain their composure when students are exhibiting challenging behavior. When teachers are overly emotional, they may not teach or respond to students' inappropriate behavior as effectively, or they may not correctly implement interventions designed to eliminate students' challenging behaviors.

- *Motivation or Accountability.* Unfortunately, some teachers are simply not motivated to help students with challenging behaviors and would rather send them to the office or refer them for special education services than work collaboratively with mental health personnel to meet their needs. A recent study (Milkie & Warner, 2011), based on interviews with more than 10,700 parents and teachers of first grade students, noted that run-down schools with inadequate supplies and teachers who were not respected by their colleagues increased first grade students' stress—especially those students living in poverty. Moreover, in a circular way, children's discipline problems increased teacher frustration and turnover and lowered their expectations, which, in turn, led to teacher exhaustion and greater difficulties with classroom management.

- *Consistency.* As noted previously, a high level of teacher inconsistency in holding students accountable for inappropriate behavior often strengthens their inappropriate behavior, making it more resistant to change and decreasing their motivation to demonstrate appropriate behavior.
- *Special Situations.* Finally, there are times when teachers are dealt or are dealing with their own special situations that affect student behavior in the classroom. For example, sometimes the mix of challenging students that a teacher was dealt at the beginning of the year are feeding off of one another, making it nearly impossible for the teacher to implement classroom instruction, behavior management, and strategic interventions on even the best of days. In addition, just like anyone else, some teachers are dealing with out-of-school situations and stressors that they bring into the classroom. This may affect the quality of their relationships and interactions with students, which, in turn, may result in inappropriate student behavior.

The curricular characteristics and factors domain involves the contents and characteristics of the academic and social, emotional, and behavioral curricula used in a classroom or that were used with specific students in the past. The most important characteristics here include how each (formal or informal) curriculum (a) identifies its instructional goals and objectives—largely through its scope and sequence and pacing charts; (b) organizes its content, instructional materials, and embedded pedagogical approaches; (c) uses its materials and approaches to facilitate teachers' differentiation or modification to address the needs of different learners; (d) assesses and monitors student learning, progress, and mastery; and (e) documents its effectiveness and efficacy in all of the areas above with different types of students.

At times, students are not learning, mastering, or demonstrating appropriate social, emotional, or behavioral skills in the classroom because of curricular factors. When this occurs, it is usually because of the absence of effective (or effectively modified) or the presence of ineffective academic or social, emotional, or behavioral curricula—either at the class or the individual student levels. When curricular factors directly impact a student's challenging behavior, there are five high-hit areas or reasons to explore and analyze (see Figure 8.3): (a) the curricula are not aligned with or do not address desired or needed academic or social, emotional, or behavioral outcomes (reasons of alignment); (b) they do not use scientifically, pedagogically, or developmentally sound instructional approaches (reasons of pedagogy); (c) they are not engaging, relevant, motivating, or organized with the learner in mind (learner-centered reasons); (d) the materials and embedded instructional approaches are not organized and consistent (reasons of inconsistency); and (e) the materials and embedded instructional approaches are not easily modified to address different students' needs and learning approaches (reasons of adaptability). Below are some specific examples or hypotheses in these high-hit areas.

- *Alignment of the Curriculum With Stated Outcomes.* At times, a social, emotional, or behavioral curriculum is not aligned with the desired external or internal goals or outcomes. For example, if a district or school (externally) wants to improve students' prosocial behavior (e.g., teaching them to appropriately ask for help, respond to teasing, discuss and resolve conflicts) and it chooses a curriculum that focuses on emotions and feelings, it is likely that the student outcomes will not be accomplished. Similarly, if a curriculum's marketing materials state that it is designed to improve students' prosocial behavior and the curriculum (internally) focuses only on emotions and feelings, once again, it is unlikely that the student outcomes will be accomplished.

- *All or Critical Parts of the Curriculum Are Not Sound.* Social, emotional, or behavioral curricula need to conform to the documented and proven developmental and cognitive-behavioral principles that facilitate student success in these areas. For example, social skills curricula need to be designed to match the cognitive-developmental and maturational status and capabilities of the students being taught (e.g., providing separate early elementary, late elementary, and middle school versions). Moreover, when a social skills program does not use social learning theory to guide its skill instruction (i.e., using a teach, model, role-play, performance feedback, and transfer of training methodology), this often undermines student outcomes.

- *Materials or Content Are Not Engaging, Relevant, or Written With the Learner in Mind.* When social, emotional, or behavioral curricula are not student-centered, student engagement and motivation diminishes, and students do not learn or master the information, skills, or applications desired.

- *Materials Are Not Instructionally Sequenced, Organized, or Consistent.* At times, social, emotional, or behavioral curricula just are not designed well. As such, the resulting instruction is not effective or efficient, lessons do not make sense, and student learning is negatively affected. For example, when more advanced social skills are taught before their prerequisite skills, they are not easily learned and mastered.

- *Materials Are Difficult to Modify or Adapt for Struggling Students.* Recognizing that not all students learn in the same way or at the same pace, social, emotional, or behavioral curricula need to suggest ways—supported by research, pedagogical approaches, and adaptable materials—to modify or adapt their instruction so that struggling learners also can succeed. Moreover, when curricula are not easily modified or adapted for different learners, they create a situation where students must fit into the curricula, rather than having curricula that can fit the students.

The student characteristics and factors domain involves characteristics and conditions that relate primarily to students' biological, physiological, cognitive, behavioral, motivational, and dispositional readiness for academic and social, emotional, and behavioral learning and mastery. These characteristics directly relate to their social competency and self-management knowledge, skills, and behaviors—including their cognitive attitudes, beliefs, and attributions toward themselves and others; their interpersonal, social problem-solving, conflict prevention and resolution, and emotional coping skills; and their self-monitoring, self-evaluation, self-correction, and self-reinforcement skills.

As discussed earlier in this chapter, one of the first critical student-focused actions in the problem-solving process is to discount the medical. That is, in collaboration with medical personnel, the possible presence of relevant physical or physiological, chemical or biochemical, hormonal or genetic, neurological or cognitive, or other circumstances or events that are causing or exacerbating a student's social, emotional, or behavioral actions or reactions must be identified or dismissed. Included here are issues of vision and hearing, speech and communication, cognitive status and processing, sleep and fatigue, and drugs and alcohol. This is an essential step in understanding why some students present with challenging behavior. When present, these medical factors must be factored into both interpreting the assessments completed and planning and implementing the interventions needed.

Beyond this, the primary reasons why students do not demonstrate appropriate and effective interactions or demonstrate inappropriate or ineffective social, emotional, or behavioral interactions relate to (a) their learning, transfer, and mastery of needed skills; (b) their motivation to demonstrate these skills and how or if they are held accountable for them; (c) the consistency of the expectations, teaching and practice, and motivation and accountability, relative to these skills, across students, staff, settings, and circumstances; and (d) special situations that involve common school settings, critical peer interactions, and unique life circumstances (see Figure 8.4). These four components were described in Chapter 1 when introducing the PBSS. They now are applied as seven high-hit reasons why students demonstrate challenging behaviors.

- *Hypothesis #1 (Skills): Skill Deficit.* A student has not been taught or has not learned and mastered the social, emotional, or behavioral skills needed to exhibit appropriate behavior and to prevent or avoid inappropriate behavior.
- *Hypothesis #2 (Skills): Speed of Acquisition.* A student is learning and demonstrating some social, emotional, or behavioral skills, but he or she is not learning and mastering these skills at the same rate or pace as other students in the classroom.
- *Hypothesis #3 (Skills): Transfer of Training/Generalization.* A student is learning and demonstrating social, emotional, or behavioral skills when they are taught, but he or she is not transferring or applying these skills independently during real or actual situations.
- *Hypothesis #4 (Skills): Conditions of Emotionality.* A student has not been taught or has not mastered the skills and behaviors to cope with situations or circumstances that trigger high levels of emotionality.
- *Hypothesis #5 (Accountability): Motivation/Performance Deficit.* A student is not motivated to learn or apply his or her social, emotional, or behavioral skills.
- *Hypothesis #6 (Consistency): Inconsistency.* Inconsistency exists somewhere in the instructional, motivational, or transfer of training process. This could involve the inconsistent teaching or prompting of social, emotional, or behavioral skills; the inconsistent use of incentives, consequences, or accountability approaches; or inconsistency that is related to different peer, staff, setting, or situational expectations, interactions, or responses.
- *Hypothesis #7 (Special Situation): Setting, Peer, Life Circumstances.* A student is experiencing or reacting to significant past or present situations or circumstances in one or more common areas of the school; with one or more peers—involving significant levels of teasing, taunting, bullying, harassment, hazing, or physical aggression; or in some school, home, or community facet of his or her life. This problem is impacting his or her (a) social, emotional, or behavioral learning, mastery, or transfer; (b) motivation to use already learned social, emotional, or behavioral skills; or (c) consistency or stability.

Step 4: Assessing to Confirm or Reject Hypotheses

Once a set of viable hypotheses has been generated, the problem-solving process proceeds as assessments are conducted to confirm or reject these hypotheses. This is done by collecting student data when the hypothesized conditions are present (the positive prediction) and absent (the converse prediction), respectively. For example, given the hypothesis that "Jason is throwing chairs because the math work is too hard for him and he gets frustrated," we need to collect data reflecting two conditions:

- *Positive Prediction:* When Jason gets math work that is too hard for him, he gets frustrated and throws chairs.
- *Converse Prediction:* When Jason gets math work that he can do, he does not get frustrated (he is calm and engaged), and he does not throw chairs (he is on-task and completes the work).

If the assessment data show a high degree of chair throwing when we give Jason math assignments that we know are well above his ability level and we see him visibly frustrated, and little or no chair throwing occurs when we give him assignments that are well within his ability level and he is engaged and on-task, then the hypothesis is confirmed. If we see chair throwing regardless of the difficulty level of the math work, then the hypothesis is rejected, and we conclude that this variable (assignment difficulty) does not explain the inappropriate behavior and should not be the foundation for an intervention. At this point, we need to generate and assess other hypotheses.

Critically, when a hypothesis for a student's inappropriate behavior relates to a skill that the student has never learned and mastered, it cannot be assessed using positive and converse prediction statements. For example, if a student has constant peer conflicts because he does not (have the skill to) recognize when they are being sarcastic with him, we cannot test the hypothesis "When Josh realizes that peers are being sarcastic, he does not get into a conflict with them." This is because Josh does not have this skill, and thus, we will never be able to observe this converse prediction condition. Given this, hypotheses involving skill deficits are confirmed when assessments confirm that a student's skill or behavior has not been mastered.

Without going into further detail, note that there are six primary approaches, summarized in the acronym *RIOTSS*, that can be used to collect the assessment data in Step 4:

Review (e.g., records, work samples, previous assessments, databases);

Interview (e.g., parents, previous teachers, previous intervention specialists, the student);

Observe (e.g., in the classroom, during assessments or interventions, in related settings);

Test (e.g., group or individual cognitive, achievement, behavioral, or personality assessments);

Survey (e.g., a class of students, a grade level of teachers); and

Self-Report (e.g., when an individual, including the student of concern, provides relevant information without prompting).

While all of these approaches have relative strengths and weaknesses, the ultimate goal is to collect the most reliable and valid data. Critically, this involves both the assessment approaches and the individuals who are selecting and conducting the assessments, and scoring and interpreting their data. For example, while many consider behavioral observations as the most direct, reliable, and valid of assessment approaches, they also could be least reliable and valid—especially, if the person conducting the assessment chooses (perhaps due to bias) the wrong target behaviors, observation approach (e.g., a momentary versus fixed-interval time sampling approach), comparison student, or time of the day or setting for the observation. Indeed, a behavioral observation could be just as biased or inaccurate as a bad interview.

Relatedly, some consider interviews and self-reports as two of the least objective and accurate assessment approaches available, unless a psychometrically valid structured interview is used. And yet, if the interview data and information are reliable and valid, they could be used to accept or reject an RTI^2 hypothesis.

A good assessment, then, begins with a good assessor. And the essence of a good assessor, ultimately, is someone who follows the primary psychometric principles of practice below.

- Assessment approaches should be selected to answer specific assessment questions, not to search for pathology where broad, undefined social, emotional, or behavioral areas are evaluated in the hope of uncovering a problem or a reason for an identified problem.
- When choosing assessment approaches to answer specific assessment questions, the most powerful, research-based approaches—that most directly answer the questions with the least amount of interpolation or interpretation—should be used.
- Assessments should involve the collection of enough data or information from enough people or sources across enough situations and settings such that their data are representative, relevant, and reliable. In saying this, overassessment must be avoided as it increases the potential of a Type 1 error, where conclusions that a problem exists or does not exist are made (a false-positive versus a false-negative conclusion, respectively), when they are inaccurate.
- As much as possible, assessments should be conducted in the settings where the concerns or problems exist, and the people, curricula, materials, and circumstances most relevant to the problem should be reflected in the assessment process to the greatest degree possible.
- In order to be valid, assessments first must be reliable. However, even when valid, assessment is conducted within a context of probabilities. That is, assessment results reflect a probability that two circumstances (as reflected in a hypothesis) are related. Rarely is there a 100% level of assurance that two circumstances or conditions will always coexist or be causally related.

In the end, assessment blends science, insight, experience, objectivity, and implementation integrity. When guided by the principles above, assessment has a high probability of accurately confirming or rejecting the hypotheses generated to explain a social, emotional, or behavioral concern. When accurate hypotheses are confirmed, we are closer to selecting the best intervention approaches so that the concern is resolved and student success is established.

Step 5: Designing Interventions and Writing the Intervention Plans

Once one or more hypotheses have been accepted, the teacher and designated consultant link them directly to relevant instructional or intervention approaches. For confirmed hypotheses in the school, teacher or instructional, or curricular areas, these approaches typically involve effective school, schooling, instructional, or curricular practices—many that are embedded in the PASS or PBSS blueprints, respectively. For confirmed hypotheses in the peer or student areas, the instructional or intervention approaches should be scientifically or research based (to the greatest degree possible) and focused on changing targeted academic or social, emotional, or behavioral outcomes. Note that when there are student-specific physical or physiological, chemical or biochemical, hormonal or genetic, or neurological or cognitive conditions that cannot be treated, the approaches will need to involve one or more of the other domains—most notably, those related to instructional or curricular modifications or accommodations, assistive supports, or compensatory strategies.

When one or more of the seven previously discussed high-hit student-specific hypotheses are confirmed, they link to distinctive instructional or intervention domains. To be more specific (see Figure 8.5), confirmed

- Skill deficit hypotheses (Hypothesis #1 from the section above) generally require approaches that involve skill teaching or instruction;
- Speed of acquisition hypotheses (Hypothesis #2) require approaches that involve increasing students' rate of skill learning and mastery;
- Transfer of training or generalization hypotheses (Hypothesis #3) require approaches that specifically train to facilitate skill transfer;
- Conditions of emotionality hypotheses (Hypothesis #4) require approaches that help students to either prevent or control their emotional reactions—physiologically, affectively, cognitively, and behaviorally—so that they can behaviorally interact or respond effectively even while some emotionality still exists;
- Motivation or performance deficit hypotheses (Hypothesis #5) require approaches that involve motivating students to demonstrate expected or desired social, emotional, or behavioral interactions or responses;
- Inconsistency hypotheses (Hypothesis #6) require approaches that isolate and decrease the inconsistency, while building and strengthening consistency and addressing the prior impact of inconsistency; and

Figure 8.5 Moving From Problem Analysis to Intervention

Goal #1/Skill Deficit:	⟶	**Teach**
Goal #2/Speed of Acquisition:	⟶	**Increase learning rate**
Goal #3/Transfer of Training/ Generalization:	⟶	**Train for the transfer**
Goal #4/Conditions of Emotionality:	⟶	**Prevent/control emotionality**
Goal #5/Motivation/ Performance Deficit:	⟶	**Motivate**
Goal #6/Inconsistency:	⟶	**Decrease inconsistency**
Goal #7/Special Situation:	⟶	**Resolve situation/target social, emotional, or behavioral skills**

Source: Project ACHIEVE Press. Dr. Howie Knoff (author).

- Special situation hypotheses (Hypothesis #7) involve preventing or resolving the setting, peer, or student-related situation, or its social, emotional, or behavioral impact, to the greatest degree possible.

While more specific instructional and intervention approaches are presented in Chapter 9, it must be recognized that virtually all of these approaches are implemented in one or more Instructional Environments somewhere (e.g., a general, special, or alternative education classroom). Thus, while these approaches are developed to directly address student-specific issues (student variables), they still involve teachers or other adults (teacher or instructional variables) and instructional or intervention approaches or treatments (curricular variables) that are applied to or with targeted students. This principle is reflected when linking the results of the problem analysis step with the seven high-hit student intervention areas (see Table 8.2).

The Academic or Behavioral Intervention Plan. Once all of the instructional or intervention approaches are chosen, an intervention plan should be written before the implementation process begins. This is to ensure that a number of important prerequisite actions are taken before formal implementation:

- Any needed parental, RTI^2, or administrative involvement or approvals are received, and any needed staff or student commitments are secured.
- All relevant evidence-based interventions have been researched, reviewed, and selected.
- All desired consultations with other experts, as needed, have occurred.

- The intervention planning and prioritization process has been completed in a deliberate and decisive way.
- Any required resources are obtained, and any implementation training is provided.
- The student (and, perhaps, peer group) are briefed or trained on the intervention.
- The classroom teacher, consultant, and significant others are all in agreement as to the intervention goals, steps, timelines, evaluations, and outcomes.

Table 8.2 Connecting Instructional or Intervention Approaches With Examples Within the Seven High-Hit Reasons for Students' Social, Emotional, or Behavioral Challenges

Identified Problem	Problem Analysis: Most Likely Instructional Environment Reasons for the Identified Problem	Target: Instructional or Intervention Approach
Problem #1. Skill Deficit Problem	Student component: Student has not been taught the skills, or has a history of absenteeism or excessive school and family moves	Likely approach: Repeating initial instruction
	Student is not attending or understanding during instruction, or has a specific within-person challenge that is impeding learning	Student-specific intervention to address the attention or student-specific circumstances or instructional modification or accommodation
	Teacher or instruction: Teacher is not teaching the skills or behaviors effectively or modifying or differentiating them effectively for the student	Likely approach: Teacher consultation focusing on more effective instruction or ways to modify or differentiate instruction for the student
	Curriculum: There is no skills instruction in the curriculum or instructional guidebook, or it is not well-matched to the needs or learning styles of the student	Likely approach: Improved curriculum selection, differentiation, or modification; adding the skills instruction to the curriculum
Problem #2. Speed of Acquisition Problem	Student Component: Student is not attending or understanding during instruction or has a specific within-person challenge that is impeding learning	Likely approach: Student-specific intervention to address the attentional or student-specific circumstances or instructional modification or accommodation

(Text continued on p. 213)

Identified Problem	Problem Analysis: Most Likely Instructional Environment Reasons for the Identified Problem	Target: Instructional or Intervention Approach
	There may be no problem here— that is, the student may be learning and mastering skills as quickly as he or she can	No intervention needed or possible
	Teacher or instruction: Teacher is not teaching the skills or behaviors effectively or modifying or differentiating them effectively for the student	Likely approach: Teacher consultation focusing on more effective instruction, or ways to modify or differentiate instruction for the student
	Curriculum: The curriculum does not provide sufficient pacing, is pacing the instruction too quickly, or is not well-matched to the needs or learning styles of the student	Likely approach: Adjusted curricular pacing, improved curriculum selection, differentiation, or modification
Problem #3. Transfer of Training or Generalization Problem	Student component: Student has not been taught how to transfer the initial skill instruction to applied situations or settings, or has missed this due to a history of absenteeism or excessive school and family moves	Likely approach: Including transfer of training instruction or repeating previous transfer of training instruction
	Student is not attending or understanding during instruction, has a specific within-person challenge that is impeding learning, does not independently recognize situations or settings where skills should be transferred, or does not cognitively understand when to apply or transfer skills	Student-specific intervention to address the attentional or student-specific circumstances or instructional modification or accommodation If the student does not have the cognitive understanding relative to the skills, there may be no student-specific intervention or teacher accommodation needed
	Teacher or instruction: Teacher is not teaching the transfer of training skills or behaviors effectively or modifying or differentiating them effectively for the student	Likely approach: Teacher consultation focusing on more effective instruction, or ways to modify or differentiate instruction for the student

(Continued)

Table 8.2   (Continued)

Identified Problem	Problem Analysis: Most Likely Instructional Environment Reasons for the Identified Problem	Target: Instructional or Intervention Approach
	Curriculum: There is no transfer of training instruction in the curriculum or instructional guidebook, or the recommended instruction is not well-matched to the needs or learning styles of the student	Likely approach: Improved curriculum selection, differentiation, or modification; adding the transfer of training instruction to the curriculum
Problem #4. Conditions of Emotionality Problem	Student component: Student has a biological or physiological condition or circumstance that is affecting his or her emotional control	Likely approach: Biological or physiological intervention or emotional control instruction that occurs outside of the classroom
	Student has not been taught how to control his or her emotionality during skill instruction or how to transfer the emotional control instruction to applied situations or settings or has missed this due to a history of absenteeism or excessive school and family moves	Including emotional control instruction or repeating previous emotional control and transfer of this training instruction
	Student is not attending or understanding during emotional control instruction, does not independently recognize situations or settings where these skills should be used, or does not cognitively understand when to apply or transfer skills	Student-specific intervention to address the attentional problems, or instructional modification or accommodation. If the student does not have the cognitive understanding relative to the skills, there may be no student-specific intervention or teacher accommodation needed
	Teacher or instruction: Teacher is not teaching the emotional control skills or process effectively or modifying or differentiating them effectively for the student	Likely approach: Teacher consultation focusing on more effective instruction or ways to modify or differentiate instruction for the student

Identified Problem	Problem Analysis: Most Likely Instructional Environment Reasons for the Identified Problem	Target: Instructional or Intervention Approach
	Curriculum: There is no emotional control instruction in the curriculum or instructional guidebook, or the recommended instruction is not well-matched to the needs or learning styles of the student	Likely approach: Improved curriculum selection, differentiation, or modification; adding the transfer of training instruction to the curriculum
Problem #5. Motivational or Performance Deficit Problem	Student component: Student is not motivated to demonstrate already-learned skills or behaviors	Likely approach: Motivational intervention (using either incentives or consequences) selected from the Behavioral Matrix (from the incentives and reward or classroom-based consequences boxes, respectively—see Figure 4.2 on page 80)
	Student is not motivated due to competing incentives and consequences—for example, between the teacher and the peer group	Motivational intervention that differentially weights the respective incentives and consequences or that changes the messages from and motivations of the peer group
	Teacher or instruction: Teacher has not identified meaningful incentives or consequences for the student, has not communicated them to the student, is not using them effectively or consistently, or is not holding the student accountable for appropriate behavior after inappropriate behavior has been demonstrated	Likely approach: Teacher consultation focusing on how to plan and accomplish these activities or tasks
	Curriculum: Largely not applicable here	Likely Approach: Largely not applicable here

(Continued)

Table 8.2 (Continued)

Identified Problem	Problem Analysis: Most Likely Instructional Environment Reasons for the Identified Problem	Target: Instructional or Intervention Approach
Problem #6. Inconsistency Problem	Student component: Student has entered the classroom and its skill or behavioral instruction having already experienced inconsistency that is causing, for example, learning, transfer of training, motivational, or other gaps	Likely approach: History of inconsistency needs to be functionally assessed, and instructional or intervention approaches—at the instruction, transfer of training, or motivational levels—need to be consistently implemented for a time that exceeds the original levels of inconsistency
	Teacher or instruction: The teacher may be demonstrating inconsistency relative to skill instruction, prompting, transfer of training, the delivery of incentives or consequences, holding the student accountable across time, settings, circumstances, or situations	Likely approach: Inconsistency needs to be functionally assessed and teacher consultation provided focusing on the specific areas of inconsistency
	Curriculum: The instructional curriculum may not have any or sufficient approaches to facilitate or maintain instructional consistency in it, or its scope and sequence or curricular materials may be causing inconsistent instruction	Likely approach: Improved curriculum selection or modification; adding needed elements of instructional consistency to the curriculum
Problem #7. Special Situations Problem	Student component: The special situation area (e.g., one or more common school areas; teasing, taunting, bullying, harassment, hazing, physical aggression; or a student-specific home, community, or other situation or issue) needs to be identified and analyzed; and the presence of a student-specific learning, transfer of training, motivational, or other gap is identified	Likely approach: Instructional or intervention approaches—at the instruction, transfer of training, or motivational levels—need to be applied and implemented in the identified special situation area

Identified Problem	*Problem Analysis: Most Likely Instructional Environment Reasons for the Identified Problem*	*Target: Instructional or Intervention Approach*
	Teacher or instruction: Teacher is not teaching the skills or behaviors for the special situation area or application effectively or modifying/differentiating them effectively for the student	Likely approach: Teacher consultation focusing on more effective instruction, or ways to modify or differentiate instruction for the student
	Curriculum: There is no skills instruction in the curriculum or instructional guidebook for the special situation area or application, or it is not well-matched to the needs or learning styles of the student	Likely approach: Improved curriculum selection, differentiation, or modification; adding the skills instruction to the curriculum

The practice of writing a formal intervention plan prior to implementation occurs in most medical settings. Indeed, when complex or multifaceted interventions are needed in a hospital, a plan is written prior to treatment so that the medical, nursing, rehabilitation, dietary, social work, and other departments are all coordinated for the benefit of the patient and the amelioration of the medical problem. More important is the fact that we don't want to undermine and lose the best and most powerful instructional or intervention approaches for a student because, for example, they were under-resourced, implemented inappropriately or inconsistently, or not implemented for a long or intense enough period of time.

Relative to the plan itself, effective intervention plans identify (a) the academic or behavioral goals or targets that will resolve or improve the student issues of concern; (b) the evidence-based instructional or intervention methods or approaches that will be used; (c) the people needed to directly or indirectly help implement or support the intervention process; (d) other needed financial, material, training, or technological resources; (e) the sequence of activities needed to fully implement the intervention from start to finish; (f) how implementation and treatment integrity and student (and other) outcomes will be formatively and summatively evaluated; (g) what short-term success will look like and how it will be formatively evaluated; and (h) what long-term success, related to the plan's explicit goals or outcomes, will look like, and how it will be summatively evaluated. Once the plan has been written and approved, and once the resources needed to implement the plan have been acquired, it is ready to be executed.

Step 6: Implementing the Intervention
Plan and Process

In order to be most successful, interventions must be (a) acceptable and realistic, (b) able to produce meaningful and needed results, (c) taught to teachers and students—as appropriate and relevant—before implementation, (d) implemented as empirically designed and with integrity and appropriate levels of intensity, and (e) useful for other students who are at risk or struggling in the classroom but have not, as yet, been identified for the RTI² process.

Relative to (c), students should be taught all facets of a social, emotional, or behavioral intervention prior to its implementation. This is comparable to what effective teachers do when they introduce a well-designed academic lesson or intervention to their students. More specifically, teachers or specialists who are implementing a strategic or intensive behavioral intervention need to discuss, teach, and practice the following with their students:

- The reason for, goals, and outcomes of the intervention;
- How the intervention will be presented, and what is expected of them (e.g., in terms of engagement, participation, response, and relevant practice);
- How they will receive feedback and what incentives or benefits are available;
- How the intervention will be evaluated (or how its progress will be monitored) for success and what success will look like at different points in time;
- How the intervention can be used in the classroom independently by the student; and
- Why the intervention will be successful in that the materials and techniques have been specially selected to maximize the student's success.

Involving Other Students in Intervention Implementation. As noted above, when preparing an intervention plan, a decision is made as to whether other at-risk or struggling students, who have not yet been identified for the RTI² process, might benefit from one or more of the planned interventions. This is an important step in the RTI² process because some interventions, especially those that focus on teaching, practicing, and reinforcing specific academic or behavioral skills, can help other, at-risk students, thereby preventing their need for more intensive future interventions. This strategy also gives classroom teachers the opportunity to impact more students at one time, to implement more classwide rather than individualized approaches, and to see how specific interventions affect different types of students with separate but related needs.

Step 7: Formative and Summative Evaluations of the Outcomes

The formative and summative evaluations for particular interventions are identified during Steps 5 and 6 of the RTI^2 process, and they have their roots in the assessment and hypothesis-testing activities in Step 4. Nonetheless, formative and summative evaluations are so important to determining the success of an intervention program that they require a step of their own.

While focused on determining the impact and success of those interventions directly targeting the initial student concerns, formative and summative evaluations also look more broadly at the entire intervention process. Indeed, formative and summative evaluations should address virtually every aspect of the intervention plan:

- The selection and training of individuals who will directly or indirectly help implement or support the intervention process
- The acquisition and use of financial, material, technological, or other needed resources
- The specificity and quality of the implementation sequence and timelines identified for the interventions
- The integrity of the intervention implementation and evaluation process
- The effectiveness of the interventions and their impact on desired or targeted student (and other) goals and outcomes
- The time, cost, and resource efficiency of the interventions
- The quality of caring, communication, collaboration, consultation, consistency, and commitment among those working on the case
- The satisfaction of students, staff, parents, and others relative to the entire process

While all of these areas are important, successfully attaining desired student outcomes clearly is the most important outcome. At the same time, if some of the other outcomes above are not present or attained, the student-focused outcomes often are not realized.

SUMMARY

Clearly, the data-based, functional assessment problem-solving process is essential to effectively identify, develop, execute, and evaluate the instructional or intervention approaches needed by students with social, emotional, or behavioral challenges. While the RTI^2 problem-solving process may seem complex, it becomes more fluid and automatic with practice and experience. At the same time, many of our most challenging students, themselves, are complex. Clearly, we need to make sure that every instructional or intervention approach needed by a student is strategically selected and effectively implemented. We cannot be satisfied with implementing just any intervention. In summary, we believe that every time we do an intervention with a challenging student, and it doesn't work, we potentially make the student more resistant to the next intervention. Given this belief, we need to do high-probability-of-success interventions with our students. To accomplish this, we need to use sound, systematic, and skillful problem identification, problem analysis, intervention, and evaluation processes.

NOTE

1. This chapter was adapted from Knoff, H. M. (2009). *Implementing Response-to-Intervention at the school, district, and state levels: Functional assessment, data-based problem solving, and evidence-based academic and behavioral interventions.* Little Rock, AR: Project ACHIEVE Press; and Knoff, H. M. (2010). The RTI^2 data-based, functional assessment, problem-solving process. In H. M. Knoff & C. Dyer, *RTI^2—Response to Instruction and Intervention: Implementing successful academic and behavioral intervention systems* (pp. 51–114). Rexford, NY: International Center for Leadership in Education.

9

Behavioral Interventions for Students With Strategic and Intensive Needs[1]

> Success is the sum of small efforts, repeated day in and day out.
>
> Robert Collier

PBSS Implementation Case Study:
NOVA Academy Alternative School, St. Bernard Parish, Louisiana

Project ACHIEVE began its relationship with the New Opportunities and Values for Achievement (NOVA) Academy in April 2002 when three of its support staff attended a four-day national Project ACHIEVE Training of Trainers sponsored by the U.S. Department of Health & Human Service's Center for Substance Abuse Prevention. NOVA Academy was the middle and high school level alternative school for the St. Bernard Parish School District, a largely poor and rural school system to the east of New Orleans, directly on the Gulf of Mexico near the Mississippi River.

Project ACHIEVE training with the NOVA staff began on-site in July 2002 and continued through August 2009.

Project ACHIEVE was implemented at NOVA to improve the school's school-wide discipline and positive behavioral support system and interventions. Especially important to this effort was the schoolwide implementation of the Stop & Think Social Skills Program, the enhancement of the school's accountability system of incentives and consequences, and the reinforcement of staff consistency relative to student and other personal and professional interactions. Unfortunately, Hurricane Katrina devastated St. Bernard Parish and its school system in September of 2009. NOVA was closed for a number of years after the Hurricane Katrina disaster.

While discipline referrals to the director decreased and attendance increased significantly during Project ACHIEVE's involvement with the school, the results below focus on the staff members' perceptions of NOVA's improved discipline, behavior management, and school safety. This is especially important because alternative school staff must feel safe within their school and confident that the school can address the intervention and crisis management needs of their students in order for them to provide the full benefits of the school's program to their students.

Staff Perceptions of School Climate and Behavior Management

NOVA staff completed the 58-item Scale of Effective School Discipline and Safety (see Chapter 10) before Project ACHIEVE began its implementation and then again after most of the program had been implemented. Staff members rated each item along a five-point scale from 1—Excellent to 5—Poor. Results were gathered from the five factors of this scale:

- Staff members believed that teachers' effective classroom management skills remained largely stable from pretest to posttest. Staff members' ratings on this factor averaged 2.80 (on the 5-point scale) at pretest and 2.91 at posttest.
- Staff members believed that students' positive interactions and respectful behavior significantly improved from pretest to posttest. Staff ratings on this factor averaged 3.93 (on the 5-point scale) at pretest and 1.75 at posttest.
- Staff members believed that the school's administrators and staff members collectively improved their ability to hold students accountable for their behavior from pretest to posttest. Staff members' ratings on this factor averaged 3.18 (on the 5-point scale) at pretest and 2.72 at posttest.
- Staff members believed that their contributions to a positive school climate remained largely stable from pretest to posttest. Staff ratings on this factor averaged 2.62 (on the 5-point scale) at pretest and 2.83 at posttest.
- Staff members believed that school safety and security, relative to staff, students, and school grounds, got somewhat safer from pretest to posttest. Staff ratings on this factor averaged 2.81 (on the 5-point scale) at pretest and 2.56 at posttest.

Staff Perceptions of Improvements in School Climate and Behavior Management

On the Scale of Effective School Discipline and Safety, NOVA staff rated certain items as significantly improved from pretest to posttest:

- It is safe to work in this school after students are dismissed.
- This school is a safe and secure place to work during the normal school day.
- Students are frequently rewarded or praised by faculty and staff members for following school rules.
- Administrators support teachers in dealing with student discipline matters.
- Students are taught the school rules.
- Administrators enforce the student rules consistently and equitably.
- Teachers have high and reasonable behavioral expectations of their students.
- Teachers at this school are
  - relaxed,
  - innovative,
  - open to change, and
  - optimistic.
- Teachers at this school willingly accept responsibility for every student in the building.
- Teachers at this school are willing to give the student peer group some responsibility for monitoring its own members.
- Teachers at this school use data (academic or behavioral) to make decisions about students.
- Teachers at this school involve students in identifying and selecting appropriate incentives and reinforcements for acceptable behavior.

INTRODUCTION

Throughout this book, we have emphasized that a school's Positive Behavioral Support System (PBSS) exists within the context of its effective school and schooling processes, and that activities related to academics, instruction, and achievement are interdependent with those focusing on discipline, behavior management, and self-management. Within Project ACHIEVE's evidence-based PBSS, the scientific principles supporting students' social, emotional, and behavioral competency have been discussed within the context of seven primary goals and six functional components. In addition, we have emphasized that some students still exhibit different intensities of inappropriate feelings, thoughts, beliefs, attributions, behaviors, and interactions, even when they are in classrooms with effective instruction and classroom management, and that we need multi-tiered systems of services, supports, strategies, and programs to address all students' social, emotional, and behavioral needs (see Chapter 1 for all).

This chapter continues the problem-solving presentation begun in Chapter 8, concentrating on the student-focused strategic and intensive instructional and intervention approaches that are identified toward the end of the problem analysis phase of the data-based functional assessment process. These approaches are linked to the seven high-hit reasons why some students do not demonstrate effective social, emotional, or behavioral self-management skills or interactions; or exhibit significant inappropriate emotions or behaviors. Because more specialized behavioral or mental health consultants (e.g., school psychologists, counselors, applied behavior specialists, special educators) typically work with classroom teachers to identify these approaches, and because they involve more strategic implementation, even in the general education classroom, they are categorized as (at least) Tier 2 interventions. As emphasized in Chapter 1, the tiers of the multi-tiered model reflect the intensity of the services and supports needed by students—not where specific interventions are delivered (e.g., inside or outside a general education classroom) or how many students (e.g., all, some, or few) are receiving them. The seven high-hit reasons involve four skill-related areas—skill deficits (Hypothesis #1), speed of acquisition (Hypothesis #2), transfer of training or generalization (Hypothesis #3), conditions of emotionality (Hypothesis #4); and three additional areas that relate to accountability, consistency, and special situations—motivation or performance deficits (Hypothesis #5), inconsistency (Hypothesis #6), and special situations (Hypothesis #7), respectively.

STRATEGIC STUDENT SUPPORT AT THE TIER 2 LEVEL

The Tier 2 instructional or intervention approaches in this section are organized using the evidence-based skill, accountability, consistency, and special situations PBSS components discussed throughout this book (see Figure 9.1). The right side of Figure 9.1 outlines representative instructional or intervention approaches in the four skill areas, the accountability and motivation and the special situations areas above (consistency is embedded in all of these approaches). The left side of the figure reminds us that all strategic instructional or intervention approaches are linked to the data-based problem-solving process and, especially, the problem analysis phase.

Peer or Adult Mentoring and Mediation. The first Tier 2 approaches involve peer or adult mentoring or meditational programs. In general, mentoring programs connect students with a valued peer or adult who provides training, guidance, motivation, or consistency within the context of a close and positive relationship. Mediation programs are a bit more

| Figure 9.1 | Tier 2: Strategic Intervention Services for Some Students |

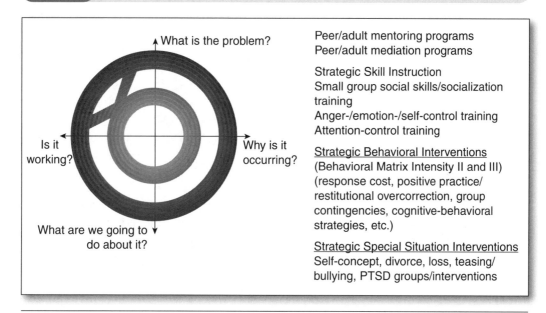

What is the problem?

Is it working?

Why is it occurring?

What are we going to do about it?

Peer/adult mentoring programs
Peer/adult mediation programs

Strategic Skill Instruction
Small group social skills/socialization training
Anger-/emotion-/self-control training
Attention-control training

Strategic Behavioral Interventions
(Behavioral Matrix Intensity II and III)
(response cost, positive practice/
restitutional overcorrection, group
contingencies, cognitive-behavioral
strategies, etc.)

Strategic Special Situation Interventions
Self-concept, divorce, loss, teasing/
bullying, PTSD groups/interventions

Source: Project ACHIEVE Press. Dr. Howie Knoff (author).

specialized as they help individual or groups of students address (usually) emotional feelings or situations by teaching or applying interpersonal relationship, social problem-solving, conflict resolution, or emotional coping skills or behaviors. Relative to students with Tier 2 needs, peer mentors or mediators may be older students who go to their school or other schools in the district. Adult mentors may be instructional or support staff employed in these students' schools, volunteers who come to the school, or volunteers who meet with the students after school or out of school. Adult mediators tend to be counselors, behavioral intervention consultants or specialists, other health or mental health support staff, or administrators who work in these students' schools. Critically, peer and adult mentors and mediators need to be strategically matched to the students they are serving; they must to be trained, supervised, and evaluated; and they must be held accountable to specific student and service goals and outcomes.

A Mentoring Program Example. Check and Connect (Christenson & Carroll, 1999; Sinclair, Hurley, Christenson, Thurlow, & Evelo, 2002) is an evidence-based example of a mentoring program that originally targeted dropout prevention by connecting At-Risk students with an in-school mentor who would check on them, often on a daily basis. During the check component, for example, the mentor and student meet a few minutes before and after each school day to informally discuss (and, hopefully, reinforce) the student's school and classroom attendance and behavior, academic and social engagement, and academic and behavioral progress. As part of the connect component, the mentor develops a positive, supportive, and ongoing in-school relationship with the student, providing a level of individualized attention, reinforcement, and validation, and a potential sounding board when challenging situations arise. The formal Check and Connect program has been used primarily at the middle and high school levels. A Check and Connect adaptation at the elementary school level is being used to similarly target students' academic and behavioral progress while fostering mentor-mentee relationships and social-emotional connections within the school.

Selecting a Mediation Program. There are a number of informal and formal mediation programs available. When selecting a mediation program, it is recommended that a district or school form a task force to review the science of mediation, the goals and desired outcomes of the approach in general, and at least three evidence- or research-based programs (Johnson & Johnson, 1996; Office of Juvenile Justice and Delinquency Prevention, 1998). By integrating these three activities, the task force hopefully will choose the best program with the highest probability of meeting the school's or district's student needs and organizational goals. It is strongly recommended that districts with multiple elementary or secondary schools choose a single mediation program at one or both levels. This facilitates more consistent staff and student communication across schools, increases service delivery success in districts with high student mobility, and eases the transition process when students move from elementary to secondary school levels.

STRATEGIC SKILLS INSTRUCTION AND INTERVENTION AT THE TIER 2 LEVEL

Based on functional assessments and analyses, when students are not demonstrating social, emotional, or behavioral skills due to skill deficits (Hypothesis #1), a slower speed of skill acquisition or mastery (Hypothesis #2), difficulties with generalizing or transferring skill training (Hypothesis #3), or due to conditions of emotionality (Hypothesis #4), more specialized instruction is needed. At the Tier 2 level, this often involves (a) a behavioral intervention specialist or mental health practitioner (e.g., counselor, school psychologist, school social worker) (b) working with a student (or a group of students with similar or related strategic needs) and (c) consulting with classroom teachers in specific, targeted skill and outcome areas. A different Tier 2 approach to accomplish the same goal might involve (a) a general classroom teacher

(b) working with students from one class or pooled from across an entire grade level (c) in a targeted skill group (d) that is learning or practicing specific, targeted skills at a special time each week.

In most cases, students in targeted skills groups will continue to participate in the ongoing Tier 1 skills instruction that is occurring in the regular classroom. In fact, the skills group students actually may be learning and practicing the same skills as in their regular classroom—just in a more adapted way to facilitate their learning, mastery, and application. For example, for skill deficit students, the instruction may need to occur more individually, with greater specificity, and with more modification of the curriculum. For speed of acquisition students, more positive practice opportunities may be necessary along with specific accommodations within the learning environment. For transfer of training or generalization students, previously learned skills may need to be directly taught in different settings, with different people, and under different circumstances so that students more automatically generalize their skill use when actually needed. Finally, for conditions of emotionality students, the smaller and more individualized skills group setting allows students to engage in supervised role-plays that simulate the specific emotional conditions or circumstances where students have difficulty executing certain skills. This increases the appropriate transfer and use of these skills in actual situations where different levels of emotionality exist.

Targeted skills groups also can strategically sequence the instruction and reinforcement of certain skills. For example, the skill deficit and speed of acquisition students may learn specific skills in their skills groups three to four weeks before the same skills are introduced and taught for the first time in the general education classroom. Transfer of training or generalization and conditions of emotionality students may receive additional, targeted practice of specific skills in their skills groups one or two weeks after they were initially taught in the general education classroom. In this way, students who need more individualized or intensive advanced or follow-up instruction, respectively, in order to benefit from regular classroom instruction, receive it as well as students who need more positive practice opportunities in order to master their skills.

Finally, based on student-specific functional assessments, there will be times when behavior intervention specialists or mental health practitioners will need to teach students more specialized skills in such areas as attention and attention control, socialization, or anger-, emotion-, or self-control (see Kazdin, 2001; Kerr & Nelson, 2010; Knoff, 2010c; Sprick & Garrison, 2008). While this instruction typically occurs on an individual or small group level in the specialist's office, it also needs to be systematically transferred to the general education classroom to ensure skill generalization and self-management. To facilitate the transfer, teachers need to know the essential elements of these more specialized approaches so that they can monitor, prompt, reinforce, or correct students' use of these skills in real-life situations. Relative to accountability and consistency, students also need to know—perhaps as the result of a transfer of training meeting with the student, teacher, and behavioral specialist—that their teachers know about and how to use these more specialized approaches.

In summary, while teaching or instruction is the primary approach needed to address the four skill-related reasons for students' difficulties, the results of the problem analysis help to determine who, when, where, how often, and how long the instruction will occur (see again Chapter 8, Table 8.2). While a Tier 2 level of instructional intensity was described above, schools that do not have behavioral or mental health specialists, or specialists with the expertise in these strategic instructional approaches, may need to involve out-of-school consultants, experts, or service providers. Whether the need for outside experts changes the designation of these services to Tier 3 services is not the compelling issue. The compelling issue is that the targeted students receive the needed instructional services so that, with the involvement of the general education staff, they can be successful in the classroom, school, and elsewhere.

Two Examples of a Skills-Based Intervention. Critically, some students with skills-based difficulties need specific, targeted cognitive or behavioral interventions rather than the instructional approaches reviewed above. For example, these students may need stimulus control or prompting and cuing interventions where they are taught to respond to specific verbal, nonverbal, setting, or situational prompts, cues, conditions, or other stimuli that are connected (conditioned) to appropriate cognitive-behavioral social interactions, emotional reactions, or behavioral responses (see Kazdin, 2001; Kerr & Nelson, 2010). At times, these interventions also focus on decreasing inappropriate interactions, reactions, or behaviors and replacing them with appropriate ones.

Typically, stimulus control prompts involve verbal or nonverbal prompts between a teacher (or other adult) and a target student that trigger a desired skill or behavior. Examples of teacher or adult prompts might include a specific word or phrase agreed upon by the teacher and the student, a finger snap or shoulder touch, a nonverbal gesture, or putting a cue card on a student's desk. Through behavioral training, these external prompts are transferred to situational or environmental cues (e.g., being in a specific setting, seeing a peer's specific behavioral response, feeling a specific emotion) that trigger the target student's appropriate social, emotional, or behavioral response. The training involves skills-based instruction—using the teach, model, role-play, performance feedback, and transfer of training steps previously discussed—that links or conditions specific responses to specific triggers. Eventually, the goal is for students to recognize and respond to specific conditions or stimuli with appropriate, self-managed behavior. Significantly, when teachers learn and use the same prompts or cues used when students are taught this intervention by behavioral intervention or mental health specialists at the Tier 2 level, then the generalization or transfer of training process typically occurs more quickly, naturally, and successfully for the students involved.

Still other students need skill-based interventions to facilitate their emotional control. For example, one key to emotional control is a student's ability to maintain a physiological level of control so that he or she still can make appropriate decisions and choices. When students are emotionally out of control, this is actually a physiological state where the concentration of adrenaline in the bloodstream passes a specific threshold. In order to maintain self- or physiological control, some students need to learn how to relax in the face of emotional conditions or triggers (thereby keeping the adrenaline concentration below their thresholds). While many students learn how to do this as part of Tier 1 social, emotional, and behavioral training at school or at home, some students need more strategic training (Tier 2) with this, and others need more intensive therapy and even drug intervention (Tier 3). Whether at the Tier 2 or 3 levels, some students need progressive muscle relaxation training or therapy (Lopata, Nida, & Marable, 2006). This clinical intervention typically is implemented by trained mental health practitioners, and it helps students to immediately return to or maintain a physiological state of emotional stability and control. Requiring parental permission, this intervention often is integrated into a broader intervention program for a student that includes specific goals, expected outcomes, and ongoing progress monitoring.

Another behavioral intervention in this area is called thought stopping. This cognitive-behavioral intervention helps some students to disrupt or stop certain thoughts or feelings that lead to a physiological loss of self-control. Once again, this is a clinical intervention that is implemented by trained mental health practitioners.

STRATEGIC MOTIVATIONAL INTERVENTIONS AT THE TIER 2 LEVEL

Some student challenges occur not because of skill deficits, but because of motivational or performance deficits. In contrast with the can't do students discussed immediately above, the Tier 2 interventions in this section focus on the Hypothesis #5: accountability won't do students. Once again, depending on the functional assessment results, the goals of some of the interventions here are to increase appropriate student social interactions, emotional reactions, or behavioral responses, while other interventions are designed to also or exclusively decrease inappropriate student behavior so that it can be replaced with appropriate behavior.

Interventions to Increase Student Behavior. While there are a number of Tier 2 motivational interventions that increase appropriate student behavior, we will briefly describe two: (a) positive reinforcement and (b) group contingencies (see Kazdin, 2001; Kerr & Nelson, 2010; Knoff, 2010c). While these approaches are often used in general education classrooms (even at the Tier 1 level), it is crucial to implement them in ways consistent with their underlying scientific principles. Indeed, when implementation ignores or violates the underlying science that makes these interventions work, or when implementers do not know how to modify these interventions as different levels of appropriate behavior emerge, the interventions will not work, their success will not be sustained, or student dependency—rather than self-management—will result. Thus, these are interventions that require training, supervision, and experience, whether used at a Tier 1 or Tier 2 level. Unless trained and experienced, general education teachers need the consultative support of a behavioral or mental health specialist when considering and implementing these interventions.

Positive Reinforcement. The goal of this intervention is to motivate and increase positive, prosocial, and other appropriate or replacement behaviors. Positive reinforcement involves a tangible or intangible, extrinsic or intrinsic thought, event, or object that follows or is contingent on a behavior, and that helps to increase the frequency, duration, or intensity of that behavior over a period of time or in the future. Reinforcers occur naturally or are delivered, by design, in schedules of reinforcement. The basic reinforcement schedules focus on how many desired behaviors have occurred (frequency), how long they have occurred (duration), or how quickly they have occurred (latency). For behaviors that are measured by their frequency, reinforcement may be scheduled after every behavior (a continuous schedule), consistently after a specific number of behaviors (a fixed ratio schedule), or after a specific average number of behaviors (a variable ratio schedule). Comparably, for behaviors measured by duration, reinforcement may be scheduled continuously, or in either fixed or variable interval formats. For behaviors related to latency, reinforcement typically is scheduled by how quickly the target behavior occurs with a goal of reinforcing progressively quicker behavioral responses over time.

Positive reinforcement interventions are used for students who are not motivated to demonstrate appropriate behavior or who are motivated to demonstrate inappropriate behavior. In order for positive reinforcement to work, the student needs to have mastered the desired or expected behavior, and the positive (extrinsic or intrinsic) reinforcement, or incentives, need to be meaningful and powerful to the student. Over time and by strategically varying the reinforcement schedules, positive reinforcement interventions should result in more automatic or self-motivated behavior. At the Tier 2 level especially, it is the strategic use and progression of different incentives and reinforcement schedules—matched to a specific student's behavioral and reinforcement history, status, current conditions, and needs—that most determine the success of this intervention.

In order to implement this intervention effectively, the teacher, behavioral consultant or specialist, or mental health practitioner should follow a specific sequence of steps:

1. Identify the behavioral goal or target specifically (i.e., the appropriate behavior to demonstrate or the inappropriate behavior to stop or eliminate).

2. Validate that the student has mastered the target behavior in multiple settings and under multiple conditions (if mastery has not occurred, instruction is needed).

3. Discuss and identify with the student a range of possible meaningful and powerful tangible (actual or symbolic or exchangeable) and intangible, extrinsic and intrinsic reinforcers.

4. Choose the reinforcer to be received for the target behavior, determine the reinforcement schedule, and specify how the reinforcer will be delivered.

5. Role-play to mastery the behavior and reinforcement process (student/teacher).

6. Develop a monitoring and evaluation protocol.

7. Transfer the training, implement, and apply.

8. Evaluate, thin, and move to self-management.

Ultimately, the keys to using positive reinforcement at the Tier 2 level include the following: (a) ensure that the student has the ability to perform the expected behavior; (b) teach and practice the intervention with the student; (c) set up the reinforcement contingencies at the beginning so that the student has almost a 100% chance of success; (d) pair any extrinsic reinforcement with social, intrinsic, and self-reinforcement over time; (e) thin the reinforcement schedule as the student consistently demonstrates the expected behavior and earns the reinforcement over time, so that more behavior is expected for less reinforcement; and (f) move the intervention from reinforcement to self-management.

A token economy is a specific positive reinforcement approach where students earn points, checkmarks, or tokens for demonstrating a wide range of appropriate classroom behaviors—using the points at different times to purchase backup reinforcers. When this method is used comprehensively, students earn points throughout the day for virtually every classroom and school activity. When it is used more selectively, specific behaviors are targeted to receive a certain number of points each day.

As discussed above, the goal of this approach is to initially shape and establish the target behaviors, and then to change the reinforcement contingencies so that more appropriate behavior is occurring for fewer, and eventually no, tokens. Four basic steps are needed to implement a token economy: identifying the target behaviors, selecting the tokens and the backup reinforcers, establishing the ratio of exchange and the procedures for when and how tokens will be dispensed and exchanged, and field testing the system. Token economies have been successful with a wide range of students, including those with specific disabilities and social, emotional, and behavioral concerns. This approach is one of the most positive strategic motivational interventions at the Tier 2 PBSS level.

Group Contingencies: Independent, Dependent, and Interdependent. The goal of this intervention is to motivate and increase positive, prosocial, and other appropriate or replacement target student behavior, or to decrease mild to moderate inappropriate behavior by involving the peer group in specific reinforcement contingencies. This intervention is especially helpful when the peer group is not reinforcing appropriate target student behavior, or when it is reinforcing inappropriate behavior.

Group contingency approaches typically begin as the target student and other students, for example in a classroom, are organized into groups or teams (cf. McKissick, Hawkins, Lentz, Hailley, & McGuire, 2010). Three different reinforcement contingencies can be used: (a) where all students must meet a set level of behavioral expectations in order for each student to individually earn an identified reinforcement (independent group contingencies); (b) where one or more target students must meet a set level of behavioral expectations in order for the group to earn an identified reinforcement (dependent group contingencies); or (c) where every student in the group must meet a set level of behavioral expectations in order for the group to earn an identified reinforcement (interdependent group contingencies).

In order to implement this intervention effectively, the teacher, behavioral consultant or specialist, or mental health practitioner should follow a specific sequence of steps:

1. Strategically select the groups for the goals of the intervention. When organizing the entire classroom into groups, change the student makeup of the groups at least every marking period.

2. Identify the behavioral goal or target specifically (i.e., the appropriate behavior to demonstrate or the inappropriate behavior to stop or eliminate).

3. Validate that the target students have mastered the target behavior in multiple settings and under multiple conditions (if mastery has not occurred, instruction is needed).

4. Discuss and identify with the group a range of possible meaningful and powerful tangible (actual or symbolic or exchangeable) and intangible, extrinsic and intrinsic reinforcers.

5. Choose the reinforcer to be received for the target behavior, determine the reinforcement schedule, and specify how the reinforcer will be delivered.

6. Role-play to mastery the behavior and reinforcement process (relative to the student, group, and teacher).

7. Prior to the implementation of this intervention, teach students in the group how to
   a. appropriately talk about and motivate each other's appropriate behavior,
   b. monitor and provide appropriate positive and corrective prompts and feedback to each other and the target student, and
   c. deal with and effectively discuss or respond to times when they reach or do not reach a criterion for reinforcement.

8. Develop a monitoring and evaluation protocol.

9. Transfer the training, implement, and apply.

10. Evaluate, thin, and fade reinforcement contingencies, and move to group self-management.

While group contingencies effectively use the peer group to motivate appropriate behavior and eliminate inappropriate behavior for one or more target students, it is essential to ensure that the target students can successfully demonstrate the expected skills or behaviors and that the reinforcers and contingencies truly are motivating. This is because the target student's failure to earn the reinforcement, especially within the dependent and interdependent group contingencies, can result in excessive levels of peer pressure, negative feedback, or scapegoating by the peer group (which has not received the reinforcement) toward the target student (who has lost the reinforcement for the peers). When used strategically and successfully, group contingencies not only use the natural impact of the peer group on individual student behavior but also can enhance the social status of the targeted student and potentially decrease peer teasing, taunting, bullying, harassment, hazing, and physical aggression.

The Good Behavior Game is a specific, evidence-based interdependent group contingency intervention that dates back to 1969 (Barrish, Saunders, & Wolf, 1969). It has a number of variations, and it has been used in kindergarten through high school classrooms (e.g., Donaldson, Vollmer, Krous, Downs, & Berard, 2011; Kleinman & Saigh, 2011; Leflot, van Lier, Onghena, & Colpin, 2010; Tingstrom, Sterling-Turner, & Wilczynski, 2006), as well as in certain common areas of the school (libraries and cafeteria; McCurdy, Lannie, & Barnabas, 2009). Most typically, the Good Behavior Game involves separating a classroom into teams of four to five members (some applications have separated the class into halves), identifying the appropriate behavior expected and the inappropriate behavior that will be counted against the team, and specifying the time period involved (from 30 minutes to a week or a month). Some studies using this intervention identified the criteria for earning a reinforcer ahead of time; others kept the criterion secret—revealing it only at the end of the specified time period. Some studies had the teams competing against each other; others had the teams competing against a criterion where all of the teams could earn a reinforcer. Overall, the Good Behavior Game has demonstrated a high degree of success in increasing on-task behavior, hand raising and waiting to be called on, keeping hands and feet to oneself, in-seat behavior, and following directions the first time, and in decreasing talking-out, talking without permission, and out-of-seat and aggressive behavior.

Interventions to Decrease Inappropriate Student Behavior. Clearly, some students exhibit significantly high, prolonged, intense, unpredictable, or resistant inappropriate behavior that requires a Tier 2 level of intervention. When students are choosing to demonstrate this behavior, motivational and accountability-focused interventions are among the needed strategies. A number of these strategies are described briefly below. They include (a) differential reinforcement of low, other, incompatible, or alternative behavior; (b) extinction or planned ignoring; (c) overcorrection—positive practice and restitutional; (d) response cost; and (e) time-out (see Kazdin, 2001; Kerr & Nelson, 2010; Knoff, 2010c).

Differential Reinforcement of Low (DRL), Other (DRO), Incompatible (DRI), or Alternative (DRA) Behavior. These interventions use different reinforcement approaches and schedules to directly or indirectly decrease or eliminate inappropriate student behavior, while increasing and solidifying appropriate behavior (cf. LeGray, Dufrene, Sterling-Turner, Olmi, & Bellone, 2010). Among the least aversive or intrusive interventions that target inappropriate student behavior, there are three primary differential reinforcement approaches: (a) one, where the student receives positive reinforcement for engaging in progressively lower rates of an inappropriate target behavior to the point where it is eliminated (DRL); (b) a second, where the student receives positive reinforcement for engaging in one or more appropriate behaviors such that he or she substitutes and eliminates an inappropriate target behavior (DRO); and (c) a final one, where the student receives positive reinforcement for engaging in behaviors that either are incompatible with or cannot coexist with (that is, they are alternative to) an inappropriate target behavior (DRI, DRA). As with any positive reinforcement approach, powerful and meaningful (to the student) reinforcers are needed to motivate the student to change his or her inappropriate behavior, and the student's inappropriate behavior must be conscious and intentional.

In order to implement this intervention effectively, the teacher, behavioral consultant or specialist, or mental health practitioner should follow a specific sequence of steps:

1. Identify the inappropriate behavior that needs to be decreased or eliminated.

2. Identify the replacement or other (DRO) behavior, the replacement behavior (DRL), or the incompatible or alternative (DRI, DRA) behavior desired, depending on the differential reinforcement strategy chosen for use.

3. Collect the baseline data relative to the frequency (duration, intensity) of the inappropriate behavior and of the replacement or appropriate behavior.

4. Validate that the student has mastered the replacement or appropriate behavior in multiple settings or under multiple conditions (if mastery has not occurred, instruction is needed).

5. Identify the differential reinforcement approach and criterion (based on frequency, duration, intensity) to be used:
   a. DRO: How much other behavior, in the absence of the inappropriate behavior, will be reinforced?
   b. DRL: What low rate of behavior over what time period will be reinforced?
   c. DRI/DRA: How much incompatible or alternative behavior, in the absence of the inappropriate behavior, will be reinforced?

6. Discuss and identify with the student a range of possible meaningful and powerful tangible (actual or symbolic or exchangeable) and intangible, extrinsic and intrinsic reinforcers.

7. Develop a monitoring and evaluation protocol.

8. Teach and discuss with the student
   a. the behavioral expectations,
   b. the incentives and consequences and their delivery, and
   c. the charting or evaluation system.

9. Role-play to mastery and provide application practice sessions in the setting where the behavior generally occurs.

10. Transfer the training, implement, and apply.

11. Evaluate, thin, and move to self-management.

DRO is generally successful when there are a high number of appropriate other behaviors to reinforce (e.g., reinforcing on-task and work completion behavior to decrease off-task peer socialization). DRL can be used to address inappropriate behaviors whose frequency needs to be decreased but not necessarily eliminated (e.g., making jokes or adding unnecessary stories when answering content questions). In addition, DRL requires adults and students in the intervention setting to be able to tolerate a certain amount of continuing inappropriate behavior (even though it is systematically decreasing), thereby sustaining this intervention over the time period needed for success. Finally, relative to DRI/DRA, the best incompatible or alternative behaviors are ones that the student already does and that cannot physically coexist with or be performed at the same time as an inappropriate behavior (e.g., reinforcing in-seat behavior to decrease classroom wandering). In addition, these incompatible or alternative behaviors must be socially acceptable and not embarrassing to the student.

Conversely, these four differential reinforcement approaches are not good options (a) if the target student demonstrates a number of inappropriate behaviors that cannot be ignored or tolerated; (b) if these inappropriate behaviors happen so frequently that they might inadvertently be reinforced as another behavior; (c) if appropriate reinforcers cannot be found or used; or (d) if teacher-delivered reinforcers are not more powerful than other reinforcers (e.g., peer attention) that are maintaining the inappropriate behavior.

Extinction or Planned Ignoring. This intervention often is considered when a student is using inappropriate behavior (e.g., persistent whining, complaining, clinging, calling or blurting out in class) to attract adult or peer attention. When he or she receives this attention (usually from adults in the form of a corrective response or a mild consequence—see Intensity I and II on the Behavioral Matrix in Chapter 4, page 80, Figure 4.2), the inappropriate behavior is reinforced and may actually be strengthened. Thus, with a goal of eliminating the inappropriate behavior and replacing it with appropriate behavior, this intervention involves the planned ignoring of the student's inappropriate behavior. At the same time, the appropriate behavior of others near the student is positively reinforced, and appropriate behavior by the target student is progressively shaped and reinforced in direct contrast to the inappropriate behavior. Over time, the inappropriate behavior is eliminated (or extinguished), but this often occurs after (a) a significant increase in the student's inappropriate behavior during the first part of the intervention (typically during the first five to eight days), and (b) the teacher (and the peer group) have consistently ignored the student's continuing inappropriate attention-seeking behavior past the time frame in which this behavior was inappropriately attended to and reinforced in the past.

In order to implement this intervention effectively, the teacher, behavioral consultant or specialist, or mental health practitioner should follow a specific sequence of steps:

1. Identify the target behaviors to decrease specifically.

2. Identify the replacement behaviors to increase or reinforce specifically.

3. Validate that the student has mastered the replacement behavior in the settings and conditions desired.

4. Teach the student

   a. the language (how you ignore or reinforce),
   b. the behavioral expectations, and
   c. the incentives and consequences (connect with the Behavioral Matrix).

5. Role-play to mastery.

6. Identify the short-term and long-term definitions of success.

7. Identify the student's history of inconsistency and the time frame needed for short-term and long-term success.

8. Train the peer group (how to ignore or reinforce the student; their incentives and consequences).

9. Develop a monitoring and evaluation protocol.

10. Transfer the training, implement, and apply.

11. Evaluate and move to self-management.

As with most behavioral interventions, the goals, outcomes, contingencies, and interactions embedded in the planned ignoring approach need to be discussed by the teacher, student (and his or her parents), peer group (separately), and behavioral consultant or specialist or mental health practitioner. The student needs to understand that escalating inappropriate behavior will still be ignored, but it may involve an additional consequence or an office discipline referral (depending on the intensity of the escalation). Critically, if a primary reason underlying the inappropriate behavior involves the student wanting to be exited from the classroom (e.g., to escape a difficult assignment, to attain some bad boy or girl status within the peer group, to communicate some anger with parents or others) and not for attention, this intervention would not be used. Once again, this reinforces the importance of completing a functional assessment before prematurely moving to an intervention. Given this, and some other factors, the following questions should be asked before considering or implementing this intervention.

Critical Pre-Intervention Questions:

- Can the teacher or class tolerate the initial increase in the frequency or duration of the inappropriate behavior while maintaining the integrity of the intervention?
- Does the student, and the rest of the class (to the degree needed), understand the intervention?
- Are the incentives and consequences meaningful and powerful?
- Is the inappropriate behavior likely to be imitated by others (for attention) and can this be discouraged?
- Is there enough time available to implement the intervention to its desired end?
- Is the teacher or class prepared to respond to any spontaneous recovery of the inappropriate behavior?

Positive Practice and Restitutional Overcorrection. The basic principle underlying overcorrection is that students will decrease or eliminate inappropriate behavior and replace it with appropriate behavior when, after demonstrating an inappropriate target behavior, they are required either (a) to positively practice the appropriate replacement behavior to an excessive degree; or (b) to fix, replace, or remediate—to an excessive degree—the damage or harm caused by the inappropriate behavior. In applying these principles through research and practice, these two related intervention approaches have demonstrated success with such problems as teasing, refusing to share materials, physical aggression, disruptive behavior, and self-injurious behavior. They also are designed, in general, to reduce other mild through severe inappropriate behaviors that have not responded to more positive behavioral interventions (including vandalism, sexual or other harassment, bullying). Critically, depending on the number, duration, or degree of overcorrection used with a student, these interventions can be aversive in nature. Thus, they typically need parent and administrative permission before being used as well as supervision by a trained psychologist, behavioral consultant, or mental health practitioner.

In positive practice overcorrection, the student must excessively practice the appropriate or replacement behavior that is the opposite of the inappropriate behavior exhibited. This intervention increases the probability of future appropriate behavior (because of the excessive positive practice), and it motivates the student to discontinue the inappropriate behavior in the future (to avoid the need for future overcorrection). Examples of positive practice overcorrections include making a student excessively practice making positive and supportive statements instead of ongoing negative, hurtful, or critical statements; silently walking in the hallway instead of running and screaming; or raising one's hand with mouth closed, instead of blurting out answers.

In restitutional overcorrection, the student must repair, fix, and/or apologize and make amends—far beyond the initial harm, damage, or hurt—for an inappropriate act or action. This intervention holds the student accountable (and then some) for the original offense, helps the student to remember the consequences for specific behaviors, and motivates the student to avoid such consequences in the future, knowing that they will be applied again if the inappropriate behavior is re-exhibited. While the remediation in this intervention is logically connected to a student's inappropriate behavior, once again, this intervention is consciously and strategically implemented as an aversive technique. Examples of restitutional overcorrections include making a student wash all of the desks in a classroom or the bathroom walls in a school for marking up desks or writing graffiti, respectively; performing community service hours working with younger students for earlier incidents of teasing, taunting, or harassing these students; or apologizing to the entire class for an offense to a smaller group of students.

In order to implement this intervention effectively, the teacher, behavioral consultant or specialist, or mental health practitioner should follow a specific sequence of steps:

1. Identify the specific behavior or offense that needs to be decreased or eliminated.

2. Complete a functional assessment of the behavior, including a history of when, where, how often, and with whom the behavior has occurred in the past, while determining why the inappropriate behavior is occurring (e.g., emotional control problems, attention, power or control, revenge, escape, etc.).

3. Determine which overcorrection approach will be used and what replacement behavior (for the positive practice overcorrection approach) or remediation or restorative behavior (for the restitutional overcorrection approach) will be used—along with when, where, how, with whom, and how long the intervention will occur.

4. Develop a monitoring and evaluation protocol.

5. Discuss the entire situation with the student, including the inappropriate behavior, the appropriate behavior that should have occurred, what the overcorrection consequence will be, and how it will be monitored and evaluated.

6. Validate that the student has mastered the skill needed to perform the replacement behavior for the positive practice overcorrection approach, or the physical (and other) capacity to perform the remediation for the restitutional overcorrection approach.

7. Implement and evaluate the intervention.

8. Debrief the situation and intervention again with the student, emphasizing the expected future appropriate behavior as well as the potential consequences for a reoccurrence of the inappropriate behavior.

For both of these interventions, it is important that the overcorrections act not as punishments but as aversive conditions that are logically connected to the original offenses and that motivate the student to make appropriate choices in the future. Once again, it is important that these interventions be linked to the outcomes of a functional assessment. Finally, it is likely that students will resist or refuse to engage in this intervention. This should be anticipated, and responses to this resistance or other contingency plans need to be in place. If, for example, the student begins this intervention and then is allowed to default or discontinue it without being held fully accountable, this inconsistency may again strengthen the student's inappropriate behavior and reinforce his or her success in resisting the process of behavioral change.

Response Cost. This intervention is designed to systematically decrease or eliminate mild to moderate inappropriate behavior by providing a student with a strategically selected number of tokens, points, or coupons that the student loses or must spend whenever he or she exhibits the targeted inappropriate behavior. The explicit goal for the student is to complete a specific period of time where he or she has one or more tokens remaining that can be cashed in for a desired reinforcement. The number of tokens initially given to the student is determined first, by how often the inappropriate behavior is exhibited before the intervention is begun (i.e., the baseline of the behavior) and thereafter, by the number of tokens remaining (i.e., the student's level of success) as the intervention is implemented over time. Thus, as the student exhibits the inappropriate target behavior less and less often (i.e., keeping more and more tokens over time), the teacher decreases the number of tokens such that the inappropriate behavior is systematically decreased and eventually eliminated. This intervention has been useful in decreasing or eliminating such persistent inappropriate behavior as aggression, inappropriate verbalizations, hyperactivity, fire setting, self-injurious behavior, and tantrums. As with any motivational intervention, the student must have the ability to demonstrate the appropriate behavior and must be motivated to earn the positive reinforcement made available.

In order to implement this intervention effectively, the teacher, behavioral consultant or specialist, or mental health practitioner should follow a specific sequence of steps:

1. Identify the specific behavior or offense that needs to be decreased or eliminated while identifying the appropriate behavior that helps the student to avoid performing the inappropriate behavior.

2. Complete a functional assessment of the behavior, including a history of when, where, how often, and with whom the behavior has occurred in the past, while determining why the inappropriate

behavior is occurring (e.g., emotional control problems, attention, power or control, revenge, escape, etc.).

3. Through this functional assessment, determine the baseline frequency of inappropriate behavior across a specific period of time (e.g., per hour, per period, per day).

4. Validate that the target student has mastered the appropriate behaviors that will help him or her to be successful in multiple settings and under multiple conditions of concern (if mastery has not occurred, instruction is needed).

5. Discuss and identify with the student a range of possible meaningful and powerful tangible (actual or symbolic or exchangeable) and intangible, extrinsic and intrinsic reinforcers.

6. Choose the reinforcer to be received for the target behavior, determine the reinforcement schedule, and specify how the reinforcer will be delivered.

7. Role-play to mastery the behavior and reinforcement process (student/teacher), especially focusing on times when the student is unsuccessful and a token needs to be taken away (i.e., the accepting a consequence skill, and the "If you consequate, you must educate" principle).

8. Choose the number of tokens that will be given to the target student and select a time period for implementing the intervention. Initially, the number of tokens should give the student a near 100% probability of success.

9. Develop a monitoring, charting, and evaluation protocol, and explain it to the student.

10. Transfer the training, implement, and apply.

11. When the student has had three successful time periods (e.g., days) where he or she earned the reinforcement, decrease the number of tokens based on both the number of tokens earned during the period of success and the need to maintain the student's success during the first part of the intervention.

12. On a weekly (or more frequent, as needed) basis, meet with the student to evaluate his or her progress and discuss future targets and reinforcers.

13. Evaluate, thin, and fade the reinforcement contingencies over time, and move to student self-management.

In addition to response cost, there are two other variations of this intervention: bonus response cost and the response cost lottery. In the first variation, students can earn bonus tokens when they retain a specific number of tokens during a prescribed period of time. In fact, the number of bonus tokens can be tiered. That is, if students have ten tokens at the beginning of a specified period, they might earn one bonus token if they have three to five tokens left after the period, two bonus tokens if they have six to eight tokens left, and three bonus tokens if they have nine or ten tokens left. By tiering the bonus tokens, there is an additional built-in incentive to demonstrate more appropriate behavior over time, higher levels of appropriate behavior may result, the total number of tokens available can be decreased more quickly over time, and the intervention's complete success and fading can similarly occur more rapidly.

The response cost lottery can be used when a group of students is involved in the intervention. Here, after the prescribed period of time, each student puts his or her remaining tokens into a lottery, which is used to select which students will receive a backup reinforcer. Assuming that students want to enter the largest number of tokens so they have the greatest probability of winning, students should demonstrate higher levels of more appropriate behavior more quickly. This again will result in the teacher being able to decrease the total number of tokens given to the students during the forthcoming time periods and a faster level of intervention success overall.

Time-Out. This is a behavioral intervention that is used in most schools—especially at the elementary school level—to the degree that it could be considered a Tier 1 intervention. At the same time, schools rarely implement this scientifically based intervention in a consistent, strategic, and educative fashion, and the implementation typically is not consistent across grade-level teams, much less the entire building. Indeed, very few educators have been formally trained to understand how to apply the underlying scientific, behavioral principles that make the time-out process work or which behavioral problems are most responsive to this intervention. Instead, many use this intervention based on an oral history that has been passed down from one educator to another. For example, many educators believe that a student should stay in the time-out chair for the same number of minutes as his or her age—even though there is no research to support this. In addition, most educators do not have the student positively practice the replacement behavior as he or she is exiting from the time-out chair (thereby holding the student accountable for appropriate, expected behavior). Instead, most teachers let the student return to his or her homeroom chair simply after completing a specified amount of time in the chair.

When used correctly and as scientifically designed (see Knoff, 2007b), time-out effectively discourages inappropriate student behavior, or it serves as a meaningful, powerful, and multilevel consequence if it does occur. In fact, where the time-out occurs extends from the homeroom classroom (Levels 1 and 2), to another teacher's classroom (Level 3), to the principal's office (Level 4) or another designated setting (e.g., in an in-school suspension or responsibility room). At a Level 1 time-out (in the student's homeroom classroom or the setting where the offense occurred), the student stays in the time-out chair for two to three minutes, regardless of age, as long as he or she is behaving appropriately. At a Level 2 time-out (still in the student's homeroom classroom or the setting where the offense occurred), the student receives an additional consequence, because he or she has either acted out while in the Level 1 time-out or demonstrated a more serious original offense than a Level 1 offense.

If students commit an even more serious offense or continue to act out in the Level 2 time-out, they proceed either to a Level 3 or Level 4 time-out. At these levels, additional consequences are applied (e.g., loss of time at recess commensurate with the total time in time-out, the need to write a behavioral contract, a parent call or conference), and when they are ready to return to their classroom, they must backward chain down the time-out levels—for example, from Level 4 to Level 3 to Level 2/1 and back to their homeroom seat. During this backward chaining process, they need to demonstrate two to three minutes of appropriate time-out behavior in each level's timeout chair.

Significantly, this time-out process represents an educative intervention. Its goal is to reinforce and motivate future appropriate behavior—not to punish already-exhibited inappropriate behavior. For students needing Tier 2 intervention, it is the consistent and educative use of time-out and the ongoing collection of progress monitoring data that demonstrate a student's (hopefully) positive response to the intervention through a decrease of inappropriate and increase of appropriate behavior over time. Critically, when a time-out process is used unscientifically, idiosyncratically, or inconsistently by individual teachers (or administrators) across a school, these practices diminish the potential to change student behavior, and they may reinforce or strengthen some students' inappropriate behavior over time.

In order to implement this intervention effectively, the teacher, behavioral consultant or specialist, or mental health practitioner should follow a specific sequence of steps:

1. Identify the specific behavior or offense that needs to be decreased or eliminated while identifying the appropriate behavior that helps the student to avoid performing the inappropriate behavior.

2. Complete a functional assessment of the behavior, including a history of when, where, how often, and with whom the behavior has occurred in the past, while determining why the inappropriate

behavior is occurring (e.g., emotional control problems, attention, power or control, revenge, escape, etc.).

3. Through this functional assessment, determine the baseline frequency of inappropriate behavior across a specific period of time (e.g., per hour, per period, per day).

4. Validate that the target student has mastered the appropriate behaviors that will help him or her to be successful in multiple settings and under multiple conditions of concern (if mastery has not occurred, instruction is needed).

5. Ensure that the intervention's prerequisites exist: a grade-level Behavioral Matrix, a designated time-out chair, a coordinated Level 3 time-out teacher and a Level 4 location, and the time-out log and tracking pass for the Level 3 and 4 time-out.

6. Teach and role-play to mastery the time-out process with the student (and classroom); ensure that he or she understands the language, expectations, contingencies, and teacher, student, and administrator responses.

7. Develop a monitoring, charting, and evaluation protocol (using the time-out log and tracking pass), and explain it to the student.

8. Transfer the training, implement, and apply.

9. On a weekly (or more frequent, as needed) basis, meet with the student to evaluate his or her progress and discuss future targets and reinforcers.

10. Continue to evaluate the intervention over time.

To summarize, when time-out is used (inappropriately) as a punishment, it often is implemented in a retributional manner (i.e., an eye for an eye, a tooth for a tooth), the student is sentenced to a certain (or progressive) amount of time (sometimes not specified) in the time-out chair, the sentenced time typically extends beyond the teachable moment, and when the time is served, the student returns to his or her seat without needing to perform any positive practice actions relative to accountability. Using the recommended educative process, the student is taught and understands the entire procedure before the intervention is implemented, the time-out is delivered in a predictable and matter-of-fact manner when needed, the student is required to positively practice the replacement behavior after the time-out is served, and the student knows that continued inappropriate behavior in time-out will result in additional consequences (and levels of time-out). All of this focuses the responsibility for inappropriate and appropriate behavior on the student. Moreover, when implemented with integrity and intensity, a student's response to this intervention provides a good test of his or her potential for, or resistance to, change.

STRATEGIC SPECIAL SITUATION INTERVENTIONS AT THE TIER 2 LEVEL

The last set of Tier 2 interventions (see Figure 9.1 once again) involve strategic interventions needed by individual students to address their social, emotional, or behavioral actions, reactions, or interactions (a) in the common areas of a school; (b) due to or involving their own teasing, taunting, bullying, harassment, hazing, and physical aggression; or (c) that relate to current or past life events or crises, traumatic experiences, or physical or emotional conditions (e.g., parents' divorce, the loss of a parent or sibling, being homeless or adopted, physical or sexual abuse, having a disability). Many of these interventions involve cognitive-behavioral interventions or therapies that are delivered by mental health practitioners (usually psychologists) in individual or small group settings as part of a more comprehensive treatment plan. The goal of these interventions is to change the social, emotional, or behavioral feelings, thoughts, beliefs, expectations, attributions, reactions, and interactions that relate to a student's inappropriate or maladaptive response to one or more of the three special situations described above. These interventions might also focus on helping students to resolve issues related to anger or emotional control, loss or grief, need for control or feelings of powerlessness, social inhibition or low self-esteem, anxiety or fear, or posttraumatic stress syndrome.

As the functional analysis results link to a student's intervention needs and desired outcomes, it is essential to note that putting students into counseling or cognitive-behavioral therapy groups or sending them to a mental health professional is not the intervention. The intervention is the strategy, intervention, therapy, or program that is delivered in the group or by the professional. Said another way, we should not be satisfied that a student is going to counseling. We should be satisfied only if the student is going to the right professional, who is delivering the right intervention, resulting in the right outcomes, achieved in the right amount of time, cost, and effort.

Moreover, given the devastating impact of some especially traumatic special situations, the right outcomes will need to be defined in realistic, short-term goals that are individualized and tailored to the student, the history, and the prevailing dynamics of the situation. Recognizing that change often is relative and personal relative to special situations, a student's ability to emotionally and cognitively cope with a past trauma often is prerequisite to the behavioral changes that others want to see. At the same time, when designed and implemented with integrity by the right mental health professional, some strategic special situation interventions are so successful that the student's emotional coping and control skills generalize quickly, resulting in high levels of social and behavioral competence, self-management, and independence.

SOCIAL, EMOTIONAL, AND BEHAVIORAL INSTRUCTION/INTERVENTION AT THE TIER 3 LEVEL

Tier 3 instructional or intervention supports, strategies, services, or programs are used with students (a) who do not respond to Tier 2 interventions (that are implemented with integrity and monitored over time through the collection of reliable and valid data), or (b) who demonstrate a significant, immediate need for intensive intervention. In the latter case, Tier 2 processes and interventions may be expedited, reduced, or even bypassed, as determined by the building-level School Prevention, Review, and Intervention Team (SPRINT). Once identified, Tier 3 instruction and intervention involve the most specialized, intensive, or multifaceted approaches. Typically, they involve multidisciplinary experts, consultants, supports, and resources and integrated home, school, community collaboration and treatment. While not a requirement or criterion for Tier 3 services, if a disability is present and is significantly contributing to or causing a student's difficulties, the instructional or intervention services, supports, strategies, or programs could be delivered as part of a 504 plan or an Individual Education Plan (IEP).

Relative to students with Tier 3 social, emotional, or behavioral needs, part of a comprehensive instructional or intervention plan will involve one or more of the services outlined in Figure 9.2. Critically, it must be noted that some or many of these students will still be in their general education classes receiving Tier 1 and Tier 2, in addition to Tier 3, services. Once again, this is determined by the functional assessments, the students' specific needs, and where the school or district categorizes its different services or supports across their three-tiered continuum. Most important is the fact that Tier 3 services generally focus on individual student strategies and services, and that classroom teachers and other school staff, while not primarily responsible for implementing these services, need to understand their implications and applications relative to instructional processes in their classrooms. Indeed, while some elements of Tier 3 services need to be confidential, teachers and other school staff still need to know (a) how the information learned during the problem analysis and student-focused intervention steps relate to a student's classroom and school functioning and success and (b) how to prompt or use the social, emotional, or behavioral approaches being taught, for example, in therapy so that they transfer

Figure 9.2 Tier 3 Crisis Management and Intensive Need Services

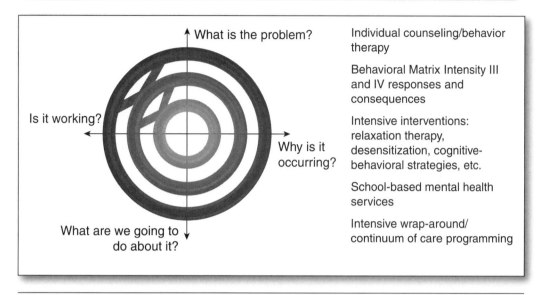

Source: Project ACHIEVE Press. Dr. Howie Knoff (author).

to classroom and other school settings. While a detailed discussion of the services in Figure 9.2 is beyond the scope of this book, a brief description does follow below.

When counseling or social, emotional, or behavioral therapy is needed by a student at the Tier 3 level, there are critical questions for the SPRINT team to ask and answer:

- What are the social, emotional, or behavioral goals, skills, or changes needed by the student?
- What evidence- or research-based therapeutic strategies or techniques will most effectively help the student (and others) to attain these goals?
- Who is the best therapist within the school, district, or community to provide the therapy?

As noted earlier, sending a student to counseling or therapy—or to a counselor or psychologist—is not the intervention. The intervention is the delivery of the right therapeutic strategies or techniques during the counseling or psychotherapy sessions that are needed by a student to facilitate change. And so, as in Figure 9.2, examples of the right strategies typically are the cognitive-behavioral or behavior therapy strategies like progressive muscle relaxation therapy, thought stopping, systematic desensitization, cognitive-control strategies, or aggression replacement therapy.

In order to find the right therapist to meet a student's needs, schools and their SPRINT teams need to know the training backgrounds, skills, areas of licensure or certification, and areas of expertise and specialization of all of the mental health practitioners (counselors, psychologists, social workers, etc.) in their school and district and in the surrounding districts and communities. This helps them to quickly and accurately match a student and his or her needs to the right therapist who can deliver the right interventions.

All of this needs to occur so that a coordinated and integrated home-school-community treatment plan is executed. That is, it is essential that all of the professionals working with a student at the Tier 3 level are working in complementary—rather than in isolated—ways. When coordination does not occur, there is a distinct potential that the community and school services might end up being either redundant or even contradictory. None of this benefits the student or those working with that student. When school-based mental health services are provided, this potential can be minimized because everyone is working in the same setting. When school-linked mental health services are provided in the community and away from the school, time and distance can create problems that are only minimized by high and conscious levels of communication and coordination by both school and agency or community personnel.

Finally, some students require such intensive crisis-oriented Tier 3 services that these need to be coordinated and delivered more in the community than at the school. These wrap-around services involve extensive community mental health services to students and their families, and these services often are strengthened by other family supports, services, and caregivers. In extreme cases, these services involve psychiatric inpatient care. When this is needed, the school often is not directly responsible or involved in the social, emotional, or behavioral components of the student's care. At the same time, the school may still be responsible to ensure that the student is receiving appropriate academic instruction and services, and it needs to have a transition plan in place for when the student is ready to return.

SUMMARY

This chapter focuses on the social, emotional, and behavioral instructional or intervention supports, strategies, services, or programs that some students need when they are not responding to effective classroom instruction or management. Integrating the evidence-based PBSS blueprint with the data-based, functional assessment problem-solving process, Tier 2 instructional and intervention approaches were emphasized. Reinforcing the importance of using a problem solving-consultation-intervention service delivery model, it is critical that all schools have professional (related services and other) support staff who are trained and available to consult with classroom teachers to help deliver the Tier 2 supports and programs. In addition, all districts should know what mental health professionals and agencies are available in their communities to provide the intensive interventions and wrap-around services needed by some students at the Tier 3 level of need.

A number of important principles have been infused throughout the discussions on social, emotional, and behavioral intervention in this chapter:

1. You can't motivate a student out of a skill deficit.

2. Students do not learn behavioral interventions through discovery learning.

3. Students must be taught, must learn, and must master most behavioral interventions prior to implementation, at least in the following areas:
   a. the language (verbal, nonverbal, symbolic),
   b. the expectations, and
   c. the contingencies.

4. Most skill instruction involves cognitive scripts that translate into behavioral skills.

5. Skill mastery occurs when students can demonstrate their skills under conditions of emotionality.

6. Most emotional behavior is conditioned.

7. Incentives and consequences only motivate when they are meaningful and powerful to the student.

8. Sometimes, incentives and consequences compete with each other—especially when students triangulate with adults and peers.

9. When inconsistency is the underlying reason for a student's difficulties, the intervention must be implemented past the history of inconsistency.

10. Intervention plans should be completely written, planned, resourced, and trained for prior to implementation.

11. Interventions must be implemented with the appropriate integrity and the needed intensity.

12. The severity of a student's behavioral problem does not necessarily predict the intensity of the intervention.

In the end, the ultimate success of the social, emotional, and behavioral PBSS side of a multi-tiered initiative is its ability (a) to strengthen students' prosocial skills, resilience, and protective factors; (b) to prevent student problems from occurring or reoccurring; and (c) to address the strategic and intensive needs of challenging, unresponsive, and unsuccessful students. This is not an impossible task—but it sometimes is a complex task. Indeed, it takes vision, commitment, coordination, funding, and personnel management. Many of the blueprints needed for success have been discussed in this chapter and book. At this point, the blueprints need planning, resources, training, personnel, and action in order to take shape. Only then can the blueprints move from vision to reality.

NOTE

1. This chapter was adapted from Knoff, H. M. (2009). *Implementing Response-to-Intervention at the school, district, and state levels: Functional assessment, data-based problem solving, and evidence-based academic and behavioral interventions.* Little Rock, AR: Project ACHIEVE Press; and has sections taken directly from Knoff, H. M. (2010). Social, emotional, and behavioral interventions. In H. M. Knoff & C. Dyer, *RTI²—Response to Instruction and Intervention: Implementing successful academic and behavioral intervention systems* (pp. 255–314). Rexford, NY: International Center for Leadership in Education.

10

Evaluating and Sustaining PBSS Outcomes[1]

The most important thing is to never stop questioning.

Albert Einstein

PBSS Implementation Case Study: The Arkansas Department of Education's State Improvement Grant, Little Rock, Arkansas

On October 1, 2003, the Arkansas Department of Education, Special Education Unit (ADE-SEU) began implementing a five-year $1.6 million per year State Improvement Grant (SIG) awarded to it from the U.S. Department of Education, Office of Special Education Programs (OSEP). The overall purpose of the SIG was to enhance student outcomes by improving their literacy, social-behavioral, and self-management skills through the implementation of

- Research-based literacy instruction strategies and interventions for At-Risk, under-achieving, and unsuccessful elementary through high school students (Goal 1)
- Schoolwide discipline, behavior management, and school safety (Positive Behavioral Support) strategies and interventions, at the elementary school

levels, for all students, especially those demonstrating significant behavioral or mental health challenges (Goal 2)

- Effective recruitment, professional development, and retention strategies so that every school in Arkansas would have fully qualified staff capable of using research-based strategies to teach students across the general education through special education continuum (Goal 3)

SIG Goal 2 focused on implementing Positive Behavioral Support Systems (PBSS) using the Project ACHIEVE blueprint in schools and districts across Arkansas as well as piloting school-based mental health partnerships between select school and community mental health center grantees over a four-year period. Selected statewide outcomes included the following:

- District Leadership Teams (DLT) from 95 Arkansas school districts attended a series of five PBSS trainings on different facets of Project ACHIEVE's PBSS and Response-to-Instruction and Intervention (RTI^2) approaches. Each DLT included a district-level administrator, elementary school principal, general and special education teachers, and at least one related services professional.
- A cadre of 110 school psychologists and counselors from across the state were parallel-trained in the same PBSS/RTI^2 content areas.
- By the end of the SIG, 40 schools representing 26 school districts were involved in the on-site implementation of the three-year PBSS process. These schools received intensive training in all facets of Project ACHIEVE's PBSS and RTI^2 and School Prevention, Review, and Intervention Team (SPRINT) approaches as well as ongoing on-site consultation and technical assistance from SIG staff. For example, during SIG Year 4, 78 on-site consultations occurred with PBSS schools, along with periodic conference calls, e-mail consultations, and off-site meetings.

Many of the evaluation tools and articulation processes outlined in this chapter were developed or refined during the SIG. Annual evaluation reports were submitted to OSEP, and the final PBSS report documented successes in the areas of strategic planning and organizational development, staff interactions and school climate, behavior management and school safety, student discipline and self-management, and classroom engagement and academic achievement.

INTRODUCTION

School improvement is a continuous process where professional development and capacity-building initiatives, activities that scale up and sustain success, and evaluations that assess short- and long-term outcomes—all at the system, school, staff, and student levels—never end. Similarly, the implementation of schoolwide PBSS is ongoing, facilitated by end-of-year activities that ensure that policies, procedures, practices, and other lessons learned are transferred systematically from one school year to the next.

As introduced in Chapter 1, Project ACHIEVE is a comprehensive pre-school through high school continuous improvement and school effectiveness program whose ultimate goal is to design and implement effective school and schooling processes that maximize the academic and social, emotional, and behavioral progress and achievement of all students. Using a strategic planning, capacity building, professional development, and technical assistance process that helps students, staff, schools, and systems to continuously improve and become independent over time, Project ACHIEVE's PBSS implementation blueprints, procedures, and strategies have been the foundation of most of the effective practices embedded throughout this book. In Chapter 2, a detailed four-year PBSS implementation blueprint was discussed. While some schools may implement it in more or less than four years, the blueprint, nonetheless, can be used to evaluate a school's progress in implementing essential activities and sustaining critical outcomes.

Consistent with the data management, evaluation, and accountability component in Project ACHIEVE's effective schools blueprint (see Chapter 1), this chapter discusses some instruments, tools, and approaches that exemplify different ways to evaluate the success of a PBSS initiative across its primary goals and objectives. It also addresses a number of systematic ways to transfer, or articulate, PBSS successes from year to year, so that every school year begins, on the first day of school, at full throttle.

REVISITING THE PRIMARY PBSS GOALS AND CONNECTING THEM TO EVALUATION

The ultimate PBSS goal of facilitating students' social, emotional, and behavioral competency and self-management has been infused and reinforced throughout this book, along with a number of complementary student, staff, and school goals (see Chapter 1). Integrating all of these goals together, a comprehensive PBSS focuses on these schoolwide outcomes:

- High levels of academic engagement and academic achievement for all students
- High levels of effective interpersonal, social problem-solving, conflict prevention and resolution, and emotional coping skills and behaviors by all students
- High levels of critical thinking, reasoning, and problem-solving skills by all staff and students
- High levels of teacher confidence relative to instruction, classroom management, and helping students with academic or behavior problems
- Consistently effective instruction and classroom management across all teachers and instructional support staff

- Low levels of classroom discipline problems, discipline problems that need to involve the principal, or discipline problems that require student suspensions or expulsions
- High levels of parent and community support and involvement in consistently facilitating, motivating, and holding students accountable for self-management

In order to evaluate the degree to which these goals are accomplished, formative (short-term) and summative (long-term, and at completion) evaluations should be integrated into all PBSS planning, preparation, and implementation processes. These evaluations help schools and staff to know when intervention decisions and plans are ready to be made and written, when strategic instructional or intervention approaches are ready to be formally implemented, whether interventions have been implemented with integrity and intensity, and whether short- and long-term goals and outcomes have been accomplished. As is evident from the PBSS goals above, evaluations occur at system, school, staff, student, and home or community levels, and at the prevention, strategic intervention, and intensive need or crisis management levels.

In the data-based, functional assessment problem-solving presentation in Chapter 8, the six ways to collect data were introduced through the acronym *RIOTSS*. Critically, these data collection approaches are the same whether they are used during functional assessment or formative and summative evaluation. In fact, the only difference involves the questions that the data help to answer. During functional assessment, the question is, "Why are the problems we are concerned about occurring?" During evaluation, the question is, "Are our interventions to solve the problems working (formative evaluation), and have they successfully resolved the problem (summative evaluation)?" Thus, formative and summative evaluations utilize data that can be collected in the following ways:

Review (e.g., records, work samples, planned assessments, databases);

Interview (e.g., parents, current teachers, current intervention specialists, the student);

Observe (e.g., in the classroom, during assessments or interventions, in related settings);

Test (e.g., group or individual cognitive, achievement, behavioral, or personality assessments);

Survey (e.g., a class of students, a grade level of teachers); and

Self-Report (e.g., when an individual, including the student of concern, provides relevant information without prompting).

As noted in Chapter 8, all of these approaches have relative strengths and weaknesses depending on the focus of the evaluations. Ultimately, what is needed are reliable and valid data that are collected from multiple settings and sources, using different instruments and approaches.

EVALUATING PBSS OUTCOMES: A SAMPLE OF NEWER TOOLS AND APPROACHES

Addressing some of the PBSS outcomes cited above, a number of newer evaluation tools and approaches are presented below. They include tools that provide information on (a) staff interactions and collaborations across the school, (b) staff perceptions and beliefs relative to student management and school safety, (c) office discipline referrals, (d) discipline-related classroom observations of students and staff, and (e) staff expertise relative to implementing different behavioral interventions. This is not an exhaustive list as other PBSS evaluation tools and resources are available from other sources and should be considered and reviewed.

Evaluating Perceptions of Staff Interactions and School Cohesion. In order to accomplish any of the seven PBSS goals above, the staff interactions across a school (and district) need to be collaborative, trusting, mission-driven, and based on a shared commitment to the students, the school, the community, and each other. *The Scale of Staff Interactions and School Cohesion* (Knoff, 2007g; SSISC) is a 25-item survey that measures these areas by asking the staff in a school to "rate these items based on the last two months of interactions across the staff in your school (or the last two months of the last school year, if it is now the beginning of a new school year)." Each item is rated along a five-point scale from 1—Excellent to 5—Poor (see Table 10.1), and the data can be pooled and analyzed (a) for the entire staff, (b) by different grade or instructional levels of staff, (c) by instructional versus administrative versus support staff, or (d) in some other functional way.

It is critical to note that this survey measures staff members' perceptions and the interactions that they have observed (or heard about) over the previous two months. These perceptions may not be accurate, and individual staff members' observations may not be representative of those across the entire staff and school. At the same time, for many staff members, perception is reality, and their behavior and interactions with colleagues are often driven by their beliefs, attitudes, attributions, and relationships. When staff members complete and receive the results from this tool, they have one assessment of their collective perceptions of the quality of the interactions and cohesion across the school. This feedback may initiate discussions and a greater understanding as to how these affect grade level, committee, and school culture, climate, and success, and what needs to be

Table 10.1	Scale of Staff Interactions and School Cohesion: Factor Analyzed Items and Rating Scale Used to Complete Items

Factor 1: Staff Understanding of the School's Mission and Expectations

1. Understanding of the school's mission
2. Understanding of their roles in the school
3. Understanding of expected instructional outcomes within the school
7. Impact of the school's mission on staff's instructional activities

Factor 2: Staff Collaboration and Cohesion

17. Staff communication
18. Staff collaboration
20. Staff celebration of accomplishments
19. Staff commitment
21. Commitment to shared or collaborative leadership
22. Focus on progress and the growth and development of people
4. Commitment to staff cohesion, support, and positive morale
5. Interpersonal effectiveness

Factor 3: Effective Staff Practices and Interactions

12. Focus on problem solving, not blaming
10. Willing to take risks/thrives on new challenges
11. Focus on outcomes, principles, and doing the right thing
13. Focus on skills and outcomes, not on hierarchies, power, and positions
14. Create options for mutual (win-win) gain
15. Ability to appropriately delay, at times, some decisions so that more options can be developed
9. Respond to and use timelines or deadlines effectively
24. Willing to model behavior
25. Able to deal with problems and problematic colleagues
8. Self- or independently motivated and enthusiastic
16. Insist on using data and objective criteria to make decisions
23. Able to set high, yet realistic, expectations
6. Commitment to a staff or building agenda, not a personal agenda

1	2	3	4	5
Excellent	Very Good	Good	Fair	Poor

Source: Project ACHIEVE Press. Dr. Howie Knoff (author).

done to improve and strengthen positive and prosocial staff-to-staff, staff-to-student, and student-to-student interactions.

The SSISC was developed by asking school staff from across the country to complete a longer, draft version of the survey. After a series of statistical analyses, three factors were identified for the resulting 25 items: Factor 1: Staff Understanding of the School's Mission and Expectations (4 items); Factor 2: Staff Collaboration and Cohesion (8 items); and Factor 3: Effective Staff Practices and Interactions (13 items). Factor 1 evaluates staff members' perceptions of their colleagues' understanding of the school's mission, and how the mission impacts instruction and instructional outcomes. Factor 2 evaluates staff members' perceptions of their colleagues' interpersonal and interprofessional collaboration and their commitment to professional growth, shared leadership, and staff cohesion. Factor 3 evaluates staff members' perceptions of their colleagues' focus on shared organizational goals, their commitment to contributing to and supporting others in meeting these goals, and their use of problem solving to identify new or needed changes when things are not going well.

From an evaluation perspective, a pre-post-post approach is typically the best way to use the SSISC. For example, the SSISC can be administered to a school's staff in early May as a pre-intervention assessment either (a) to help determine areas of concern relative to staff interactions or school cohesion, so that these can be analyzed over the summer and addressed at the beginning of the new school year; or (b) to measure the current status of the school in these areas, so that the impact of a schoolwide PBSS implemented during the next school year can be formally evaluated (pretest or baseline administration Year 1). After the implementation of needed interventions or a schoolwide PBSS during the next school year, the SSISC could be administered again as a posttest in either December or May (intervention implementation posttest Year 1), and the results would be compared and contrasted with the pretest or baseline assessment completed the May before. Finally, the SSISC could be administered in December or May of the next school year (intervention implementation post-test Year 2) and, again, compared and contrasted with the first two administrations to track continued improvement or to identify continuing areas of concern.

Whenever the SSISC is administered, feedback typically is provided using three formats: (a) summary scores and a discussion of the three SSISC factors; (b) individual item scores and a discussion of specific SSISC items that reflect school strengths and other items that reflect areas in need of further analysis, staff attention, or school improvement; and (c) a combination of (a) and (b) above. Strategically, SSISC feedback is given in a way that best facilitates the staff members' understanding of the results and the planning and intervention processes that may need to follow. This feedback might occur initially with the school's leadership team, then in small grade- or instruction-level teams, then followed up by a broader discussion at a faculty meeting. Or the feedback might occur initially at a faculty meeting, allowing the staff to then decide what needs to be done (if anything) to further validate the results, to address the concerns, and to sustain the strengths.

Regardless of the meeting format or discussion and planning sequence, a written report of the SSISC results often is helpful. This report could be distributed prior to any of the planned meetings as an advanced organizer or after the meetings as a summary of the results presented. It also is important to decide who will present the results and how the school's strengths and weaknesses will be reported. Clearly, there are a number of strategic decisions to make after analyzing and interpreting the SSISC's results. These decisions, and their effective execution, may contribute as much to the productive use of the SSISC as the results themselves.

Evaluating Perceptions of Effective School Discipline and Safety. In order to track the processes that facilitate PBSS success, schools need to periodically survey their staff as to their perceptions and beliefs relative to PBSS implementation and whether they are seeing selected PBSS outcomes. *The Scale of Effective School Discipline and Safety* (Knoff, 2007f; SESDS) is a 58-item survey that helps measure a number of the research- and practice-based PBSS processes discussed throughout this book. Once administered and analyzed, its results provide information about the first six of the seven PBSS goals above. To complete the SESDS, school staff members are asked to "rate the discipline and behavior management statements below on your level of agreement based on your general and specific experiences at your school within the past two months (or based on last year if this question-naire is being completed prior to the beginning of the school year)." Each item is rated along a five-point scale from 1—Strongly Agree to 5—Strongly Disagree (see Table 10.2), and the data are pooled and can be analyzed (a) for the entire staff, (b) by different grade or instructional levels of staff, (c) by instructional versus administrative versus support staff, or (d) in some other functional way. Like the SSISC, the SESDS is a staff perception tool, its results need to be cross validated with other assessments, and all of the information needs to be synthesized into an integrated profile of school strengths, weaknesses, and areas of PBSS concern.

The SESDS was developed by asking school staff from across the country to complete a longer, draft version of the survey. After a series of statistical analyses, five factors were identified for the resulting 58 items: Factor 1: Teachers' Effective Classroom Management Skills (24 items); Factor 2: Students' Positive Behavioral Interactions and Respect (11 items); Factor 3: Holding Students Accountable for Their Behavior: Administration and Staff (7 items); Factor 4: Teachers' Contribution to a Positive School Climate (9 items); and Factor 5: School Safety and Security: Staff, Students, and School Grounds (7 items). Factor 1 evaluates staff members' perceptions of their colleagues' social, emotional, and behavioral expecta-tions of students—especially when they are in their classrooms; to what degree they consistently teach the behaviors representing these expectations; how they attend to and provide incentives, consequences, and feedback for

Table 10.2	Scale of Effective School Discipline and Safety: Factor Analyzed Items and Rating Scale Used to Complete Items

Factor 1: Teachers' Effective Classroom Management Skills (24 items)

55. Teachers at this school provide appropriate incentives to both individual students and groups of students.

53. Teachers at this school provide consistent, immediate, and appropriate responses for acceptable student behavior.

51. Teachers at this school continuously monitor students' academic and social behaviors.

54. Teachers at this school provide consistent, immediate, and appropriate responses for unacceptable student behavior.

58. Teachers at this school attend and acknowledge both acceptable and unacceptable student behaviors.

52. Teachers at this school use data (academic or behavioral) to make decisions about students.

56. Teachers at this school involve students in identifying and selecting appropriate incentives and reinforcements for acceptable behavior.

49. Teachers at this school believe that students' problems must be assessed within the context of the student, the classroom, the instruction within the classroom, and the curriculum.

57. Teachers at this school involve students in identifying and selecting appropriate consequences for unacceptable behavior.

29. Teachers have high and reasonable behavioral expectations of their students.

50. Teachers at this school believe that students' problems must be functionally assessed before appropriate interventions can be identified and implemented.

24. Students are taught school and classroom routines before being held accountable for them.

46. Teachers at this school are willing to look at students' strengths as well as their weaknesses.

28. Teachers have high and reasonable academic expectations of their students.

48. Teachers at this school are willing to give the student peer group some responsibility for monitoring its own members.

31. Students are provided multiple opportunities to practice and apply new social skills in both group and individual settings.

15. Students are frequently rewarded or praised by faculty and staff for following school rules.

(Continued)

Table 10.2   (Continued)

47. Teachers at this school are willing to tolerate some negative behavior as long as it is decreasing over time.

22. Teachers treat students with respect.

19. Students are taught the school rules.

10. Student at the school are prompted and encouraged to reinforce themselves when appropriate.

8. Students at the school experience five positive interactions from teachers and other staff for each negative interaction.

45. Teachers at this school willingly accept responsibility for every student in the building.

34. Class starts promptly at the beginning of each instruction period.

Factor 2: Students' Positive Behavioral Interactions and Respect (11 items)

26. Students have the behavioral skills needed to work in cooperative learning groups.

25. Students have the behavioral skills needed to work independently when required.

27. Students consistently demonstrate appropriate levels of academic engagement and time on task.

32. Students participate appropriately in all learning activities until the end of each instructional period.

33. Class is rarely interrupted to discipline students.

9. Students at the school experience five positive interactions from their peers for each negative interaction.

11. Students treat each other respectfully and are not subject to verbal abuse by other students.

17. Staff members are treated respectfully by students and not subject to verbal abuse.

30. Time is allocated for social skill instruction consistently during each week.

18. Most students in this school are eager and enthusiastic about learning.

35. Students here care about the school.

Factor 3: Holding Students Accountable for Their Behavior: Administration and Staff (7 items)

23. Administrators enforce the student rules consistently and equitably.

16. Administrators support teachers in dealing with student discipline matters.

1. Students at this school are held accountable for maintaining school rules throughout the year.

14. Staff members enforce the student rules consistently and equitably.

20. Teachers, administrators, and students share responsibility for maintaining discipline in this school.

13. Few discipline problems are referred to the office.

6. There is a positive school spirit.

Factor 4: Teachers' Contribution to a Positive School Climate (9 items)
Teachers at this school are:

37. . . . cohesive

41. . . . productive

38. . . . enthusiastic

44. . . . optimistic

43. . . . open to change

40. . . . satisfied

36. . . . involved

42. . . . innovative

39. . . . relaxed

Factor 5: School Safety and Security: Staff, Students, and School Grounds (7 items)

12. This school is a safe and secure place to work during the normal school day.

5. It is safe to work in this school after students are dismissed.

2. Property of staff members is secure.

7. Students and staff members take pride in the school and help to keep buildings and grounds clean and attractive.

21. Students generally believe that school rules are reasonable and appropriate.

3. Vandalism or destruction of school property by students is not a problem.

4. Property of students is secure.

1	2	3	4	5
Strongly Agree	Agree	Uncertain	Disagree	Strongly Disagree

Source: Project ACHIEVE Press. Dr. Howie Knoff (author).

appropriate and inappropriate behavior, respectfully; and whether they treat students with respect and accept responsibility to support all students.

Factor 2 evaluates staff members' perceptions of their students' social, emotional, and behavioral skills and interactions with staff and peers in both academic and social situations as well as their students' enthusiasm, engagement, and cooperation during learning opportunities. Factor 3 evaluates staff members' perceptions of how well their administrators and colleagues hold students accountable for appropriate behavior, how consistently school rules are encouraged and enforced, and whether there is positive school spirit and low numbers of office discipline referrals. Factor 4 evaluates staff members' perceptions of whether their colleagues contribute to a positive school climate due to their satisfaction, involvement, cohesiveness, and productivity. Finally, Factor 5 evaluates staff members' perceptions of how safe and secure the school is during and after school and whether students and staff work together to keep the school clean and attractive.

Like the SSISC, the SESDS often is used in a pre-post-post format, and its results are reported to the faculty using one of the three feedback approaches described above. Finally, the feedback and discussion sessions may highlight the need to further validate the results, to address identified concerns, and to take specific actions to sustain the recognized strengths. Ultimately, any recommended actions or interventions should be consistent with the school's current PBSS goals, action plans, and existing initiatives.

Evaluating Office Discipline Referrals. One of the important goals of a schoolwide PBSS is to decrease school suspensions and expulsions, discipline referrals to the principal's office, the need for classroom time-outs, and other minor classroom disruptions that disrupt the academic program and process. Beyond simply documenting the frequency of these disciplinary events over time, it is essential to collect contextual data that can help the functional assessment process. For example, rather than knowing the finite number of office discipline referrals (ODR) that occurred across a school or for a specific grade level last month, it is better to also know (a) when and where the discipline problems occurred; (b) whether the infractions involved one student, a small group, or a large group of students; (c) what led up to or triggered the event; (d) who sent the students to the office; and (e) what consequences followed the event. In this way, ODR patterns can be identified and further analyzed, high-problem settings and times can be discerned, and classroom or special situation analyses and interventions can be conducted and implemented.

The Automated Discipline Data, Review, and Evaluation Software System (ADDRESS) is a free downloadable software application that uses Microsoft Access to help schools track and analyze ODRs and other classroom or school discipline events (go to the Data Analysis Warehouse at www.arstudentsuccess.org). The ADDRESS comes with preset fields that include the name of the student, date of the incident, referring adult, time of the incident, specific infraction, context for the incident (e.g., individual student, small group, large group, substitute teacher, teacher assistant), location of the incident, administrative/staff response or action, and a place for comments. Critically, many of these preset fields do not come with predetermined variables or descriptors that are locked into the program (for example, a preset list of infractions or administrative responses that cannot be adapted or modified). Instead, users can add their own variables or descriptors in the different ADDRESS fields during its initial setup and, later, as needed. Even where the ADDRESS has predetermined or preloaded specific variables, users can always delete them and add others of their own. This allows the ADDRESS to be customized completely to the needs or desires of the school and its staff.

The ADDRESS also allows staff to run a wide variety of prearranged data analysis reports or to create custom reports by clicking on and dragging desired variables onto the analysis screen. These reports pool different variables of interest (e.g., the number of discipline referrals last month is the sixth grade, organized by place and time of the day), presenting them in data tables, graphs, or diagrams. The ADDRESS also organizes data from year to year, and it can provide cross-year comparisons and analyses. Finally, the ADDRESS has a reporting function such that data can be e-mailed to other parties so that they can view and track a school's ODR outcomes.

The ADDRESS possesses additional advantages:

- It can be downloaded on any number of computers in a school and networked so that data entry and utilization are dependent on a single computer. The ability to utilize the ADDRESS across a closed network also allows a school or district to use it flexibly for specific strategic purposes. For example, teachers from one grade level could load and track their own data, or individual teachers could use the ADDRESS to collect and analyze their own classroom data.
- It is not web-based or dependent on the internet. This is especially important for schools that are technologically challenged (especially those in rural areas or that have limited budgets). In addition, as ADDRESS data are housed on a local computer or server, all data remain the property of the school or district, and the security and confidentiality of the data can be locally assured.
- Its files can be saved and are transportable, and they can be archived and recovered easily from year to year.
- It was designed to be user-friendly. Data entry, in particular, is highly efficient, and repetitive data entries are not required.

- It comes with a sample ODR form (see Table 10.3) used by staff when sending misbehaving students to the office that is adapted to reflect the specific variables or descriptors chosen by an individual school for tracking and entered into the software during its initial setup. Because the form is largely organized in check-off boxes, it can be completed quickly, it provides more information (at the office) than forms that ask for written descriptions of the discipline problem, and the data are easily transferred from the form into the ADDRESS database (for later cumulative analysis).

Observing and Evaluating Classroom Discipline and Behavior Management. During the past decade, walk-throughs have been recommended as a brief, time-effective way to evaluate the quality of instructional interactions within a classroom (Downey, Steffy, English, Frase, & Poston, 2004; Skretta, 2007). Typically involving three- to five-minute observations of specific classroom interactions, most of the published walk-throughs have focused on academic engagement or effective instruction. In 2008, staff from the Arkansas Department of Education's State Personnel Development Grant developed a behaviorally oriented walk-through protocol focusing on classroom management to extend the ADE's work with Teachscape, a company involved in applying technology to school improvement and success. Based on much of the behavioral and classroom management research and work cited in this book, the *Effective Classroom Management Classroom Walk-Through* (CWT) was developed for principals or others to evaluate the degree of positive, effective, and proactive classroom management approaches in classrooms across their school.

As designed, the Effective Classroom Management CWT protocol involves 23 items organized in three areas (see Table 10.4):

- The Evidence of Teacher's Effective Classroom Management area (9 items) looks at whether teachers specifically identify their behavioral expectations for students in the classroom, and then monitor, evaluate, and reinforce students for appropriate or prosocial behavior while responding to and correcting inappropriate or antisocial behavior. Students' academic engagement also is tracked here, as is the degree of respect demonstrated by teachers toward students.
- The Students' Positive Behavioral Interactions and Respect area (9 items) looks at the degree to which students are positive, prepared, engaged, and on-task throughout a class period along with how well they interpersonally relate to peers and adults and treat them with respect.
- The Classroom Safety and Security area (5 items) looks at the organization and arrangement of a school's classrooms, and whether emergency procedures are posted and can be physically and logistically followed.

(Text continued on page 268)

Table 10.3 ADDRESS Student Office Referral Form

STUDENT: _____ DATE: _____ / _____ / _____

REFERRING ADULT: _____ TIME OF INCIDENT: _____

INFRACTION: *Behavior Prompting Referral*		
☐ Significant refusal to follow adult directions ☐ Verbal abuse toward staff ☐ Taunting/physically threatening behavior (adult or student) ☐ Overt/defiant swearing ☐ Inappropriate racial/sexual language	☐ Throwing dangerous objects/furniture ☐ Other hazardous/unsafe behavior ☐ Vandalism/damage to property ☐ Stealing ☐ Physical abuse toward staff ☐ Fighting/closed fist punching	☐ Sexually inappropriate behavior (touching/exposing body parts) ☐ Sexual harassment ☐ Leaving the building without permission ☐ Possession of tobacco/drugs/alcohol ☐ Possession of weapon or look-alike	☐ Possession: other restricted item

CONTEXT OF THE INCIDENT	LOCATION:	ANTECEDENT: *Event(s) prior to incident*	INITIAL RESPONSES: *by teacher/other adult*

☐ Individual student incident
 ☐ Student with one other student
 ☐ Student in small group
 ☐ Student in large group
	☐ Bus stop/bus/walking to school
	 ☐ On school grounds/outside building
	 ☐ Coming into building
	 ☐ Hallways
	 ☐ Cafeteria: breakfast
	 ☐ Classroom: at seat
	 ☐ Classroom: cooperative/other group
		Student:
		 ☐ Was asked to do something
		 ☐ Was asked to transition to a new activity
		 ☐ Could not get desired item
		 ☐ Was emotional or upset
			☐ Verbal redirection
			 ☐ Physical redirection
			 ☐ Required to continue activity
			 ☐ Ignoring
			 ☐ Time-out (duration:____)
			   ☐ Within room
			   ☐ To another room/office

(Continued)

Table 10.3 (Continued)

CONTEXT OF THE INCIDENT	LOCATION:	ANTECEDENT: Event(s) prior to incident	INITIAL RESPONSES: by teacher/other adult
☐ Student-teacher interaction ☐ Student-other adult interaction ☐ Student-substitute teacher ☐ Student-support staff ☐ Other (specify):	☐ Classroom: activity transition ☐ Transition between classes: line/hall ☐ Bathroom break ☐ Cafeteria: lunch ☐ Recess ☐ Special activity: _____ ☐ Dismissal to bus/loading onto bus ☐ Bus ride home/walking to home ☐ Other (specify):	☐ Was provoked by another student ☐ Other (specify): Setting: ☐ Quiet, orderly environment ☐ Loud, disruptive environment ☐ Adult attending to other students ☐ Free/unstructured time between activities ☐ Cooperative learning groups ☐ Other (specify):	☐ Interruption/blocking ☐ Separation of students ☐ Gave student additional task to complete ☐ Response cost: ☐ Lost time on recess ☐ Lost access to activity ☐ Lost access to items ☐ Parent Contact ☐ Other (specify):

RESPONSES: Subsequent Actions Taken by Administration

CONFERENCE with:	Date	REFERRAL to:	Date	Student Assignment	Date	COMMUNICATION DOCUMENTATION	Date	Detention:	Date
☐ Student ☐ Student and teacher ☐ Parent ☐ Student and parent ☐ Peer mediation ☐ All of the above		☐ Counselor ☐ SPRINT team ☐ Mental health ☐ Superintendent ☐ Community resources:		☐ Letter ☐ Written summary ☐ Contract ☐ School assignment ☐ Call parent		☐ Parent ☐ Teacher ☐ SPRINT team ☐ Superintendent ☐ Other (specify):		☐ Recess ☐ Half day ☐ Full day ☐ After school Suspension: # days: ☐ In-school ☐ Out of school	

Source: Project ACHIEVE Press. Dr. Howie Knoff (author).

| Table 10.4 | The Effective Classroom Management Classroom Walk-Through: Items and Rating Format |

Teacher's Name: Grade Level:

School:

Date of Observation: Observer's Name:

Classroom Walk-Through Observations

Teacher's Effective Classroom Management	Ratings
Observation 1: The teacher's instruction or activities keep the students attentive and academically engaged. ○ 4—To a High Degree ○ 3—To a Moderate Degree ○ 2—To a Low Degree ○ 1—To No Degree ○ No—No opportunity to observe	
Observation 2: The teacher specifically states the behavioral expectations for students when introducing classroom tasks or activities. ○ 4—To a High Degree ○ 3—To a Moderate Degree ○ 2—To a Low Degree ○ 1—To No Degree ○ No—No opportunity to observe	
Observation 3: The teacher continuously monitors students' on-task and academic engagement behavior. ○ 4—To a High Degree ○ 3—To a Moderate Degree ○ 2—To a Low Degree ○ 1—To No Degree ○ No—No opportunity to observe	

(Continued)

Table 10.4 (Continued)

Teacher's Effective Classroom Management	Ratings
Observation 4: The teacher monitors student behavior as related to interpersonal interactions, classroom discipline, and student self-management. ○ 4—To a High Degree ○ 3—To a Moderate Degree ○ 2—To a Low Degree ○ 1—To No Degree ○ No—No opportunity to observe	
Observation 5: The teacher consistently provides specific feedback to students for appropriate/acceptable behavior along with periodic praise or rewards. ○ 4—To a High Degree ○ 3—To a Moderate Degree ○ 2—To a Low Degree ○ 1—To No Degree ○ No—No opportunity to observe	
Observation 6: The teacher consistently provides specific corrective prompts to students for mild inappropriate or unacceptable behavior. ○ 4—To a High Degree ○ 3—To a Moderate Degree ○ 2—To a Low Degree ○ 1—To No Degree ○ No—No opportunity to observe	
Observation 7: The teacher consistently provides specific consequences to students for moderate to severe inappropriate or unacceptable behavior. ○ 4—To a High Degree ○ 3—To a Moderate Degree ○ 2—To a Low Degree ○ 1—To No Degree ○ No—No opportunity to observe	
Observation 8: The teacher treats students with respect. ○ 4—To a High Degree ○ 3—To a Moderate Degree ○ 2—To a Low Degree ○ 1—To No Degree ○ No—No opportunity to observe	

Teacher's Effective Classroom Management	Ratings
Observation 9: Students in the classroom experience five positive interactions from teachers for each negative interaction. ○ 4—To a High Degree ○ 3—To a Moderate Degree ○ 2—To a Low Degree ○ 1—To No Degree ○ No—No opportunity to observe	
Notes:	

Students' Positive Behavioral Interactions and Respect	Ratings
Observation 10: Students demonstrate appropriate behavioral and interpersonal skills when the teacher is directly providing classroom instruction. ○ 4—To a High Degree ○ 3—To a Moderate Degree ○ 2—To a Low Degree ○ 1—To No Degree ○ No—No opportunity to observe	
Observation 11: Students demonstrate appropriate behavioral and interpersonal skills when working in cooperative learning groups. ○ 4—To a High Degree ○ 3—To a Moderate Degree ○ 2—To a Low Degree ○ 1—To No Degree ○ No—No opportunity to observe	
Observation 12: Students are prepared and on-task at the beginning of the instructional period or activity. ○ 4—To a High Degree ○ 3—To a Moderate Degree ○ 2—To a Low Degree ○ 1—To No Degree ○ No—No opportunity to observe	

(Continued)

Table 10.4 (Continued)

Students' Positive Behavioral Interactions and Respect	Ratings
Observation 13: Students demonstrate appropriate on-task behavior when working independently. ○ 4—To a High Degree ○ 3—To a Moderate Degree ○ 2—To a Low Degree ○ 1—To No Degree ○ No—No opportunity to observe	
Observation 14: Students are on-task until the end of each instructional period or activity. ○ 4—To a High Degree ○ 3—To a Moderate Degree ○ 2—To a Low Degree ○ 1—To No Degree ○ No—No opportunity to observe	
Observation 15: Students treat each other respectfully and no students are subject to inappropriate, negative, or verbal abuse by another student. ○ 4—To a High Degree ○ 3—To a Moderate Degree ○ 2—To a Low Degree ○ 1—To No Degree ○ No—No opportunity to observe	
Observation 16: Students treat the teacher with respect and do not subject the teacher to inappropriate, negative, or verbal abuse. ○ 4—To a High Degree ○ 3—To a Moderate Degree ○ 2—To a Low Degree ○ 1—To No Degree ○ No—No opportunity to observe	
Observation 17: Students in the classroom are eager and enthusiastic about learning. ○ 4—To a High Degree ○ 3—To a Moderate Degree ○ 2—To a Low Degree ○ 1—To No Degree ○ No—No opportunity to observe	

Students' Positive Behavioral Interactions and Respect	Ratings
Observation 18: Student misbehavior rarely interrupts classroom learning. ○ Yes ○ No	
Notes:	

Classroom Safety and Security	Ratings
Observation 19: Classroom desks and other furniture, equipment, and materials are in good repair and organized in a safe and secure manner. ○ Yes ○ No	
Observation 20: The classroom is clean. ○ Yes ○ No	
Observation 21: The classroom is organized with sufficient space for students to move and walk around. ○ Yes ○ No	
Observation 22: Appropriate emergency procedures are visibly posted. ○ Yes ○ No	
Observation 23: The classroom has clear pathways to the exit in case of a fire (drill) or other emergency. ○ Yes ○ No	
Notes:	

Source: Project ACHIEVE Press. Dr. Howie Knoff (author).

Relative to use, the individual completing this classroom walk-through typically goes into the classroom and observes for 5 to 15 minutes. Because some teachers and students behave differently when an administrator or adult observer first enters a classroom, the first five minutes of the observation are not used in the evaluation, thereby allowing time to diminish any behavioral reactivity. After the observation, which may focus on one or more of the three areas above, the observer completes the ratings on the CWT protocol and describes any other relevant observations.

CWT data provide information on individual teachers and their students as well as observed classroom management approaches and outcomes. The CWT process and protocol should be discussed with classroom teachers before their use so that they understand why specific behaviors are being observed and what represents effective behavior. After enough observations have occurred—so that the data are both reliable and valid—the CWT results are pooled, analyzed, reported, and discussed with individual teachers (or even classrooms). These discussions focus on reinforcing the effective classroom management interactions that were observed, increasing nonexistent or lower levels of appropriate behavior, and eliminating or changing inappropriate behavior. CWT data from individual teachers also may be combined across time and classrooms with other observation or behavior rating data to get a global sense of how a grade level of teachers, or an entire school, is doing relative to the first six PBSS goals outlined at the beginning of this chapter. Thus, this tool can be used in both formative and summative assessments to facilitate classroom management improvements and to document that they have occurred.

Evaluating Staff Expertise in Behavioral Interventions. It is essential that schools and districts have a wide range of strategic and intensive social, emotional, and behavioral interventions available for students demonstrating challenges in these areas and enough experts to facilitate their implementation. In Chapter 9, a number of these interventions were outlined in the context of the seven high-hit reasons why some students do not demonstrate effective self-management or social competency behaviors and skills. These, and other, interventions can be integrated into a *Behavioral Intervention Survey* that is used to evaluate the consultation and intervention expertise of the school or district staff members who are most responsible for developing social, emotional, or behavioral interventions for challenging students.

A sample Behavioral Intervention Survey is provided in Table 10.5. The survey has brief descriptions of a range of interventions that should be available in any district (additional ones can be added at any time). Related services professionals (e.g., school psychologists, counselors, social workers), special education teachers, and other behavioral intervention specialists individually complete the survey, rating their ability to consult on and independently implement each intervention along a five-point scale from 1—Expert in Both Consulting and Independently Implementing This Intervention to 5—No Knowledge of This Intervention.

Table 10.5 The Behavioral Intervention Survey

Behavioral Intervention Survey

Howard M. Knoff, Ph.D.
Director, Project ACHIEVE

Directions: Below is a list, with brief descriptions, of a number of specialized classroom or school behavioral interventions. All SPRINT teams need to have consultants on (or available to) the team who are able to implement (and work with teachers to assist their implementation of) these interventions in the classroom with specific students. Please read the description of each intervention below and rate your ability to consult on and independently implement each intervention along the following scale:

1	2	3	4	5
Expert in Both Consultation & Implementation	Very Skilled in Both Consultation & Implementation	Skilled Only in Implementation	Questionable Even in Implementation	No Knowledge of Intervention

Rating	Intervention
	Positive Reinforcement Schedules: Understanding the types of positive reinforcement schedules (continuous versus intermittent; ratio versus variable) helps teachers to increase student responses for less and less reinforcement over time.
	Extinction: A procedure where inappropriate behavior that has been previously reinforced is no longer reinforced resulting in a decrease and then elimination of the behavior.
	Stimulus Control and Cuing Procedures: Procedures where students are taught to respond to specific cues, conditions, or other stimuli (e.g., the presence of a specific person), thereby behaving in a desired way with a minimum of teacher effort.
	Task Analysis and Backward Chaining: The process of breaking a desired behavior that must be taught into specific subbehaviors and then the teaching process where the last steps of the behavior are taught first.
	Positive Approaches to Reducing Inappropriate Behavior: Using different reinforcement approaches, these interventions involve reinforcing low rates of behavior, other behavior, and competing behavior.

(Continued)

Table 10.5 (Continued)

1	2	3	4	5
Expert in Both Consultation & Implementation	Very Skilled in Both Consultation & Implementation	Skilled Only in Implementation	Questionable Even in Implementation	No Knowledge of Intervention

Rating	Intervention
	Peer/Adult Mentoring and Mediation: In general, mentoring programs connect students with a valued peer or adult who provides training, guidance, motivation, or consistency within the context of a close and positive relationship. Mediation programs are more specialized as they help individual or groups of students address (usually) emotional feelings or situations by teaching or encouraging interpersonal relationship, social problem-solving, conflict resolution, or emotional coping skills or behaviors.
	The Educative Time-Out Process: A procedure where students who are demonstrating significantly disruptive through dangerous behavior are asked to sit in a time-out chair—either in their homeroom, in another teacher's classroom, or in the principal's office or administrative setting—as a consequence (not punishment) for their inappropriate behavior. After demonstrating appropriate behavior in time-out, they must positively practice the appropriate behavior that they should have done as part of their re-entry into the classroom and their seat.
	Response Cost/Bonus Response Cost: An intervention approach that decreases inappropriate behavior by having students pay for the privilege of exhibiting the inappropriate behavior while they are positively reinforced for exhibiting fewer and fewer of these inappropriate behaviors over time.
	Overcorrection—Positive Practice and Restitutional: Two related intervention procedures that help to reduce inappropriate behavior where students either must practice an appropriate response (which is the opposite of an undesired behavior) or must make amends for an already performed undesired behavior.
	Group Contingency Interventions: Behavior management approaches where students in a classroom are organized into teams and they work for reinforcement as a team. Three different approaches can be used here: where all students must meet a set level of behavioral expectations; where any student can lose or earn points on behalf of a team; or where a specific student (rotating) can lose or earn points on behalf of a team.

1	2	3	4	5
Expert in Both Consultation & Implementation	Very Skilled in Both Consultation & Implementation	Skilled Only in Implementation	Questionable Even in Implementation	No Knowledge of Intervention

Rating	Intervention
	Behavioral Contracting: An approach where a teacher and student (and parent) literally write a contract to specify a specific set of expected (and low rates of undesired) behavior.
	Intensive or Individualized Social Skills or Socialization Training: More intensive or individualized small group instruction in the area of social skills or socialization using an evidence-based training program. This instruction focuses on more frequent or intensive training opportunities with more positive practice repetitions of targeted interpersonal, social problem-solving, conflict prevention and resolution, and emotional coping cognitions and behaviors. The specialized instruction includes supervising students in role-plays that simulate the emotionally charged situations that are problematic for them, better preparing them to handle a diverse range of real-life social-emotional circumstances.
	Thought Stopping Approaches: Techniques that condition students to stop focusing on certain inappropriate, negative, or off-task thoughts or though patterns.
	Self-Awareness, Self-Instruction, Self-Monitoring, Self-Evaluation, and Self-Reinforcement Approaches: Techniques that teach students how to increase the self-management approaches listed above.
	Emotional Self-Control Approaches: Techniques that condition students to increase their emotional and physiological awareness to emotional situations and to increase or maintain appropriate levels of emotional self-control.
	Cognitive-Behavioral Interventions/Behavior Therapy Related to Post Traumatic Stress Syndrome or Similar Emotional Responses Related to Divorce, Loss, Trauma, Harassment, or Abuse. Cognitive-behavioral techniques that assist students in being able to physiologically, emotionally, and behaviorally cope with past or present situations, circumstances, or events that impact their social, emotional, and behavioral control on a regular basis and at an extreme level.

Source: Project ACHIEVE Press. Dr. Howie Knoff (author).

From a formative evaluation perspective, a school or district could pool the results of these self-evaluations to determine the current intervention expertise across its multidisciplinary professionals. When contrasting these results with the intervention needs of the school or district, this evaluation helps identify intervention gaps that need to be closed, for example, by hiring additional personnel or short-term consultants, or by investing in strategic training, professional development, and clinical supervision for existing personnel. From a summative evaluation perspective, this survey could be completed one or more years after, for example, a professional development initiative with existing intervention staff. After comparing the initial and second set of individual and pooled ratings, the school or district can determine its progress in the intervention areas evaluated, and the impact of the professional development on student behavior and staff satisfaction.

SUSTAINING PBSS OUTCOMES: IMPLEMENTING SYSTEMATIC ARTICULATION PROCESSES

In addition to evaluating PBSS outcomes, it is important that schools use an organized and transparent process so that effective system, school, staff, and student processes are transferred systematically from one school year to the next. In this way, the lessons learned during each school year—especially about students and how they most effectively learn—are articulated so that every new school year begins, on the first day of school, at full PBSS capacity. Effective articulation processes also minimize the wasted time and effort that sometimes occur when teachers do not receive important student information at the beginning of the school year (or receive it late), such that they end up reinventing the wheel. At times, this results in a delay of effective instruction, services, and supports for some students that, in turn, exacerbates their problems or delays their success.

In education, the term *articulation* refers to the planned and systematic transfer of school, staff, and student information, interventions, and other lessons learned from one school year to the beginning of the next school year. Typically, this transfer occurs from one classroom teacher to next year's classroom teacher, from one grade-level team to the next year's grade-level team, from the members of each building-level committee to the next year's members on the same committees, from one administrative team to the next year's administrative team, or from one school staff to the next year's school staff.

Unfortunately, many schools do not organize their articulation processes as planned, annual events. Indeed, at a school or committee level, organizational goals are discussed and determined, strategies are planned and implemented, outcomes are evaluated and attained, and progress is realized and celebrated every year. However, when these strategies and successes are not transferred systematically and systemically to the next school year, organizational progress is disrupted, professional momentum is interrupted, productive time and energy are wasted, and staff become disenchanted and burned out. This lack of coordination and articulation represents organizational inefficiency.

Similarly, at the grade or teacher level, professional development, supervision, and technical assistance is delivered in most schools every year—often focused on evidence-based practices, differentiated instruction, and effective classroom management for all students. Yet, when the knowledge, skills, and confidence that teachers obtain because of this training are not shared across teachers and grade- or instruction-level teams, are not progressively built on from year to year, and are not provided to new staff at the beginning of each new school year, instructional collaboration, consistency, effectiveness, and efficiency are undermined and school success becomes more transitory. This lack of coordination and articulation results in a loss of information, experience, time, and success, and reflects professional inefficiency.

Finally, at the classroom or student levels, functional assessment, data-based problem solving, consultation, and strategic intervention are delivered every year—focused on students with significant academic or behavioral challenges who need these more intensive interventions and supports. Yet, when the academic or behavioral progress that teachers make with these challenging students is not shared, and when the lessons learned about how to effectively reach and teach them are not systematically transferred to the next year's grade-level team or teachers, these students may not receive the best, most proven approaches or materials required for their immediate success at the beginning of the new school year. When this occurs, student progress and achievement is disrupted, student motivation may be impaired, and student success may be compromised. This lack of coordination and articulation represents student services and support inefficiency.

Articulation, then, is a critical process that helps staff to evaluate the accomplishments of the current year, to plan smooth transitions to the next school year (at the school, staff, and student levels), and to maintain and extend the momentum of school and classroom academic, behavioral, and RTI^2 and SPRINT processes. But to be most successful, articulation activities need to occur at the end of a current school year so that schools are best prepared for the beginning of the next school year. Thus, the organizational principle underscoring all articulation processes is "the beginning of the new school year starts in April."

While there are many areas of articulation that schools need to plan and execute, this section focuses on those that are directly related to PBSS processes:

- The school discipline/PBSS committee membership, and its annual strategic planning activities
- The Get-Go process

- Student Briefing Reports
- Special Situation Analysis
- Resource needs assessments, results, and planning

Prior to beginning these articulation activities in April, however, the documents and data detailed below need to be collected and available to those who will be involved in the respective articulation processes.

For the Committee Membership and Strategic Planning Activities

- The school discipline/PBSS committee's current membership and terms of offices and a roster of all of the staff in the school, including those who served on the school discipline/PBSS committee during the past six years
- The school's current School Improvement Plan (SIP), its current PBSS-related section or activities, the draft of the school's SIP for the coming school year, and blank copies of a SIP and a committee action plan form used by the school

For the Get-Go Process

- A roster of all IEP and 504 students in the school (or students who will likely be receiving such services on the first day of school in the new year)
- Student attendance printouts that differentiate the data by grade, by excused versus unexcused, and by student being absent or tardy, respectively. The data should be organized as follows: students absent/tardy: 0–4 times, 5–9 times, 10–14 times, 15 to 19 times, 20–29 times, more than 30 times
- Data, printouts, and charts documenting and analyzing the ODR, suspensions, and expulsions for the school year
- From each grade level and teacher, a functional assessment of the instructional or mastery level of each student in his or her class on the state's or school's curricular benchmarks or scope and sequence objectives and outcomes—at least in the areas of literacy, mathematics, and language arts
- From each grade level and teacher, a summary of students having attendance, medical, behavioral, social-emotional, or other difficulties with indications of their response to classroom interventions and the current severity status of the problem

For the Student Briefing Reports

- All of the descriptive information on the Get-Go and At-Risk students including any information on interventions implemented, progress monitoring data collected, and conclusions drawn

For the Special Situation Analysis

- All of the descriptive information and data related to the special situations that have been addressed during the current school year, and those that still exist

For Resource Mapping: General, Academic, and Behavioral Intervention Surveys

- Any resource maps completed in prior years along with a list of the resources that were acquired or developed during the current year as a result of SIP or school discipline/PBSS committee activities or initiatives
- A list of the resource needs identified by the school discipline/PBSS committee and other committees in the school for the next year's SIP
- A detailed list of all of the academic, behavioral, or other interventions needed by the Get-Go and At-Risk students after they have been identified through the Get-Go process
- A list of the resources needed by the school discipline/PBSS committee to successfully implement the special situations intervention plans written for the next school year
- A list of all of the professional development activities attended by (all, many, or some) staff in the school and on the school discipline/PBSS committee and how these activities were shared with the entire staff (if relevant) or used at the classroom level
- The results of all completed Behavioral Intervention Surveys across the school or district

THE SCHOOL DISCIPLINE/PBSS COMMITTEE MEMBERSHIP AND ITS ANNUAL STRATEGIC PLANNING

Activities. During its April meeting, the school discipline/PBSS committee looks at its current membership, analyzes its accomplishments during the current school year, and begins to address both areas relative to planning for the next school year. Relative to the first area, the committee looks at its current members' terms of office and identifies which individuals will be replaced by new members (see Chapter 3). If these new members can be chosen and confirmed in April, then they can attend the May and June meetings of the committee, giving them an early orientation to the committee and how it works and functions. During these meetings, they also can contribute to the committee's strategic planning discussions as the discipline/PBSS section of the new SIP is drafted for the next school year. Critically, the SLT needs to coordinate the new member selection process for all of the school's committees so that a smooth, seamless transition occurs for everyone involved.

As noted above, the school discipline/PBSS committee also collects and evaluates the data and outcomes for all of the goals written in its section of the current SIP. Committee members then determine what goals, objectives, and activities need to continue into the new school year and what new goals and activities should be added. All of these projected goals and activities are documented on a SIP or committee action plan, and they are submitted to the School Leadership Team (SLT) for consideration and inclusion in the next formal SIP.

As part of the April planning process, the school discipline/PBSS committee also completes a number of tasks so that certain PBSS activities are ready to begin immediately at the start of the next school year. Relative to these tasks, the committee should

- prepare next year's Stop & Think Social Skills calendar, including an outline of the classroom and building routines that need to be taught at the beginning of the school year and that need to be reinforced after any vacations or significant breaks from school,
- look at and fine-tune (if needed) anything on the grade-level Behavioral Matrices, and prepare for the schoolwide and grade-level rollout of the Behavioral Matrices on the first day and weeks of school,
- identify what new or booster training will be needed for new and returning staff prior to the beginning of the next school year—especially in the area of social skills instruction, the implementation of the time-out process, and the response system that is built into the Behavioral Matrices, and
- take stock of what materials need to be ordered or prepared (e.g., social skill manuals and support materials; Behavioral Matrix posters; time-out logs, trackers, and passes), and what activities (e.g., getting the Behavioral Matrices printed into the school's student/ parent handbook, updating the school's website) need to be accomplished during the summer so that PBSS activities can begin on the first day of school.

The Get-Go Process. The Get-Go process is a student review process where the progress and current status of every student in the school is discussed at the end of the school year to determine if he or she needs services, supports, strategies, or programs on the first day of the new school year or soon thereafter. Using this process, information and lessons learned about students during the current school year are systematically transferred to the teachers and others who will have them in their classrooms after the summer break. While this process is largely coordinated by the building-level SPRINT team in collaboration with each grade- or instruction-level team, the school discipline/PBSS committee is informally involved as it shares (a) the results of the most recent ADDRESS (or other ODR) data—analyzed by student, teacher, and grade level for each quarter of the school year and cumulatively across the entire school year; (b) what social, emotional, and behavioral skills were actually taught at each grade level during the present school year; and (c) the results of any special situation analyses that were completed and implemented. Because there is at least one grade- or instruction-level team representative on the school discipline/PBSS committee, these representatives can discuss this information during the separate grade- or instruction-level Get-Go sessions.

When implemented, a Get-Go review generally takes no more than two to three minutes per student. Typically, representatives from the building-level SPRINT team and all of the instructional staff on a grade- or instruction-level teaching team simply go down a prepared list of all of their students, deciding together if each student is a Get-Go, At-Risk, Check-In, or No Problem student. The names of students identified in one of the first three categories are placed on a Get-Go Review and Analysis Form, and the specific areas of concern and any needed instructional or intervention approaches are briefly described. For the Get-Go and At-Risk students, these entries are more fully documented by teachers' completion of a Student Briefing Report (see the next articulation activity below). No Problem students are those students who the team believes will have no academic or social, emotional, or behavioral problems during the transition to the new school year. The names of these students do not appear on the Get-Go Review and Analysis Form.

By definition, a Get-Go student needs immediate instructional or intervention services, supports, strategies, or programs in place on the first day of the new school year. Students on IEPs, 504 Plans, and any other state- or district-mandated academic or behavioral intervention plan are automatically Get-Go students as their services or supports, by law or regulation, must be ready for implementation on the first day of the new school year.

An At-Risk student has received interventions during the past school year that were so successful that they are not needed to start the new school year, and yet, the staff at the meeting feel that the student may still be at risk for further difficulties. Given this and the intervention time and effort already invested, students are designated At Risk so that the instructional staff who teach these students during the next year can be systematically briefed as to each student's academic and behavioral history, and the reasons for and results of previous interventions. This briefing occurs both verbally, at the end of the current or prior to the beginning of the new school year, and through the written Student Briefing Report.

Check-In students are identified because staff want someone to check in with them at some point during their transition into the new school year. Some of these students have received and completed one or more successful interventions during the current year, and (unlike the At-Risk students) the staff feel that there is no need to extensively brief their next year's teachers. Other students simply have a specific issue that the staff need or want to track into the next year. For all of these students, their check-in status puts an articulation safety net in place so that one or more designated individuals will look in on them at some point during the first quarter of the school year.

When identifying Check-In students, the SPRINT and grade-level team specifies and documents the areas of concern, when the check-in should occur (e.g., just prior to the beginning of the school year, or after Week 1, 2, 4, or 9), and who should complete and record the check-in and with whom. For some students, the check-in may involve calling the parents before the first day of school to remind them that the school year starts in two days, checking to see if they are in school on Day 1, and then running attendance reports after Weeks 1, 3, and 5. For others, it involves a scan of their report cards at the end of the first marking period to check their grades and progress. For still others, it involves asking a teacher to comment on their performance in the classroom at the end of the second week of school.

Ultimately, the goal of the Get-Go process is to make sure that specific students' instructional or intervention history, information, status, and needs are effectively and efficiently communicated to new teachers and support staff so that they will successfully transition into the new school year. Prior to each Get-Go meeting, the grade-level and building-level SPRINT teams need to review all of the students whose challenges were formally analyzed through the data-based functional assessment problem solving or who received early intervening services. Similarly, as noted above, any student on an IEP, 504, or academic or behavioral intervention plan should be designated as a Get-Go student prior to the meeting. Finally, it must be recognized that some students will be identified during the Get-Go process not because of academic or social, emotional, or behavioral concerns but because of (a) attendance issues (including being persistently late), (b) medical conditions that teachers and others need to know about, or (c) current or historical family issues that impact their performance at school. Depending on the severity of these conditions or the need for teacher training or briefing, these students could be identified as Get-Go, At-Risk, or Check-In students, respectively.

Student Briefing Reports. These reports are summaries of the most essential information about specific students as learned by their classroom teachers and teaching teams during a specific school year. Written primarily by students' general education teachers, these Briefing Reports could be included as part of a computerized student record database and organized as a cumulative, year-to-year running record to document specific students' academic and behavioral progress over time. As noted above, Student Briefing Reports must be written by every teacher and staff person who has worked with a student designated as a Get-Go or At-Risk student for the next school year. For students with IEPs, or 504 or academic or behavioral intervention plans, these plans may substitute for the Briefing Report as long as all of the essential student information is present. Beyond this, any teacher can write a Briefing Report on any student to share any information that would help another colleague to understand, teach, motivate, or assist a student at the beginning of the next school year.

The primary goal of a Student Briefing Report, then, is to provide a functional overview of a selected student's academic and behavioral history and the lessons learned over the recent school year. As such, the Briefing Report should include the

- academic and behavioral background of the student—including critical factors (physical, medical, social, supportive) that impact or contribute to this background,
- academic and behavioral strengths and progress during the past school year,
- academic and behavioral weaknesses and the functional reasons why they exist,
- a description of successful strategies or interventions to address the student's needs and how they were implemented,
- a description of less successful or unsuccessful strategies or interventions for the student,
- keys to helping this student be successful, and
- other information of note.

When teachers have to write Student Briefing Reports for Get-Go or At-Risk students, we suggest that the reports be part of the check-out process whereby principals formally release their teachers for the summer at the end of the school year. In addition, we also strongly recommend that principals discuss a number of critical issues with staff before they begin writing their Briefing Reports—for example, confidentiality, maintaining objectivity, documenting data, keeping reports secure (especially if they are on an on-line computer database), and informing parents.

Once written, the Student Briefing Reports can be kept by the building principal or the chair of the building-level SPRINT team over the summer. During the week before the new school year, these reports are given to the new classroom teachers (and relevant others), and a series of meetings can be scheduled to provide additional information, consultation, and training (especially for the Get-Go students) so that all teachers are prepared for all of their students as the new year begins. For Get-Go students, the Student Briefing Reports provide the context and history that make the necessary before-school training (so that the interventions are available for Day 1 implementation) more meaningful. For At-Risk students, the Student Briefing Reports may provide all of the information needed by a teacher to effectively and successfully approach these students on the first day of school.

Special Situation Analysis. In April, the school discipline/PBSS committee needs to review and evaluate the special situations (see Chapters 6
and 7) that they have addressed during the current school year and those
that still exist. For the former situations, the committee needs to ensure
that the strategies, supports, and interventions implemented to resolve
any setting- or student-specific special situations are systematically transferred to ensure their continued success into the new school year. For the
latter situations, the school discipline/PBSS committee might prioritize
any still-existing special situations and conduct a Special Situation Analysis on one of them prior to the end of the school year. In this way, the committee systematically articulates the school's special situation successes
from one year to the next. It also implements or prepares to implement
interventions for at least one additional special situation so that it might be
prevented or resolved on the first day of the new school year.

In order to accomplish both of these outcomes, a possible chronology
is suggested:

1. At the March meeting of the school discipline/PBSS committee,
   identify the special situations that have been addressed successfully
   during the current school year. Ask different members of the committee to prepare their suggestions as to what needs to occur to
   transfer these successes systematically into the new school year.

2. At the same meeting, identify one or more special situations that
   continue to exist, but have not been addressed during the current
   year. Ask different members of the committee to prepare a discussion of these situations for the April meeting so that one of them can
   be chosen to address by the end of the current school year.

3. At the April meeting of the committee, hear and discuss the suggestions as to how to transfer the current special situation successes
   into the new school year, and agree on a specific action plan.

4. At the same meeting, decide which new special situation will be
   addressed before the end of the current school year, and choose the
   leader and task force that will conduct the Special Situation Analysis
   and intervention planning process.

5. In April and May, the Special Situation Analysis is completed (see
   Chapters 6 and 7).

6. At the May meeting of the committee, the analysis and an intervention
   action plan for the new special situation is presented and approved.

7. From May through the first day of the new school year, those relevant aspects of the intervention action plan are implemented.

8. During the planning days immediately before school starts, on the
   first day of school, and during the weeks to follow, the intervention
   action plan continues to be implemented and outcomes are evaluated.

During some years, there are special situations that cannot be resolved until the current year ends or the new school year begins. This may occur, for example, because their interventions require money that was not budgeted during the current school year but that will be available when the new fiscal year begins in July. Or the special situation may require changes—for example, the redesign of the daily schedule, hallway traffic patterns, the physical organization of the cafeteria—that can only occur during the summer. The school discipline/PBSS committee needs to make note of these circumstances and integrate them into their articulation processes toward the end of every school year.

Resource Needs Assessments, Results, and Planning. Based on all of the articulation activities above, the school discipline/PBSS committee should compile a list of the resources and funds needed to complete them. The chair of the committee then should bring this list to the SLT meetings that focus on developing the goals, activities, and funding of the next SIP—meetings that typically occur toward the end of every school year. To make the strongest case possible, the committee and committee chair also need to analyze the PBSS resources provided and used during the past three years, and determine their return on investment relative to student, staff, and school outcomes. If fully funded, the committee will be ready to implement all of its planned activities in a timely way. If underfunded, the committee needs to analyze all of its activities, the resources needed, and once again, their relative return on investment, and select which articulation activities should be funded and implemented.

SUMMARY

Processes that evaluate short- and long-term PBSS outcomes and activities that scale up and sustain its success—at the system, school, staff, and student levels—never end. This chapter discussed a selected number of instruments, tools, and approaches that help to evaluate the success of a PBSS initiative across its primary goals and objectives. These tools included the *Scale of Staff Interactions and School Cohesion*, the *Scale of Effective School Discipline and Safety*, the *Automated Discipline Data, Review, and Evaluation Software System* (ADDRESS), the *Effective Classroom Management Classroom Walk-Through* (CWT), and the *Behavioral Intervention Survey*.

The chapter also addressed a number of systematic ways to transfer, or articulate, PBSS successes from year to year, so that every school year begins, on the first day of school, at the highest level of effectiveness and efficiency. More specifically, articulation activities were described in the following areas: school discipline/PBSS committee membership and strategic planning, the Get-Go process, the development of Student Briefing Reports, year-end special situation analyses, and resource needs assessments and planning.

In the end, like businesses, schools are usually successful on the strength of their strategic planning and effective execution of sound policies, procedures, and implementation activities—not because of good luck. Evaluation and articulation activities are essential to help schools, committees, and staff members evaluate the accomplishments of the past year, to plan for smooth transitions into the next school year, and to maintain and extend the momentum of the school's academic and behavioral successes. While every school committee engages in articulation processes to some degree, those completed annually by the school discipline/PBSS committee refocus the school's attention on its PBSS goals and outcomes and on the social, emotional, and behavioral self-management progress and proficiency of all students. Attending to evaluation and articulation processes is good business. Ultimately, good business in schools translates into staff effectiveness and productivity, and short- and long-term student success.

NOTE

1. Sections of this chapter were adapted from and/or taken directly from Knoff, H. M. (2010). End-of-year transition activities that sustain the RTI^2 process. In H. M. Knoff & C. Dyer, *RTI^2—Response to Instruction and Intervention: Implementing successful academic and behavioral intervention systems* (pp. 315–335). Rexford, NY: International Center for Leadership in Education.

References

Allan, E., & Madden, M. (2008). *National study on student hazing*. Orono, ME: National Collaborative for Hazing Research and Prevention.

Arkansas Department of Education, State Personnel Development Grant. (2009, October). *School-wide discipline, behavior management, and student self-management: Focusing on social skills instruction and selecting an evidence-based social skills program*. Little Rock, AR: Author.

Bandura, A. (1977). *Social learning theory*. Englewood Cliffs, NJ: Prentice-Hall.

Barrish, H. H., Saunders, M., & Wolf, M. M. (1969). The Good Behavior Game: Effects of individual contingencies for group consequences on disruptive behavior in a classroom. *Journal of Applied Behavior Analyses, 2*, 119–124.

Batsche, G. M., & Knoff, H. M. (1994). Bullies and their victims: Understanding a pervasive problem in the schools. *School Psychology Review, 23*, 165–174.

Bender, D., & Losel, F. (2011). Bullying at school as a predictor of delinquency, violence, and other antisocial behavior in adulthood. *Criminal Behaviour and Mental Health, 21*, 99–106.

Benson, P. L. (2006). *All kids are our kids: What communities must do to raise caring and responsible children and adolescents* (2nd ed.). San Francisco, CA: Jossey-Bass.

Blum, R. W., & Libbey, H. P. (2004). School connectedness—Strengthening health and education outcomes for teenagers. *Journal of School Health, 74*, 229–299.

Bosworth, K., Espelage, D. L., & Simon, T. (1999). Factors associated with bullying behavior in middle school students. *Journal of Early Adolescence, 19*, 341–362.

Branigan, H. M., & Jones, R. D. (2006). *Leadership for rigor, relevance, and relationships*. Rexford, NY: International Center for Leadership in Education.

Brock, S., Nickerson, A., Reeves, M., Jimerson, S., Lieberman, R., & Feinberg, T. (2009). *School crisis prevention and intervention: The PREPaRE model*. Bethesda, MD: National Association of School Psychologists.

Card, N. A., & Hodges, E. V. E. (2008). Peer victimization among schoolchildren: Correlations, causes, consequences, and considerations in assessment and intervention. *School Psychology Quarterly, 23*, 451–461.

Cartledge, G., & Milburn, J. F. (1995). *Teaching social skills to children: Innovative approaches* (2nd ed.). New York, NY: Pergamon.

Cartledge, G., & Milburn, J. F. (1996). *Cultural diversity and social skills instruction*. Champaign, IL: Research Press.

Cawalti, G. (Ed.). (1995). *Handbook of research on improving student achievement*. Arlington, VA: Educational Research Service.

Christenson, S., & Carroll, E. B. (1999). Strengthening the family-school partnership through Check and Connect. In E. Frydenberg (Ed.), *Learning to cope: Developing as a person in complex societies* (pp. 248–273). London: Oxford University Press.

Christenson, S. L., Rounds, T., & Franklin, M. J. (1992). Home-school collaboration: Effects, issues, and opportunities. In S. L. Christenson & J. C. Close-Conoley (Eds.), *Home-school collaboration: Enhancing children's academic and social competence* (pp. 19–51). Silver Spring, MD: National Association of School Psychologists.

Conzemius, A., & O'Neill, J. (2002). *The handbook for SMART school teams.* Bloomington, IN: National Education Service.

Cook, C. R., Williams, K. R., Guerra, N. G., Kim, T. E., & Sadek, S. (2010). Predictors of bullying and victimization in childhood and adolescence: A meta-analytic review. *School Psychology Quarterly, 25,* 65–83.

Craig, W. M., Pepler, D. J., & Atlas, R. (2000). Observations of bullying in the playground and in the classroom. *School Psychology International, 21,* 22–36.

Doll, B. J., & Swearer, S. M. (2006). Cognitive-behavioral interventions for participants in bullying and coercion. In R. B. Mennuti, A. Freeman, & R. W. Christner (Eds.), *Cognitive-behavioral interventions in educational settings* (pp. 184–201). New York, NY: Routledge.

Donaldson, J. M., Vollmer, T. R., Krous, T., Downs, S., & Berard, K. P. (2011). An evaluation of the Good Behavior Game in kindergarten classrooms. *Journal of Applied Behavior Analysis, 44*(3), 605–609.

Downey, C. J., Steffy, B. E., English, F. W., Frase, L. E., & Poston, W. K. (2004). *The three-minute classroom walkthrough: Changing school supervisory practice one teacher at a time.* Thousand Oaks, CA: Corwin.

Dunst, C. J., Trivette, C. M., & Johanson, C. (1994). Parent-professional collaboration and partnerships. In C. Dunst, C. Trivette, & A. Deal (Eds.), *Supporting and strengthening families: Vol. 1. Methods, strategies, and practices* (pp. 197–211). Cambridge, MA: Brookline Books.

Durlak, J. A., Weissberg, R. P., Dymnicki, A. B., Taylor, R. D., & Schellinger, K. B. (2011). The impact of enhancing students' social and emotional learning: A meta-analysis of school-based universal interventions. *Child Development, 82*(1), 405–432.

Dwyer, K., & Osher, D. (2000). *Safeguarding our children: An action guide.* Washington, DC: U.S. Departments of Education and Justice, American Institutes for Research.

Dwyer, K. P., Osher, D., & Warger, W. (1998). *Early warning, timely response: A guide to safe schools.* Washington, DC: U.S. Department of Education.

Espelage, D. L., & Holt, M. K. (2001). Bullying and victimization during early adolescence: Peer influences and psychosocial correlates. *Journal of Emotional Abuse, 2,* 123–142.

Glew, G. M., Fan, M. Y., Katon, W., Rivara, F. P., & Kernic, M. A. (2005). Bullying, psychosocial adjustment, and academic performance in elementary school. *Archives of Pediatric Adolescent Medicine, 159*(11), 1026–1031.

Goldstein, A. (1988). *The prepare curriculum: Teaching prosocial competencies.* Champaign, IL: Research Press.

Goodman, S. D., & Schaughency, E. (2001, September/October). Schools address correlation between behavior and reading difficulties: Data driven decision making practices inform about what does and does not work. *CEN Newsline.* Michigan State Department of Education.

Hinduja, S., & Patchin, J. W. (2010). *Cyberbullying: Identification, prevention, and response.* Eau Claire, WI: University of Wisconsin–Eau Claire.

Hinduja, S., & Patchin, J. W. (2012, February). *Bullying and cyberbullying laws fact sheet* [web post]. Retrieved from http://www.cyberbullying.us/index.php

Huesmann, L. R., & Reynolds, M. A. (2001). Cognitive processes and the development of aggression. In A. C. Bohart & D. J. Stipek (Eds.), *Constructive and destructive behavior: Implications for family, school, and society* (pp. 249–269). Washington, DC: American Psychological Association.

January, A. M., Casey, R. J., & Paulson, D. (2011). A meta-analysis of classroom-wide interventions to build social skills: Do they work? *School Psychology Review, 40,* 242–256.

Johnson, D. W., & Johnson, R. T. (1996). Conflict resolution and peer mediation programs in elementary and secondary schools: A review of the research. *Review of Educational Research, 66,* 459–506.

Kazdin, A. E. (2001). *Behavior modification in applied settings* (6th ed.). New York, NY: Wadsworth.

Kerr, M. M., & Nelson, C. M. (2010). *Strategies for addressing behavior problems in the classroom* (6th ed.). Boston, MA: Pearson.

Kilian, J. M., Fish, M. C., & Maniago, E. B. (2006). Making schools safe: A system-wide school intervention to increase student prosocial behaviors and enhance school climate. *Journal of Applied School Psychology, 23*(1), 1–30.

Kleinman, K. E., & Saigh, P. A. (2011). The effects of the Good Behavior Game on the conduct of regular education New York City high school students. *Behavior Modification, 35*(1), 95–105.

Klem, A. M., & Connell, J. P. (2004). Relationships matter: Linking teacher support to student engagement and achievement. *Journal of School Health, 74,* 262–273.

Knoff, H. M. (2000). Organizational development and strategic planning for the millennium: A blueprint toward effective school discipline, school safety, and crisis prevention. *Psychology in the Schools, 37,* 17–32.

Knoff, H. M. (2001). *The Stop & Think Social Skills Program* (Preschool–Grade 1, Grades 2/3, Grades 4/5, Middle School 6–8). Longmont, CO: Cambium Learning/Sopris West.

Knoff, H. M. (2005a). *Character education vs. social skills training: Comparing constructs vs. behavior.* Little Rock, AR: Project ACHIEVE Press.

Knoff, H. M. (2005b). *The Stop & Think parent book: A guide to children's good behavior.* Little Rock, AR: Project ACHIEVE Press.

Knoff, H. M. (2007a). Best practices in strategic planning, organizational assessment, and school effectiveness. In A. Thomas & J. Grimes (Eds.), *Best practices in school psychology—V.* Bethesda, MD: National Association of School Psychologists.

Knoff, H. M. (2007b). *Changing student behavior by linking office discipline referrals to a strategic time-out process: A step-by-step implementation guide to the effective use of classroom consequences.* Little Rock, AR: Project ACHIEVE Press.

Knoff, H.M. (2007c). *Developing and implementing the Behavioral Matrix: Establishing school-wide behavioral standards and benchmarks for student accountability.* Little Rock, AR: Project ACHIEVE Press.

Knoff, H. M. (2007d). *Holding students responsible for their school and classroom behavior: Developing a school-wide accountability system to encourage student self-management and staff consistency.* Little Rock, AR: Project ACHIEVE Press.

Knoff, H. M. (2007e). *More Stop & Think Social Skills and Steps: Classroom and building routines and scripts from preschool to high school.* Little Rock, AR: Project ACHIEVE Press.

Knoff, H. M. (2007f). *The scale of effective school discipline and safety.* Little Rock, AR: Project ACHIEVE Press.

Knoff, H. M. (2007g). *The scale of staff interactions and school cohesion.* Little Rock, AR: Project ACHIEVE Press.

Knoff, H. M. (2007h). Teasing, taunting, bullying, harassment, and aggression: A school-wide approach to prevention, strategic intervention, and crisis management. In M. J. Elias, J. E. Zins, & C. A. Maher (Eds.), *Handbook of prevention and intervention in peer harassment, victimization, and bullying.* Binghamton, NY: Haworth Press.

Knoff, H. M. (2009a). *Implementing effective schoolwide student discipline and behavior management systems: Increasing academic engagement and achievement, decreasing teasing and bullying, and keeping your school and common areas safe.* Little Rock, AR: Project ACHIEVE Press.

Knoff, H. M. (2009b). *Implementing Response-to-Intervention at the school, district, and state levels: Functional assessment, data-based problem solving, and evidence-based academic and behavioral interventions.* Little Rock, AR: Project ACHIEVE Press.

Knoff, H. M. (2010a). End-of-year transition activities that sustain the RtI^2 process. In H. M. Knoff & C. Dyer, *RtI^2—Response to Instruction and Intervention: Implementing successful academic and behavioral intervention systems* (pp. 315–335). Rexford, NY: International Center for Leadership in Education.

Knoff, H. M. (2010b). The RtI^2 data-based, functional assessment, problem-solving process. In H. M. Knoff & C. Dyer, *RtI^2—Response to Instruction and Intervention: Implementing successful academic and behavioral intervention systems* (pp. 51–114). Rexford, NY: International Center for Leadership in Education.

Knoff, H. M. (2010c). Social, emotional, and behavioral interventions. In H.M. Knoff & C. Dyer, *RTI^2—Response to Instruction and Intervention: Implementing successful academic and behavioral intervention systems* (pp. 255–314). Rexford, NY: International Center for Leadership in Education.

Knoff, H. M., & Batsche, G. M. (1995). Project ACHIEVE: Analyzing a school reform process for at-risk and underachieving students. *School Psychology Review, 24,* 579–603.

Knoff, H. M., & Dyer, C. (2010). *RtI^2—Response to Instruction and Intervention: Implementing successful academic and behavioral intervention systems.* Rexford, NY: International Center for Leadership in Education.

Knoff, H. M., Finch, C., & Carlyon, W. (2004). Inside Project ACHIEVE: A comprehensive, research-proven whole school improvement process focused on student academic and behavioral outcomes. In K. Robinson (Ed.), *Advances in school-based mental health: Best practices and program models* (pp. 19-1 to 19-28). Kingston, NJ: Civic Research Institute, Inc.

Knoff, H. M., Haley, L., & Gonzales, J. (2011, September). *Integrating the School Prevention, Review, and Intervention Team (SPRINT) and Response-to-Instruction/Intervention (RtI²) process: A model implementation guidebook for schools and districts.* Little Rock, AR: Arkansas Department of Education—Special Education, State Personnel Development Grant.

Ladd, G. W., & Mize, J. (1983). A cognitive-social learning model of social skill training. *Psychological Review, 90,* 127–157.

Leff, S. S., & Crick, N. (Eds.). (2010). Special series: Relational aggression interventions in schools: Innovative programming and next steps. *School Psychology Review, 39.*

Leflot, G., van Lier, P. A. C., Onghena, P., & Colpin, H. (2010). The role of teacher behavior management in the development of disruptive behaviors: An intervention study with the Good Behavior Game. *Journal of Abnormal Child Psychology, 38*(6), 869–882.

LeGray, M. W., Dufrene, B. A., Sterling-Turner, H., Olmi, J., & Bellone, K. (2010). A comparison of function-based differential reinforcement interventions for children engaging in disruptive classroom behavior. *Journal of Behavior in Education, 19,* 185–204.

Lopata, C., Nida, R., & Marable, M. A. (2006). Progressive muscle relaxation: Preventing aggression in students with EBD. *Teaching Exceptional Children, 38*(4), 20–25.

McCurdy, B. L., Lannie, A. L., & Barnabas, E. (2009). Reducing disruptive behavior in an urban cafeteria: An extension of the Good Behavior Game. *Journal of School Psychology, 47*(1), 39–55.

McKissick, C., Hawkins, R. O., Lentz, F. E., Hailley, J., & McGuire, S. (2010). Randomizing multiple contingency components to decrease disruptive behaviors and increase student engagement in an urban second-grade classroom. *Psychology in the Schools, 47*(9), 944–959.

McNeely, C., Nonemaker, J., & Blum, R. (2002). Promoting school connectedness: Evidence from the National Longitudinal Study of Adolescent Health. *Journal of School Health, 72,* 138–146.

Meichenbaum, D. (1977). *Cognitive-behavior modification: An integrative approach.* New York, NY: Plenum.

Merrell, K. W., Gueldner, B. A., Ross, S. W., & Isava, D. M. (2008). How effective are school bullying intervention programs? A meta-analysis of intervention research. *School Psychology Quarterly, 23,* 26–42.

Milkie, M. A., & Warner, C. H. (2011). Classroom learning environments and the mental health of first grade children. *Journal of Health and Social Behavior, 52,* 4–22.

Morris, A. (2011). Cyberbullying in Texas: Reform is necessary to keep the virtual playground safe. *Baylor Law Review, 63*(2), 498–525.

Nansel, T. R., Overpeck, M., Pilla, R. S., Ruan, W. J., Simons-Morton, B., & Scheidt, P. (2001). Bullying behaviors among U.S. youth: Prevalence and association with psychosocial adjustment. *Journal of the American Medical Association, 285*(16), 2094–2100.

Office of Juvenile Justice and Delinquency Prevention. (1998). *Guide for implementing the comprehensive strategy for serious, violent, and chronic defenders.* Washington, DC: U.S. Department of Justice, Office of Justice Programs.

Payton, J., Weissberg, R. P., Durlak, J. A., Dymnicki, A. B., Taylor, R. D., Schellinger, K. B., & Pachan, M. (2008). *The positive impact of social and emotional learning for kindergarten to eighth-grade students: Findings from three scientific reviews.* Chicago, IL: Collaborative for Academic, Social, and Emotional Learning.

Pellegrini, A. D., Bartini, M., & Brooks, F. (1999). School bullies, victims, and aggressive victims: Factors relating to group affiliation and victimization in early adolescence. *Journal of Educational Psychology, 91,* 216–224.

Pöyhönen, V., Juvonen, J., & Salmivalli, C. (2010). What does it take to stand up for the victim of bullying? The interplay between personal and social factors. *Merrill-Palmer Quarterly, 56,* 143–163.

Raffaele, L., & Knoff, H. M. (1999). Improving home-school collaboration with parents of children at-risk: Organizational principles, perspectives, and approaches. *School Psychology Review, 28,* 448–466.

Rigby, K. (2000). Effects of peer victimization in schools and perceived social support on adolescent well-being. *Journal of Adolescence, 23,* 57–68.

Rigby, K. (2001). Health consequences of bullying and its prevention in schools. In J. Juvonen & S. Graham (Eds.), *Peer harassment in school: The plight of the vulnerable and victimized* (pp. 310–331). New York, NY: Guilford Press.

Rigby, K. (2002). Bullying in childhood. In P. K. Smith & C. H. Hart (Eds.), *Blackwell handbook of childhood social development* (pp. 549–568). Malden, MA: Blackwell.

Rosenfeld, S. (1987). *Instructional consultation.* Hillsdale, NJ: Lawrence Erlbaum Associates.

Sinclair, M., Hurley, C., Christenson, S., Thurlow, M., & Evelo, D. (2002). Connections that keep kids coming to school. In R. Algozzine & P. Kay (Eds.), *Preventing problem behaviors: A handbook of successful prevention strategies.* Thousand Oaks, CA: Corwin.

Skretta, J. (2007). Using walkthroughs to gather data for school improvement. *Principal Leadership, 5,* 16–23.

Sprick, R., & Garrison, M. (2008). *Interventions: Evidence-based behavioral strategies for individual students* (2nd ed.). Eugene, OR: Pacific Northwest.

Stokes, T. F., & Baer, D. M. (1977). An implicit technology of generalization. *Journal of Applied Behavior Analysis, 19,* 349–367.

Swearer, S. M., & Doll, B. (2001). Bullying in schools: An ecological framework. *Journal of Emotional Abuse, 2,* 7–23.

Swearer, S. M., Espelage, D. L., & Napolitano, S. A. (2009). *Bullying prevention and intervention: Realistic strategies for schools.* New York, NY: Guilford Press.

Swearer, S., Espelage, D. L., Vaillancourt, T., & Hymel, S. (2010). What can be done about school bullying? Linking research to educational practice. *Educational Researcher, 39,* 38–47.

Texas School Safety Center. (2008). *Campus safety and security audit toolkit.* Austin, TX: Attorney General's Office.

Tingstrom, D. H., Sterling-Turner, H. E., & Wilczynski, S. M. (2006). The Good Behavior Game: 1969–2002. *Behavior Modification, 30*(2), 225–253.

Tolan, P. H., Gorman-Smith, D., & Loeber, R. (2000). Developmental timing and onsets of disruptive behaviors and later delinquency of inner-city youth. *Journal of Child and Family Studies, 9,* 203–220.

Trump, K. S. (2011). *Proactive school security and emergency preparedness planning.* Thousand Oaks, CA: Corwin.

Ttofi, M. M., & Farrington, D. P. (2009). What works in preventing bullying: Effective elements of anti-bullying programs. *Journal of Aggression, Conflict and Peace Research, 1,* 13–24.

U.S. Department of Education, Office of Planning, Evaluation and Policy Development, Policy and Program Studies Service. (2011). *Analysis of state bullying laws and policies.* Washington, DC: Author.

U.S. Department of Health and Human Services, Substance Abuse and Mental Health Services Administration. (2010). *National registry of evidence-based programs and practices* [Web registry]. Retrieved from http://www.nrepp.samhsa.gov/ViewIntervention.aspx?id=70

Virginia Department of Education. (2000). *School safety audit.* Richmond, VA: Author.

Vreeman, R. C., & Carroll, A. E. (2007). A systematic review of school-based interventions to prevent bullying. *Archives of Pediatric Adolescent Medicine, 161,* 78–88.

Wang, M., Haertel, G., & Walberg, H. (1993/1994). What helps students learn. *Educational Leadership,* December/January, 74–79.

Ysseldyke, J., & Christenson, S. (1993). *The Instructional Environment System-II* (TIES-II). Longmont, CO; Sopris West.

Zins, J., Elias, M., & Maher, C. (Eds.). (2007). *Bullying, victimization, and peer harassment: Handbook of prevention and intervention in peer harassment, victimization, and bullying.* New York, NY: Haworth Press.

Zins, J. E., Weissberg, R. P., Wang, M. C., & Walberg, H. J. (Eds.). (2004). *Building academic success on social and emotional learning: What does the research say?* New York, NY: Teachers College Press.

Index

NOTE: Page numbers with tables and figures are identified as (fig.) and (table).